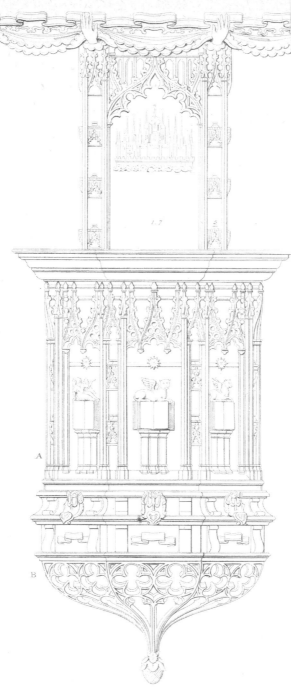

1. Worcester: the early 17th-century pulpit,
with its strange tester, held up by
disembodied hands, and a carved relief of the
Heavenly Jerusalem on the back (engraving
from Britton, 1835). The pulpit remains, but
the tester disappeared in the 19th century,
though the back carving survives.

2. St Saviour's, Southwark, later Southwark Cathedral: a view of
1818 looking west from the choir. Within twenty years the nave
was in ruins (see pl. 8), and today all that remains of the
furnishings seen here are the chandelier and the wooden roof-
bosses, now exhibited at the west end.

GERALD COBB

English Cathedrals

THE FORGOTTEN CENTURIES

RESTORATION AND CHANGE
FROM 1530
TO THE PRESENT DAY

With 291 illustrations

THAMES AND HUDSON

Dedicated with grateful thanks
to
Sir Nikolaus Pevsner

without whose encouragement and happy suggestion of a
publisher this book might never have materialized

I must thank Mr Arthur Sabin, Hon. Archivist to the Dean and Chapter of Bristol Cathedral, for much interesting information and references about the cathedral reredos, etc., and the Rev. Louis Ward for Mr Sabin's address. My thanks are due to the College of Arms for permission to reproduce drawings of Lichfield monuments in Visitation of Staffs, 1634 (pls 240–243), and to the Society of Antiquaries for allowing me to include pls 95 and 206 from items in their collection.

I must also thank Mr Francis Greenacre, Curator, Fine Art, Bristol Museum and Art Gallery; the Librarian of Bath Reference Library, Queen Square, and Mr V. J. Kite, Area Librarian; and Mr F. B. Stitt of the William Salt Library, Stafford, for their kind help in supplying photographs and useful information.

I must especially thank Mr A. Colin Cole, Garter King of Arms, for kindly allowing access to his copy of Gough's *Sepulchral Monuments*, and Mr John A. Goodall for photographing plates from those immense volumes – some job!

Lastly I am grateful to my close friend, Nicholas Redman for very useful suggestions, reading of proofs, and general help.

Grateful acknowledgment is made to the following owners of the copyright of photographs:
Bath Reference Library 17, 27, 29, 34; Bristol Museum and Art Gallery 22, 44, 52, 54; F. Frith and Co. 73, 193, 195, 201, 218, 220; Robert Harrison 114; Martin Hurlimann 179; Institute of Advanced Architectural Studies, York (NMR) 219; Judge's, Ltd 121, 142, 259; A. F. Kersting 225; J. Loughton (NMR) 97, 98; National Monuments Record 81, 183, 188, 196, 226, 256, 282; Photochrom Co. Ltd 25, 143; M. H. Ridgway (Courtauld Institute) 246; Salt Library, Stafford 224; Walter Scott 87; E. A. Sweetman and Son 36; Valentine's 110, 162; Reece Winstone 43, 53, 57, 62, 65, 69, 71, 74.

Filmset and printed in Great Britain by
BAS Printers Limited, Over Wallop, Hampshire
Bound in Great Britain by
Webb Son & Co, Ltd., Glamorgan

Contents

3. Bristol: an engraving published in 1839, showing a tomb built
against the medieval sedilia. The complete sedilia were restored
by Pearson.

Introduction

THE PURPOSE of this book is to draw attention to the many mutilations and restorations of our Greater Churches during the last four centuries, and so demonstrate the necessity for at least a superficial knowledge of their architectural history since the Dissolution of the monasteries if we are to assess their true value as legacies of medieval building and craftsmanship. In order to keep the work to manageable proportions, ten churches (seven cathedrals, plus Beverley Minster, Bath and Selby Abbeys) have been chosen as representative examples to be examined in depth. But equally rewarding accounts could be written of almost all the other cathedrals in the country, and it is to be hoped that these may eventually go to the making of another volume.

From my own very extensive collection of works on our cathedrals and minsters, and individual guide-books from the 18th century onwards, I have been able to construct a meaningful narrative of the changes that have taken place in these great churches. The text is illustrated with some of the very numerous views – drawings, engravings and particularly old photographs – that I have been amassing for over fifty years. This combination of text and illustrations will make it possible, perhaps for the first time, for the craftsmanship of fabric and fittings to be properly assessed.

As an example of how ignorance of these changes may mislead an otherwise knowledgeable writer, mention may be made of Dr F. J. Allen who, in his *Great Church Towers of England* (1932) discusses the alterations to Newbury parish church and the south-west tower of Bridlington Priory as if they were ancient work, albeit restored. Evidently he did not know that at Newbury the pinnacles he admired were Victorian additions where none had been before, while the Bridlington tower was heightened by Sir George Gilbert Scott to his own design.

What do we mean by 'Greater Churches'? From an architectural as well as an ecclesiastical viewpoint, there are roughly two categories of churches – parish churches and chapels of ease, and those of cathedral, monastic and collegiate establishments. Those of the second category are known as Greater Churches, for as a rule they are larger and more complex than the parochial ones, though not always so. But although some of the smaller Greater Churches look very like parish churches, for instance, St Asaph's Cathedral or Dorchester Abbey, I know of only two old parish churches built at all like a cathedral. These are the chancel (only) of Hythe church, which is, it seems, unique (for a parish church) in having all three storeys of main arcade, triforium and clerestory (the clerestory and vault restorations by J. L. Pearson); and the splendid St Mary Redcliffe, Bristol, with its double-aisled transepts (a rare feature, even in cathedrals), Lady chapel at the east end and stone-vaulting throughout. But even there the position of the single tower – a magnificent one (spire 1872) – at the west end of the north aisle is distinctly parochial.

The Greater Churches of England which before the Reformation were extraordinarily numerous – as many as 698 dated foundations have been numbered – have suffered under five main periods of adversity. Firstly, at the Dissolution of the monasteries, when about nine-tenths of them were destroyed, either wholly or in part, or allowed to go to ruin, followed in those that remained by plunder of their treasures.[1] Secondly, in the Civil War (and the lax period leading up to it) when Cromwell's soldiers wrought great havoc in cathedrals and other churches, especially damaging the furniture and fittings. Thirdly, during the long period of neglect engendered by Baroque contempt for the Gothic, which lasted until the late 18th century; followed, fourthly, by the succession of necessary and well meant, but usually unfortunate,

---

4, 5. Westminster Abbey: photographs taken from the Victoria Tower, Houses of Parliament, before and after Scott's restoration in the 1860s. His most obvious changes are the new windows and conical roof to the chapter house and the gable and pinnacles at the end of the south transept.

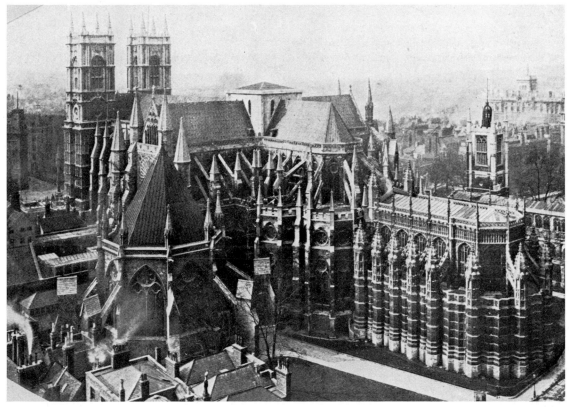

'restorations' with the destruction and renovation which they involved, which have persisted until modern times. And, lastly, the hazards of the 20th century – war, traffic, pollution and inflation. But the third and fourth of these periods of adversity also had their credit side.

In these days of multiplying graphic and photographic material, it is hard to realize that in Henry VIII's time – and for long afterwards – the very existence, not to mention the appearance, of the multitude of monastic and other Greater Churches in England would be practically unknown to the ordinary man, except for those living near them. The extent of official knowledge of their number and whereabouts can be roughly deduced from the king's commissioning John Leland to make a roving survey of the religious houses and their antiquities. But his descriptions are disappointingly varied, and graphic records were extremely rare. A few architectural drawings from the 15th century onwards have survived, scattered through various libraries, besides fine etchings of some of our cathedrals by Wenceslaus Hollar.[2] But the first real series of cathedral and conventual views, by Daniel King, appeared in 1655 in Dugdale's *Monasticon* (vol. I) – the following year they were published separately by King[3] – and was on the whole pretty poor work.

After 1700 illustrated architectural works began to increase rapidly, and after 1800 improved in accuracy also, until, in the middle of the century, photography arrived to make exact images of great architecture and craftsmanship available to all. It was just in time to record attractive work of the 17th, 18th and early 19th centuries in our cathedrals before that work was ejected by the 'restorers' as 'debased' or 'pagan' (i.e. post-Gothic) in favour of new and more 'correct' fittings. However, old photographs of cathedrals placed side by side with later ones, lead sadly to the discovery that the new work was nearly always (and in our own day very often still is) inferior in design, if not in finish, to what preceded it, in a story of gradual deterioration.

In the rest of this Introduction I propose to give a brief sketch of the changes and developments that have taken place between the Reformation and the present day, drawing examples mainly from those cathedrals and Greater Churches that are not examined in detail in the body of the book.

Reformation to Civil War

Henry VIII, as a counter to his generally destructive measures, established six new cathedrals, at Westminster, Bristol, Gloucester, Oxford, Peterborough and Chester, utilizing in each case a lately dissolved abbey church for the purpose. Westminster lasted as a cathedral for only ten years; and then, after being re-established as an abbey under Queen Mary, it finally became under Elizabeth I what it is now – the collegiate church of St Peter.

At Oxford the cathedral was established to the west of the city at Oseney Abbey, which had a central and a lofty western tower, and from Anthony Wood's account appears to have been one of the most splendid sanctuaries in England. Unfortunately, after three years Henry removed the bishop's throne to St Frideswide's Priory church, the nave of which had been partly demolished by Wolsey to make way for his Cardinal College, which the King had refounded as Christchurch in 1532. Thus Oseney was deserted and we lost this grand cathedral of three years standing, the ruins of which remained until the Civil War, when they were demolished by Charles I for material to strengthen the defences of the city. Henry also destroyed another cathedral of longer standing than Oseney – that of Coventry, which from the early 13th century had been joint cathedral with Lichfield for the bishops of Coventry and Lichfield. It stood in the same church yard as the great parish churches of Holy Trinity and St Michael and, with their soaring spires, they must have formed a marvellous group. St Michael's, made a cathedral in 1918 and burnt out in the Second World War, is now a shell, with Basil Spence's new cathedral adjoining at right angles.

Between Henry VIII's reign and the Civil War the only constructive event of importance in our context was the renovation of Old St Paul's. This great cathedral, before the loss of its lofty spire in 1561, was not only the longest but also the tallest church in England, and perhaps in Europe, and one of the finest, with its magnificent Norman nave and transepts, fine Early English steeple, and superb eastern limb of the 13th century with its famous rose window. The fall of the spire caused great damage; repairs dragged on and were only partial: the spire was never replaced, although a design was prepared which is still extant, and was used by Hollar in his plate in Dugdale's *History of St Paul's Cathedral* (1658) of the cathedral as it was before 1561 – the Classical details of its spire lights betray its late date.[4]

In 1620 James I rode in state to St Paul's to hear a sermon at the cross and open the campaign for the restoration, but nothing was done until 1631 when Laud, then Bishop of London, succeeded in getting things started. From 1633 until the outbreak of the Civil War in 1642, St Paul's underwent a thorough and much needed repair, financed by a nationwide appeal which brought in about £100,000. This renovation was undertaken by Inigo Jones who, having thoroughly assimilated the principles of Renaissance architecture (hitherto little known in England), did not scruple to reclothe the exterior of the nave and transepts in Classical garb – made easy by the roundness of the Norman windows.[5] And at the west end he added the famous and beautiful Corinthian portico, the admiration of all men of taste both then and since, which was paid for by Charles I himself.

Under the Commonwealth, the cathedral was made 'a Horse-Quarter for soldiers during the whole of the late usurpation. The stately Portico . . . was converted to shops for seamstresses and other trades, with Lofts and Stairs ascending thereto . . . those stately Pillars (being) shamefully hewed and defaced and the Royal statues ''broke in pieces'' '.[6] Sir Paul Pinder's fine choir-stalls were destroyed and the retrochoir walled off as a preaching house.

After the Restoration of the monarchy the cathedral's repair was resumed and a number of houses newly built against the walls were demolished. Christopher Wren, immediately before the Great Fire of 1666, produced a design to Romanize the interior in harmony with the exterior. The central tower, which was not safe, was to be demolished and the crossing enlarged for the erection of a tall peristyle and dome surmounted by a spiring finial like an attenuated fir-cone. This design would probably have been carried out, and thus, even if there had been no Great Fire of London, we should virtually have had a new St Paul's except for the medieval eastern limb. This Gothic survival, united with the Classical nave, transept and dome, would indeed have been an odd combination, and this goes far to console one for the loss of the old cathedral. This attempt, and that at Llandaff a hundred years later, to classicize a great Gothic church are fortunately the only ones we have indulged in in this country.

Extreme laxity of behaviour and of control in our cathedrals was notorious long before the lamentable situation under the Commonwealth. The nave of St Paul's, with its two opposite doors and those in the transepts, was known as Paul's Walk, being used as a common thoroughfare, a shopping centre and a fashionable promenade – and this from long before the Reformation. In the returns at Bishop Bancroft's visitation of 1598, we

learn that 'all kinds of burden-bearing people, as Colliers with sacks of coles, Porters with Baskettes of flesh and such like' still perambulated the nave. At service time

the choristers were eager in search of spur-money[7] [and there was] suche noyse of the children and others in the side chapels and churches at the divine service that a man can scarce be hearde . . . people walked about in the upper choir where the Communion Table doth stand, with their hats on their heads, commonly, all the service time, no man reproving them . . . St Dunstan's Chapel was made a storehouse for glass, and the glass was brought in even during service time . . . the sweepings of the church lay in it three and four weeks together till the smell became 'very noysom'; the bell-singers admitted persons into the Organ loft for money, to the decay of the instrument . . . the chapels below the steps were much unglazed; in St George's Chapel lay old stones and a ladder; in Long Chapel old fir poles and other old lumber; vaults under the church were let to a carpenter; . . . houses and shops blocked up the windows of some of the chapels.[8]

Sparrow Simpson[9] also gives examples of this laxity in other cathedrals. At Salisbury, in a pamphlet appended to papers about Archbishop Laud's visitation, we read of attendance at services:

of 260 canonical howers *per ann*, they are not 60 in the church; of these 60, not 30 at second lesson, of these 30 not 10 at the confession, no not at communions. For this, though we have expresse statute agaynst it, and paenaltye, yett wee plead custome and challenge and receyve commons. According to this neglect, our quyre and church service is utterly destitute and naked of all cathedral ornaments. I might say robbed, for about 40 years agone, they were solde and fowly.

From Canterbury this account was sent to Laud in 1634:

Men both of ye better and meaner sort, mechanicks, youths and prentises do ordinarily & most unreverently walk in our church in ye tyme of divine service. . . . As also for ye . . . trudginge up & downe of youths & clamours of children to ye great disturbance of the preachers in their sermons. The vergers & other officers have had a charge to look to this but to little or no purpose. Dr Barston, Dr Hinchman & myself have byn fayne to ryse & goe out of our seates to see & staye ye disorders. But I never (to my uttermost rememberance) sawe Barfoot ye verger (who sits in my sight) to ryse at ye greatest noyse. 'Bye Me John Lee'.

At Carlisle things were also rather disordered and distinctly 'provincial', according to the Norwich Tourists in 1634:

their cathedral . . . is nothing soe fayre and stately as

those we had seene, but more like a great wild Country Church. . . . The organs and voices did well agree, the one being like a shrill Bagpipe, the other like the Scottish Tone. The Sermon in the like accent, was such, as wee would hardly bring away, though it was deliver'd by a neat Schollar . . . one of the Bishop's chaplains, to supply his lord's place that day. The Communion also was administered and receiv'd in a wild and unreverent manner.[10]

Sparrow Simpson continues:

Alas, we need not end even here. Many another grand cathedral had the same sad tale to tell; the same wearisome story of pluralities and non-residence; of overwhelming greediness and self-seeking; of rampant nepotism; of desecrated naves (as, for instance, Paul's Walk) and deserted choirs; of dignitaries receiving great revenues and rendering no service in return; of cold hearts. The way was paved for still greater desecrations, and they came. Horses neighed in Canons' stalls; and Dr Cornelius Burges, with his twenty thousand pounds of plunder, preached in the ruined choir.[11]

Nemesis indeed with such a background! – and in spite of Laud's frantic efforts to reform it. (See appendix for extracts showing the deplorable encroachments in some cathedral closes, which at York persisted until the early 19th century.)

On the triumph of the Parliament after the Civil War, episcopacy was abolished and the cathedrals were either shut up as useless or fitted up as preaching houses, generally after incredibly rough handling by Roundhead soldiers. At Lichfield, during the famous siege of the close, which had been fortified by the Royalists, the central spire was battered down by gunfire; and at Peterborough, the splendid cloisters – perhaps the finest in the country, fitted with ancient glass with scriptural subjects and portraits of the kings of England – were utterly destroyed, as was also the magnificent reredos in the choir with three spires reaching almost to the ceiling. At both these places, and at Durham, where a body of Scots soldiers was locked up in the cathedral and made a bonfire of the stalls to keep warm, terrific havoc was wrought. Again at Lichfield, the soldiers

demolished all [most of] the monuments, pulled down the curious carved work, battered in pieces the costly windows, and destroyed the evidences and records. They stabled their horses in the body of the church, kept courts of guard in the cross aisle, broke up the pavement, and polluted the choir with their excrement; every day hunting a cat with hounds through the church, and delighting themselves with the echo from the goodly vaulted roofs. And to add to their wickedness, they brought a calf into it, carried it to the font, and gave it a name in scorn and derision of that Holy Sacrament of Baptism.[12]

At St Paul's they exhibited still greater profanity. Some very repulsive details are to be found in a scarce little tract of four leaves entitled 'Newes from Powles, or a New Reformation of the Army: with a true Relation of a Coult that was foaled in the Cathedrall Church of *St Paul* in *London*, and how it was Publiquely *Baptized* by *Paul Hobson*'s souldiers, one of them p . . . . . g in his helmet, and sprinkling it in the name of the Father, Son and Holy Ghost. . . . Printed in the year 1649.'[13]

At York, on the other hand, the splendid stained glass was saved by Fairfax – a native of the county – who, although a Cromwellian, is said to have locked all the doors and suffered no one to enter; and at Winchester, the cathedral escaped with little damage.

Eighteenth-century attitudes

After the Restoration of the monarchy, the depredations of the Cromwellians were as much as possible made good, especially by such energetic prelates as Bishop Hacket (1661–71) at Lichfield and Bishop Cosin (1660–71) at Durham.[14] The repair of Westminster Abbey was, it appears, taken in hand: the Galilee porch was removed from the north transept front and the whole front made plain and ugly, except for the great rose window (which was patched with plaster and brick) and the gable above, and the south rose window was rebuilt. Later, as surveyor to the fabric, Wren greatly improved the north front, and generally refaced the abbey (except Henry VII's chapel), and designed a central dome or spire (both are shown on the one drawing). He also made drawings for towers to complete the unfinished west front, but unfortunately they are lost. The present towers were begun in 1734 from designs by Nicholas Hawksmoor and were finished after his death by John James. In 1690 Selby Abbey's central tower came to grief and destroyed the south transept – the tower was plainly rebuilt.

In the early 18th century, after two hundred years or more of neglect which had resulted in Llandaff Cathedral going to ruin, the chapter was at last aroused and, about 1732, John Wood senior of Bath was commissioned to design a smaller church in the Classical style to be erected within and to incorporate some of the ruined walls. Building was slow and it was only finished in 1752, and then without the western domed tower that had originally been intended. It seems to have been a charming design, although regarded as an unspeakable monstrosity by the restorers of a hundred years later! If the full design had been carried out, the beautiful 13th-century west front might well have been demolished.

In 1741 the spire on the south-west tower of St Margaret's, King's Lynn, was blown down and part of the early 13th-century nave demolished, after which the central wooden octagon, very similar to the central lantern at Ely, was unfortunately pulled down. The old nave was cleared away and rebuilt in a nearly flat-arched Perpendicular style (very like Wren's St Mary Aldermary in the City of London), but fitted with most splendid Classical furniture. This, alas, was all removed around 1874 – a tragic loss.[15]

The veneration we now feel for our medieval cathedrals was non-existent in the 17th and 18th centuries among the intelligentsia, whose chief regard was for Roman and later Greek architecture. Only a few antiquaries and topographers cared, such as Horace Walpole, Francis Grose (antiquities), Richard Gough (sepulchral monuments), John Carter and the Rev. John Milner (whose standard *History and Survey of the Antiquities of Winchester*, 1798–1801, proved a cat among the dove-cotes). This utter indifference to the worth of our medieval heritage (see appendix) and its subsequent neglect led to a great deal of interesting and valuable remains – architecture, painting, sculpture, stained glass, and so on – being destroyed or covered up. But whitewash also preserved; and it seems that, on the whole, more damage was wrought by the early 'restorers' in their zeal for 'neatness' and for removing the 'Gothick rudeness' of paintings, screens and chapels, so as to render the interiors of these great churches more 'up-to-date'.

The name most associated with this first phase of restoration is that of James Wyatt, whose notoriety stems from his being given jobs of repair and innovation at four important cathedrals – Hereford, Lichfield, Salisbury and Durham. But his contemporaries were similarly involved in what we now regard as vandalism, for example, James Essex at Ely, Nicholson and Morpeth at Durham, before Wyatt, and Atkinson after him.[16] And although Wyatt may have inherited the epithet 'The Destroyer' and later 'The Vandal', it must also be remembered that architects to cathedrals were never given carte-blanche (at least not in theory) to carry out a repair or alteration. They were employees of the dean and chapter, and credit for whatever improvement or vandalism was effected must be shared, in varying degrees, between architect and cathedral body;[17] whether or not an architect was

called in to advise, the ultimate responsibility remained with the dean and chapter.

The Rev. Jocelyn Perkins[18] gives a lurid picture of what might have been in Westminster Abbey in the 1770s but for the grace of God. The dean consulted with his architect Henry Keene together with Essex and Wyatt, about 'an improvement' which would have 'erected a new choir in the eastern part of the abbey, from the nave to the upper end of St Edward's Chapel', involving the destruction of the 15th-century altar-screen and the clearing away of the Confessor's Shrine. This was agreed to in chapter, but doubts about the small number of prebendaries present led to a second ballot in which, mercifully, there was no clear mandate. What an escape! But it shows indeed the cultural outlook towards our medieval heritage at that time.

Going back to 1734, the following quotation from James Ralph[19] helps us to understand how such episodes could happen. At Westminster Abbey, he says, 'the enclosure behind the altar, commonly known by the name of St Edward's Chapel, has nothing remarkable in it but certain Gothique antiquities, which are made sacred by tradition only, and serve to excite a stupid admiration in the vulgar'. (As this defeated scheme for 'improving' the choir of Westminster Abbey preceded Wyatt's similar work carried out at Salisbury and Lichfield, may we not assume that the former attempt inspired the latter fruition?)

Yet, within eighty years, the following effusion was typical of the change wrought by the Gothic Revival: 'The prospect . . . from the grand western door, through the whole extent of the lofty aisle, terminated by the magnificent window at the back of the choir, is calculated to affect the most indifferent spectator with mingled emotions of admiration and religious awe.'[20] These opposite tendencies resulted in the sacrifice not only of fine 17th- and 18th-century features and fittings, but also, in many instances, of the medieval pulpitum or other screen and, in some cases, the removal of the whole choir either eastwards, or later westwards, of its original position. At Peterborough, Ely and Chester, the choir was twice resited before 1900.

The Gothic Revival

Under the earlier phase of the Gothic Revival (c. 1770–1840s), the age of Roman cement and Coade stone, the pulpitum was usually retained or, if destroyed, a new stone screen erected, as at Ely (1770s), Salisbury (1790), Peterborough (c. 1830s),

6. Hereford Cathedral in the 18th century (engraving from Browne Willis) before the collapse of the west tower and the removal of the spire.

and Winchester (1834), for the practical consideration of keeping warm in an unheated church. But with the second phase, which reached its climax about 1870, the heating of large buildings was a practical proposition and so there was no need for a division between nave and choir, and these new screens (and some old ones), not to mention many fine Baroque altarpieces and other furniture, were in consequence swept away. It seems that the only medieval choir-screens removed in this second phase were at Hereford, Chichester, Bristol and Chester, the last two by, or on the advice of, Scott.[21]

In place of the fittings so needlessly destroyed, first, the rather attractive creations of Essex and Wyatt were set up and then, in the later phase, their places taken by the wonderful metal screens and marble reredoses which flowed so freely from the over-worked offices of Scott and others. Two of Scott's choir-screens have now, in their turn, been thrown out – at Hereford and Salisbury – for the passion to denigrate and remove one's immediate predecessor's work is still with us.

A good deal of renovation, most of it disastrous, was done in the first phase of the Revival, especially at Ely, Durham, Hereford, Salisbury, Lichfield and York. At Ely, Essex saved the cathedral from collapse, but badly refashioned the lantern and destroyed the 12th-century pulpitum – the earliest surviving in England. Durham – most unfortunate of minsters – suffered successive

indignities from about 1773 to near 1850 (after which Scott was appointed to make amends). First, the cloisters lost their old tracery, the north porch was demolished and rebuilt, losing its upper storey, and the whole of the north side of the cathedral was scraped to a depth of four inches, with new carvings and pinnacles added – all apparently under the architect George Nicholson.[22] The great Norman chapter house was barbarously destroyed by 'Mr Morpeth, under contract'[23] by order of chapter held 20 November 1795.[24] Wyatt was called in in that year, but actually did comparatively little damage[25] as his scheme for demolishing the Galilee was defeated, largely by Carter's protests. And although he made designs for adding an octagonal storey and spire to the central tower and proposed demolishing the Neville screen and constructing a new enclosure for the high altar from its materials, his intentions happily came to nothing. In about 1810, Atkinson, the cathedral architect,[26] covered the upper storey of the great tower with Roman cement and removed all seventeen of the statues, which were then ranged around the platform of St Cuthbert's shrine for many years.[27] Last but by no means least, in the 1840s Salvin displaced Bishop Cosin's fine choir-screen and the organ of 1684, thrust Cosin's choir-stalls back between the massive Norman piers (thus halving their number), removed his charming Classical font and its huge wooden canopy, and even opened the great west doorway (closed by Cardinal Langley in the 15th century) so as to create a grand vista from end to end of the cathedral – something Wyatt never did!

The restoration of Hereford was forced on the dean and chapter by the fall of the western tower in 1786. Unfortunately, they chose Wyatt to repair the damage, who not only did *not* rebuild the tower but also shortened the nave by one bay and destroyed the whole of the Norman triforium and clerestory up to the central tower (from which he removed the spire). In their place he substituted a new west front and 'Gothick' work of feeble design – so feeble, indeed, that Cottingham was later employed to improve the interior, and to him we owe the colouring of the vaults and the quite good carved corbels to the vaulting shafts and other details.

At York a less drastic but far more permanent restoration was taking place: all the decayed details of the west front were replaced in stone by a skilful mason named Shute or Shoults, who very carefully imitated the more 'perfect' remains; he also did much work on the canopies in the chapter house.

6

15
171

125
133

All his renewals seem as sound as when first done and, superficially at least, are not easy to detect from the original work. And between 1808 and 1822, Henry VII's Chapel in Westminster Abbey, woefully dilapidated, was completely refaced. This was carefully done by Gayfere, the abbey mason, and his carvers, under the general direction of Wyatt, the cost of over £42,000 being voted by Parliament.

About 1825 Rochester's central tower and spire were removed and a pinnacled tower substituted by Cottingham. In 1834 the north-west tower of Canterbury was rebuilt by Austin to match the south-west one. It was a great pity the Norman tower was destroyed but its rebuilding certainly improved the appearance of the cathedral as a whole. It would have been much better if the tower had been repaired and the spire rebuilt. This would have given us back an asymmetrical but picturesque west front – a rare feature in England, but common in France (Chartres, St Jean-de-Vigne at Soissons, Amiens, Evreux, etc.)

A little later the 13th-century nave of St Saviour's Southwark (now cathedral), was pulled down and a 'church-warden Gothic' nave substituted, the retrochoir only just escaping demolition. In 1829 the groined ceiling of the choir

8. Southwark: the nave in 1834, open to the sky (*British Magazine*). The present nave, by Arthur Blomfield, dates from 1890.

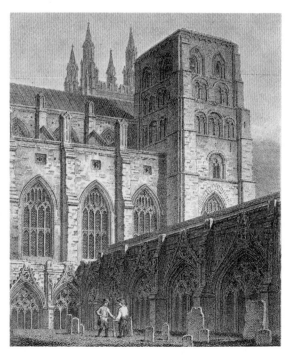

7. West end of Canterbury Cathedral (Storer) before the rebuilding of the north-west tower in 1834.

and in 1840 that of the nave at York (both of wood, imitating stone) were destroyed by fire. Again the famous glass was amazingly preserved but the fine medieval stalls were consumed. The restorations were entrusted respectively to Sir Robert Smirke and his brother, Sydney Smirke, who reproduced the old designs more or less exactly.

During the second phase of the Revival (1840s onwards) all the cathedrals were 'restored'. This was the age for vistas and for 'correctness and consistency' of style.[28]

At Wells the cathedral suffered unfortunate treatment by two architects. First, in 1842, Benjamin Ferrey was called in to remove the whitewash and so on that disfigured the interior – good! – but then he removed all the wall tablets to the cloisters where they still are. Then, in 1848–54, Salvin was let loose on the choir, where he removed the ancient stalls and erected chilly stone ones with brash carvings *between the piers* (as at Durham). He also removed Bishop Beckington's monument and

9. Chichester Cathedral shortly after the collapse of the central tower in 1861 (*Illustrated London News*).

10, 11. Canterbury: Bell Harry tower, before and after alterations to the bell-openings by W. D. Caröe in 1904.

chapel from the choir (now replaced). Lastly, around 1870, for the much decayed original blue lias shafts of the west front Ferrey substituted Kilkenny marble – which rapidly came to resemble slate pencils.

15
139
At Hereford and Ely solid choir-screens were replaced by Scott's lighter designs; and at Ely he moved the whole choir westward as at present and

reconverted Essex's lantern to its original form – a great improvement. Between 1848 and 1872 St Mary Redcliffe, Bristol, underwent a much needed restoration, culminating with the completion of its unfinished spire. This is perhaps too tall – certainly the present steeple seems less imposing than when the fine tower carried only a stump. Chichester's spire is a close copy of the original which collapsed after great efforts to save it in 1861. The Arundel screen or pulpitum was removed by Slater just before the fall and later stored in the detached bell-tower until 1960, when it was replaced under the crossing but without the fine organ that had graced it before 1860. The north-west tower is also new, its predecessor having disappeared. Both western towers are shown complete in Hollar's print in *Monasticon*, vol. III (1673), crowned with battlements (now gone). But in King's earlier engraving the north-west tower is half demolished, with the south-west tower the same as Hollar's; while still earlier, in 1610, Speed's map of Sussex shows all three towers with spires. This, with Lincoln, Lichfield and Ripon, would make four three-spired churches and there is a tradition that Coventry Cathedral, destroyed by Henry VIII, was another.

9

While some of the exteriors were conservatively treated, as at Winchester, Gloucester and Peterborough, others were largely refaced or partly rebuilt. Of these over-restorations, the most drastic were at Chester and Worcester (the towers spoiled) and Lichfield (new statues) in the 1860s and 1870s – all by Scott; the south transept at York by Street, (1871–74); and the north front of Westminster Abbey by Scott and Pearson, entirely destroying Wren's work (c. 1875–90).

The very real danger, from the aesthetic standpoint, of so-called 'restoration' of ancient buildings by other than extremely sensitive and capable architects, is illustrated by Lord Grimthorpe's treatment of St Albans Abbey between 1879 and 1895. Of course, it is realized that his taking on the repair when he did probably saved the building from partial collapse. But his transformation of the exterior was disastrous in not only the peculiarly insensitive character of his façades, with their ugly turrets and pinnacles, but also in the mere fact of raising the roofs of nave, transepts and choir. For St Albans had, by the routine modifications of its exterior during the three and a half centuries since medieval times, assumed a unique (?) uniformity of outline, with no gable anywhere at all (except the low pitch of the Lady chapel roof, which may virtually be ignored).

14

12, 13. Transformations of the Canterbury choir: (*left*) Hartover's altar-screen, etc. of 1664 (Dart, 1726) and (*right*) Burrough's altarpiece of 1732 (Wild, 1807) removed in 1826.

Every façade was one of right angles (with or without short turrets) and from whatever viewpoint the abbey was seen there was a serenity about it; its lowness giving full dignity to the splendid Norman tower. These lovable characteristics were lost by raising the roofs.

Although Canterbury was, on the whole, kindly dealt with, the Bell Harry tower there – one of the most beautiful anywhere – was tampered with and marred by W. D. Caröe around 1904, who patched the stonework and substituted four large louvres in each section of the upper windows for the former numerous small ones, which visually fragmented these elegant lights. Of other less damaging restorations, at Selby, the abbey was transformed by Sir G. G. and Oldrid Scott, *c*. 1870–1935, with, after a fire in 1906, rebuilt central and later heightened western towers; Southwark nave was again rebuilt in 1890, by Blomfield, closely following that destroyed sixty years before; at Rochester, the west front was restored by Pearson in 1894 and ten years later the tower was again rebuilt (by C. Hodgson Fowler) with a spire recalling that removed by Cottingham – quite a pleasant piece of work; and about the same time, Wyatt's west front at Hereford was replaced by one of the rather pompous designs by Oldrid Scott.

In 1884 Peterborough's low central tower, for long decrepit, had to be rebuilt,[29] and in 1896 the famous west front was found to be defective and had to be partially reconstructed. These operations raised storms of protest and much hysterical rhetoric, but actually they were very carefully done, most of the original stones being replaced as before.[30] And Winchester Cathedral, threatened with disaster owing to insecure foundations, was made safe under T. G. Jackson at a cost of £113,000 from 1906 to 1912, when the foundations were filled with concrete and flying buttresses added to the south aisle of the nave.

The changes of fashion in furniture and fitments in the last four centuries left their mark on all cathedral interiors, often transforming their appearance as choir-screen, organ, stalls and reredos were altered or superseded. Canterbury was outstanding for the many changes in its choir,[31] while Westminster Abbey ran it close with the numerous alterations to its interior, as brilliantly recorded by Perkins. Mention must also be made of Scott's restoration of the Westminster chapter house in the 1860s. After being used from time to time as the House of Commons for over two centuries before the Reformation, it continued as Crown property and does so to this day. Around 1703 it was fitted up as a Record office and filled with presses and shelves; later (*c.* 1740) the vaulted ceiling was demolished as dangerous and a wooden upper storey inserted, with box-like roof. The great Geometric windows had been destroyed and filled with brick except for smaller round-headed lights when Scott commenced his restorations, which transformed the disfigured building into a rival of the later Salisbury chapter house, its former twin except for the high pitched roof.

10
11

108–
114

148

201

12
13

4, 5

At St Paul's Cathedral the choir as left by Wren extended from the apse to the centre of the west bay of the eastern arm, where it was closed by a splendid wood and marble screen bearing the magnificent organ of 1694 by Bernard Smith. The altar was against the east wall of the apse, and the great apsidal pilasters (ranging with those between the main arcades of choir and nave) were painted to represent lapis lazuli, while twenty-one panels under the three lower windows were filled with figured crimson velvet.[32] But there was no reredos, only a temporary arrangement, according to *Parentalia* (1750) which says Wren intended a baldacchino with twisted columns. Between the choir-screen and the dome area was a considerable unenclosed space[33] and after 1858, when special services under the dome were instituted, the organ and screen were taken down to open up the choir, and the organ placed in the north choir aisle, while a larger organ (from the panopticon of Science and Art in Leicester Square) was purchased cheaply and placed in the south transept in 1860. But in 1872 the whole choir was moved west to the edge of the dome area and the old organ was divided into two and placed each side of the choir entrance as at present.

By this time the drive to decorate the interior of St Paul's was at its height, and Dean Church, Canon Gregory (later dean, who lacking knowledge of Renaissance art went to Italy to study it in 1869) and Canon Lidden, moved the chapter to appoint William Burges as superintendent – a man who detested Wren's 'abominations' as he termed that great architect's works! He produced a plan and models which, to quote the late Canon Prestige,[34] were exhibited in the Royal Academy in 1874 to 'the consternation of all beholders'. The entire interior of the cathedral was to be replaced with a veneer of polished marble, varied with a wealth of mosaic, gilding, carving, bronzes, arabesques, friezes and similar gauds: white was to pre-dominate near the ground, but as the eye rose it would observe the temperature of the pigments rising with its own angle of vision, in blacks, reds, blues, greens and gold, reaching fever-point in the saucer domes of the roof, which were to be subdivided into panels by the addition of plaster mouldings; and as the chromatic brilliance was to increase with the height above the floor, so was its intensity to be augmented in its passage eastward through the choir to the sanctuary. A 'rough estimate' set the total cost of the projected work at £400,000, of which about one-tenth was actually available. Although approved by the chapter, Burges's amazing scheme was defeated by public outcry. With the removal of the choir-screen, the lack of a reredos became acutely apparent and in 1888 a gorgeous marble altarpiece was erected from designs by Bodley and Garner. It had twisted and wreathed columns and was connected to the choir walls by curved colonnades and hailed at the time as being 'beyond praise'.[35] But later it fell into disfavour and was destroyed (see p. 18). Lastly, from 1891 to 1906, mosaic was freely applied to the ceilings and the upper choir walls to designs by Sir William Richmond.

In Wales, Bangor was largely transformed by the indefatigable Scott. He designed a lofty spire which was never built, and a recent bequest of funds for its erection has had to be put to other uses as the crossing was not considered strong enough to support it. But it seems that some sort of heightening has been accomplished. Scott also superintended the restoration of St David's Cathedral, the west front of which, altered by Nash in the 1780s, he rebuilt; and the eastern limb, which was mostly in ruins, has gradually been roofed in and refurnished. The Classical temple in the ruins at Llandaff was demolished and the whole church restored by John Pritchard, with a new Early English south tower and Bretonesque pierced spire.

Three Scottish examples should be mentioned. St Giles's High Church, Edinburgh, was entirely refaced externally, except the steeple, in 1829–38 by William Burn, and is disappointingly dull. He also removed some chapels.[36] Glasgow Cathedral, the finest Greater Church in Scotland, was rendered uninteresting outside by the stupid de-molition, in the 1840s, of its two unequal but picturesque western towers which, projecting far beyond the west front, produced an almost cavernous recess between them. The grand in-terior, first fitted with stained glass late last century from Munich, has in the last fifty years been greatly enhanced by the substitution of fine modern work by about a dozen glass-painters of first repute. Lastly, at the Priory church at Haddington, the crossing and choir which had lain open to the sky since the Dissolution, have been roofed in and 'vaulted' in fibreglass, the ribs of which, being made in slightly irregular sections, produce a most convincing impression of old work. Although frankly deceptive, this has the advantage of putting no thrust against the old walls and is comely to behold – as is, indeed, the whole interior.

The twentieth century

At Cambridge, King's College chapel choir has been devastated by the removing of the panelling and reredos (by Detmar Blow in 1911, replacing Gothic work by Essex) which carried the woodwork round the east end from stalls to stalls. This has left the walls beneath the windows absolutely and starkly bare, their whiteness vying with, instead of the woodwork setting off, the glorious glass – all this to display the newly acquired painting by Rubens of the Holy Family. Something has also been done to darken the famous Renaissance organ-screen which, when I saw it a few years ago, looked quite black and in horrid contrast to the then newly whitened fan-vaulted ceiling.

At York between the wars three memorial chapels were erected in the transept and south choir aisles, each enclosed by metal screens; and to make room for one of these, in the west aisle of the south transept, the fine Frosterley marble font with handsome cover and ironwork[37] was thrown out. Later a new font was made for the crypt. Lastly, in 1955 a huge RAF memorial clock, designed by Sir Albert Richardson, was placed in the east aisle of the north transept.

In World War II most of the cathedrals mercifully escaped serious damage. The exceptions were Llandaff, already mentioned as badly shattered; Exeter, hit by a bomb in the south choir aisle which destroyed the beautiful little St James's chapel; Manchester, partly demolished; and St Paul's, which had two high-explosive bombs through its roofs, one smashing the high altar to pieces and the other penetrating to the crypt, besides two very near misses. Westminster Abbey was also hit but, very wonderfully, in the one place that did not matter, the roof of the lantern over the crossing. But the school hall (the old dormitory), the Busby library and the deanery were gutted.

At Chichester two specimens of post-war art now brighten the interior: a flaming tapestry of abstract design behind the high altar, *The Trinity* (1966) by John Piper, certainly a splendid, although inappropriate, piece of colour; and in the south choir aisle an oil painting of Mary Magdalene and Christ as the Gardener, by Graham Sutherland (1961). The latter, apart from the curious rendering of the *dramatis personae*, is only a rough sketch, and so is quite out of place in an ancient cathedral where everything (even the 'Saxon' carvings nearby) is carefully designed and finished.

At Llandaff there is a sad example of avant-garde intrusion in a medieval cathedral. In place of

a choir-screen a monstrous concrete four-legged 'spider' (miscalled a pulpitum) now straddles the nave – the work of the late George Pace. It bears a pierced cylinder carrying many small gilt statues and a seventeen-foot high aluminium figure of Christ by Jacob Epstein. Also John Pritchard's tall stone chancel arch and fine high arched wooden roof (destroyed in the war) were replaced by a lower arch to accommodate a nearly flat panelled ceiling, probably at vast expense. But this deliberate loss of height fits into the current trend (in schooling, biblical translation, morals etc.) of levelling-down instead of up. A flat roof in a fine Gothic cathedral is surely a negation of the aspiring spirit of the Pointed style.[38]

The argument so often heard to justify the intrusion of contemporary art into historic churches is to equate it with 17th- and 18th-century additions, which, it is said, go perfectly with earlier architecture, whether medieval or later. This of course may be so, but there is one proviso that is generally ignored, that such Carolean and Georgian additions were always in a *current and living tradition*. This surely cannot be said of the multifarious forms of avant-garde art with its emphasis on pattern versus content, still less of the 'new art forms' which are so sedulously sought after these days. All this of course is hotly disputed as being reactionary and out of date but is, I believe, none the less true. How often do people say of Victorian times, let alone of earlier periods, that they were 'another world' from today. If that is true, it is illogical to thrust art of the nuclear age, with its esoteric 'symbolism', into that wonderful heritage of straightforward craftsmanship – our ancient cathedrals and churches.

After this catalogue of renewals, additions, losses and disasters, it is good to chronicle two important repairs which took place between the wars at St George's, Windsor, and St Paul's, London, apparently none too soon. At both these national shrines many structural weaknesses were revealed and made good. At Windsor the vaults had not been properly bonded into the walls, and it was marvellous they had stayed up so long. This was remedied and the King's Beasts, removed by Wren from the pinnacles as hopelessly decayed, were replaced by new ones. In the interior the organ between the nave and altar was divided to give a glimpse of the east window from the nave – a doubtful improvement. At St Paul's Wren had himself committed the mistake he condemned in the building of the old cathedral, that of filling the interior of his piers with loose rubble (or, at least, rubble that became loose). Under Godfrey Allen as surveyor, many tons of liquid cement were pumped into these piers, and a new steel chain and other reinforcements placed around the base of the dome. In consequence of this timely reparation the cathedral was able to withstand the shock of the two high explosives which struck it during the last war.

But the post-war activities at St Paul's have been less satisfactory, apart from the repairs of war damage to the fabric. The great marble reredos of 1888 by Bodley and Garner, which was a splendidly designed piece of work and only slightly damaged in the war (although the high altar before it was utterly destroyed), was deliberately demolished and a new marble baldacchino erected in its stead at vast expense. Unlike its predecessor, it is open and as a result practically invisible from the west end of the nave. The lofty Corinthian pilasters of the apse (ranging with those between the main arcades), originally painted to resemble lapis lazuli, then removed in the 1880s and replaced by darkish grey variegated marble, were again converted to stone – unadorned giants among so much glitter. And the magnificent Grinling Gibbons stalls were so treated that the contrast between the oak and pear-wood carvings was reduced to a near-uniform dark brown, while the restrained Victorian marble pulpit was replaced by a pompous 'Baroque' wooden erection.

After a lengthy and expensive cleaning, in 1963–64, of the whole exterior of the cathedral, which had settled down to contrasting white above (where washed by the rain) and dark buff below (where the soot had been), the west front has now been whitened all over. This is now unlike the rest of the exterior, to whiten which would entail still vaster expense! Lastly, in 1974 an attempt was made to replace the fine baroque statues of the Apostles and Evangelists on the parapets of the west front and transept fronts by new figures of quite different and more contemporary feeling, obviously out of place on a great Renaissance cathedral. After much publicity and criticism the scheme happily was abandoned. The original statues, by Bird, were gracefully weathering and are still very beautiful – they have now been strengthened.

Is it too much to hope that such drastic alterations and expensive fittings or refittings will soon be things of the past, and that appeals in future would be for essential repairs only? If not, we shall be unworthy guardians of these wonderful buildings.

There are two lines, one of them from Holy Writ, which seem appropriate to the present situation: 'Now that which decayeth and waxeth old is ready to vanish away', and 'The old order changeth, yielding place to new'. They may be applied respectively to the old monastic system (clubbed to death in England though it was by Henry VIII) and to the Reformation and Elizabethan settlement; and again to the neglect and disrepair of the 17th and 18th centuries and the extraordinary wave of 'restoration' in the 19th century. In that remarkable movement, the need for repair was made the excuse for those reconstructural excesses of which the theory (that of preservation) and the practice (that of drastic renewal) were contradictory.

It would be good, in our amazing day, if we could feel that we had learnt the lessons of these two sayings; but, frankly, I doubt it. In spite of the dangers from inflation, traffic and pollution, we must see to it that that which waxeth old does not necessarily decay, and that though the old order changes, these irreplaceable legacies do not vanish away or get spoilt by irresponsible meddling.

Appendix I: Structural losses

NAVES AND CHAPELS. Bristol Cathedral and Hexham Abbey lost their naves at the Dissolution, and continued without a western limb until modern times, when new naves were erected. Oxford and Carlisle are bereft of a portion of their west ends: at Oxford, demolished by Wolsey to make way for his great quadrangle, and at Carlisle, pulled down by the Cromwellians to provide materials to build up the defences of the city in the Civil War (only two bays remain).[39] Neither of these depredations has been made good.

The following Lady chapels have been destroyed: at Norwich, Tewkesbury and Romsey at the Reformation, Peterborough about 1662, Southwark in 1830,[40] and Hexham in 1858. A new chapel was erected between the wars at the east end of Norwich as a war memorial.

St Saviour's Southwark (now the cathedral) also lost its fine Early English nave and St Mary Magdalene's parochial chapel in the 1820s and 1830s. Its beautiful retrochoir only narrowly escaped a like fate after hot disputes between the 'antiquarians' and the 'progressives', not only within St Saviour's vestry itself (some members of which wanted to rebuild the whole church), but also in the pages of the *Gentleman's Magazine* and other periodicals. Besides these losses, the whole exterior, except the tower, was refashioned by George Gwilt.

TOWERS AND SPIRES. There was originally a detached campanile on the south side of Canterbury Cathedral (destroyed by an earthquake in 1382), and in the 16th century detached bell-towers were quite numerous, including important examples at St Paul's, Westminster Abbey and Salisbury; but none survive except those at Chichester, Elstow and Evesham and the ruined Gundulph's Tower at Rochester. (At Evesham the church itself has disappeared.) Others known to have existed were at Worcester, Tewkesbury, Lichfield, Norwich and Llandaff (ruins remain at Llandaff). At Cambridge a cloister and splendid campanile were designed for King's College chapel (but never built),[41] perhaps inspired by Magdalen's famous tower at Oxford. There is a more modest bell-tower at New College, Oxford.

LEAD-COVERED SPIRES formerly adorned many of our Greater Churches, ranging in size from the lofty examples at Old St Paul's and Lincoln's central towers, to the little needle spires at Ely and St Albans. It is remarkable that none at all remain – not counting those capping the two diminutive Norman towers at Canterbury and the twelve corner turrets of Lincoln's three towers (all no doubt renewed, those at Canterbury certainly so). The great spires at St Paul's and Lincoln were destroyed by storms in the mid 16th century but the smaller western spires at the latter church survived until 1807. Carlisle's small spire and Durham's two slender western ones were removed in the mid 17th century as were the three at Ripon – these last must have given the church an outline similar to that of Lichfield. Canterbury's northwest tower, of Norman date, was crowned with a great spire until it was blown down in the fearful storm that swept over England in 1703 – the tower itself survived until 1834. Other spires taken down in the 18th and 19th centuries were at St Margaret's, King's Lynn (south-west), Peterborough (north-west), Hereford and Rochester (central), the two, square on plan, at Southwell (west), and the needle spires at St Albans and Ely. After a long interval new spires have now replaced the old at Rochester and Southwell. Lastly, at Chester the lofty 16th-century western tower of St John's church fell down on Good Friday 1881, and was not rebuilt. It destroyed the Early English north porch.

14. Exeter nave about 1785, with the stalls and pulpit for nave sermons (J. Pierce).

At St Albans the great tower bore a wooden lantern from the 13th to the 15th centuries. Exeter (north), Peterborough (central) and Romsey had large wooden cages for the bells on their towers, but only the one at Romsey survives. Drake [42] tells us there was set up in 1666 on York's central tower 'a turret of wood covered with lead and glazed' as a beacon in case of a landing by the Dutch or French, with whom we were then at war. When he wrote, York also had a small prayer-bell turret on the south-west corner of the great tower; and 18th-century prints show a similar one on top of Wells' central tower. Beverley Minster's whimsical lead-covered dome was removed around 1824.

Appendix II: Liturgical and other changes

NAVE SERMONS. Before the middle of the 19th century, for purposes of comfort, cathedral services were virtually always confined to the choir which was enclosed by screens and curtains for warmth. But at a number of minsters there is evidence of the use of the nave for hearing the sermon. At Wells a fine stone pulpit was erected in the nave by Bishop Knight (1540–47), the entrance to which is through Treasurer Hugh Sugar's chantry chapel. At Bath Bishop Montague (1608–16) likewise donated a handsome stone pulpit for the nave,[43] and at Exeter an 18th-century print of the nave shows pulpit and seats for the congregation. A 'plan' of 1635 of Chichester's nave shows seating around 'the sermon place',[44] and at

7

122

14

Beverley there were carefully made nave furniture and fittings. At Ely Browne Willis's plan shows a pulpit attached to the second pier of the nave on the south side from the Norman pulpitum (see page 88). At Worcester the present choir pulpit of stone was originally at the west end of the nave, with seats for the people and dignitaries. But this was a special case, as they appear to have been used by the puritanical faction, while the choir housed the Episcopalians.[45]

This transition of the congregation from choir to nave and back again must have effectually disrupted services. Was it caused by a desire to stretch the legs during the long services then prevalent, or was it made necessary by extra people coming in only for the sermon? Only from the late 1850s were the naves of our cathedrals regularly used for services, and these were called 'special' services, i.e. other than the statutory ones (Matins, Holy Communion, Evensong).

FONTS. These seem always to have been located outside the choir, usually in the nave or occasionally in the transept. (See Boyle[46] for the movements of the Durham pre-Cromwellian font.) Was baptism a separate service from those in the choir? If not, a further disrupting of services!

OTHER USES. Portions of these Greater Churches were, at least after the Reformation, appropriated to other uses. At Ely the Lady chapel was a parish church until recent times (see page 82); at Chichester the north transept and its chapel was St Peter's the Great church until 1853.[47] Some parts of the following cathedrals have also been parochial: at Chester the wide south transept; at Carlisle the remaining two bays of the nave; at Norwich St Luke's chapel (font remains). At St Albans the Lady chapel was a school until 1870; at Chichester and Hereford the Lady chapel and at Peterborough the 'New Work' (at the east end) were libraries.[48] Since 1814 the east aisle of the south transept at Ely has also been a library.[49] There the south-west transept was partitioned off as 'The Work House' (Willis's plan 1730), and later used as a workroom for repairs until around 1845.

St Giles, Edinburgh, first parochial, then collegiate (1467), then cathedral (mid 17th century), and from 1578 until 1870 divided into three or four separate churches, was by the great restoration of 1872–83 internally unified once more – a very epitome, in its many changes, of Scottish ecclesiastical history.

134

134

Bibliography

1 EARLY ACCOUNTS

Leland, c. 1535. The Itinerary of John Leland – c. 1535–43, ed. Lucy Toulmin Smith. 4 vols, 1907–10. He has little to say about cathedrals – abbeys and priories interested him more.

Topographical Excursion, 1634. 'A Relation of a Short Survey of Twenty-Six Counties, briefly describing the Cities and their Scytuations, and the Corporate Towns and Castles therein; observed in a Seven Weekes Journey begun at the City of Norwich and from thence into the north – on Monday, August 11th, 1634, and ending at the same place. By a Captain, a Lieutenant and an Ancient (Ensign); all three of the Military Company in Norwich.' Brit. Museum Lansdowne ms, no. 213, fol. 315–45. Ed. L. G. Wickham Legg, 1904 (Stuart Series, VII). Among other places, they visited Lichfield, Worcester, Bristol and Bath. The writer, the Lieutenant, was named Hammond.

Topographical Excursion, 1635. 'A Relation of a Short Survey of the Western Counties . . . observed in a seven weekes journey. . . . By the same Lieutenant that with the Captain and Ancient of the Military Company in Norwich made a journey into the North the Yeare before.' In same ms, fol. 347–84. Ed. Wickham Legg for the Royal Historical Society, published in the *Camden Miscellany*, XVI, 1936. Includes visits to Winchester, Salisbury, Peterborough and Ely.

Ryves, 1646. Bruno Ryves, *Mercurius Rusticus; or the countries complaint of the barbarous outrages committed by the sectaries of this late flourishing kingdom.* 19 nos. from Aug. 1642. Ryves (1596–1677), Dean of Windsor, later of Chichester, was noted for 'his florid preaching'. Republished 1646, 1647, 1685, with a finely engraved frontispiece in compartments (?).

Evelyn's Diary, 1641–c. 1705. Ed. E. S. de Beer, 6 vols, 1955.

Pepys's Diary, 1659–69. Various edns.

Fiennes, 1888. Celia Fiennes, *Round England on a Side-Saddle in the Time of William and Mary 1689–1702.* Interesting but often far from reliable.

Defoe, 1724–26. Daniel Defoe, *A Tour through the Whole Island of Great Britain.* Many edns after his death in 1731, each with interesting additions and alterations.

Magna Britannia, 1727. Magna Britannia et Hibernia, Antiqua et Nova – A New Survey of Great Britain . . . By an Impartial Hand. 6 vols, 1727 & later.

2 GRAPHIC RECORDS

Dugdale, 1655. Sir William Dugdale, *Monasticon Anglicanum*, 3 vols, 1655–73, with 114 etched pls (abridged into 1 vol., 1718). Most valuable as record of drawings and etchings of the time by: (1) *Wenceslaus Hollar* (1607–77). His etchings were of high artistic quality but sometimes contained unaccountable errors of draughtsmanship, e.g. at Salisbury and Lichfield. About 42 pls drawn and etched by Hollar, and 7 etched by him from others' designs. (2) *Daniel King* drew and etched 27 pls, and etched 20 from others' designs, all for vol. I. Pls of Peterborough, Selby and Beverley are valuable. Pls both drawn and etched by him are atrocious. (3) Other lesser known artists who worked mainly as draughtsmen: *Richard Newcourt, Thomas Johnson, Richard Hall, Robert Vaughan, Richard Ralinson* and *Edward Mascall.*

English edn of *Monasticon, 1718.* Pls of original vol. I reprinted almost as before; 12 new views in II and III, inc. Bristol. All Hollars omitted or replaced by poorer ones. King had died c. 1664, but at least 14 of his views appear among the replacements. New names of draughtsmen and etchers appear.

King, 1656. Daniel King, *The Cathedral and Conventual Churches of England and Wales orthographically delineated by Daniel King.* Consisted of King's 47 etchings and the other 60 or so (inc. Hollar's) from vol. I of *Monasticon.* Did Dugdale originally commission King to make his drawings and then, disappointed with them, allow him to publish them separately by way of compensation for terminating the contract?

The following three books also contain splendid examples of Hollar's skill in drawing and etching:
Dugdale, 1658. Sir W. Dugdale, *History of St Paul's Cathedral.*
Ashmole, 1672. Elias Ashmole, *Institution, Laws and Ceremonies of the . . . Order of the Garter.*
Sandford, 1677. Francis Sandford, *Genealogical History of the Kings and Queens of England.*

Buck, 1721–49. Samuel and Nathaniel Buck, *Antiquities of England and Wales.* 3 vols of 396 pls (mostly ruined abbeys and castles), no text.

3 ILLUSTRATED HISTORICAL AND ARCHITECTURAL RECORDS

Grose, 1772–87. Francis Grose, *The Antiquities of England and Wales.* Alphabetical order. 4 vols 1772–76, 2 vols 1777–87. Said to have been issued separately (folder and plate) and that few 'sets' are alike. The 2-vol. supplement has more *unruined* churches than the others. (He also ed. *The Antiquarian Repertory, A Miscellaneous Assemblage of Topography, History . . .*, 1807–09, 4 vols, over 200 ills.)

Browne Willis, 1727, 1730. Browne Willis, *A Survey of the Cathedrals of York, Durham, Carlisle, Chester, Manchester, Lichfield, Hereford, Worcester, Gloucester and Bristol,*

2 vols, 1727. *A Survey of . . . Lincoln, Ely, Oxford and Peterborough,* 1 vol., 1730. 2nd edn 1742, 3 vols.

Wild, 1807–23. Charles Wild, *Architectural Illustrations* of the cathedrals of Canterbury (1807), York (1809), Lichfield (1813), Chester (1813), Lincoln (1819) and Worcester (1823). Splendid aquatints. (He also produced *Twelve Beautiful Specimens of Ecclesiastical Architecture of the Middle Ages . . . Cathedrals of England,* n.d., c. 1830?, magnificent aquatints, no text.)

Britton, 1814–35. John Britton, *Cathedral Antiquities,* 6 vols: Salisbury (1814), Norwich (1816), Winchester (1817), York (1819), Lichfield (1820), Canterbury (1821), Oxford (1821), Wells (1824), Exeter (1826), Peterborough (1828), Gloucester (1829), Bristol (1830), Hereford (1831) and Worcester (1835). Superb engravings. (He also issued octavos on St Mary Redcliffe, Bristol, 1813, and Bath Abbey, 1825, and 5 vols of *Architectural Antiquities,* 1807–26.)

Storer, 1814–19. James Storer, *History and Antiquities of Cathedral Churches of Great Britain,* 4 vols. 248 'highly-finished engravings . . . by James Storer'. (Includes Welsh but not Scottish or Irish cathedrals.)

Buckler, 1822. John Chessell Buckler, *Views of Cathedral Churches of England and Wales.* 42 pls (mostly accurate), with descriptions.

Winkles, 1836–42. B. Winkles, *Illustrations of the Cathedral Churches of England and Wales,* 3 vols: 1836 (2nd edn 1838), 1838, 1842. Reissue (addition of Manchester) 1860. Steel engravings by Winkles, taken from drawings by Robert Garland, architect, and other artists.

Coney, 1842. John Coney, *Ecclesiastical Edifices of the Olden Time – A Series of Etchings . . .,* 2 vols. (1st issued to ill. Dugdale's *Monasticon,* 8-vol. edn 1817–36.) 241 pls inc. beautifully drawn seals, figures of monks and nuns (some copies of Hollar), and arms of abbeys.

Vallance 1947. Aymer Vallance, *Greater English Church Screens* (1947). Very valuable and profusely illustrated.

4 19TH- AND 20TH-CENTURY GUIDES

Murray's Handbooks, 1861–79. England (6 vols 1861–69), Wales (1 vol. 1873), St Albans (1 vol. 1877), St Paul's (1 vol. 1879, abridged from Dean Milman's *Annals of St Paul's,* 1868). All ill. with careful wood engravings. Reissued later. For this book: Winchester, Salisbury (1861), Ely, Peterborough (1862), Bristol, Worcester, Lichfield (1864).

Bell's Cathedral Series, c. 1897–1914. Introductory vol. and separate vols on all English and Welsh cathedrals, and other Greater Churches. Salisbury (1896), Winchester, Peterborough, Lichfield, Beverley (1898), Worcester (1900), Bristol, Ely, Bath (1901). For details see chapter bibliographies.

Pevsner, 1951–74. Nikolaus Pevsner, *The Buildings of England*, by counties. For this book: Cambs. (1954), W. Riding Yorks. (1957), N. Somerset, Bristol and Bath (1958), Northands (1961), Wilts. (1963), Hants (1967), Worcs. (1968), E. Riding Yorks. (1972), Staffs. (1974). New edns conform to new boundaries.

Pitkin Pictorials (Pride of Britain Series), on cathedrals and Greater Churches. From the 1950s onwards, not dated until the later 1960s. New edns, with different ills, always appearing. Valuable for up-to-date pictures and information. For details see chapter bibliographies.

Annual Reports and other publications of the Friends of cathedrals. These bodies of well-wishers originated in Chester, and were soon followed by others until now, I believe, all cathedrals have their Friends. Interesting articles on aspects of cathedral life and work, and fabric and fittings – some of it of outstanding value.

5 ARTICLES IN PERIODICALS

Gentleman's Magazine, 1731–1868 (after which its interest declined, and the first fifty years show little of architectural interest). For easy reference see Sir Laurence Gomme's Gentleman's Magazine Library: *Sacred and Medieval Architecture*, 2 vols, 1890, 1891; *Ecclesiology*, 1 vol., 1894; *Topography* by counties, 14 vols, 1891–1902; *London*, 3 vols, 1904–05; and *Architectural Antiquities*, 2 vols.

The Ecclesiological Society's publications. The soc., founded in 1839 in Cambridge, had several changes of name. Its journal was known in turn as the *Transactions of the Cambridge Camden Society*, *The Ecclesiologist*, *Transactions of the St Paul's Ecclesiological Society*, and now as *The Ecclesiological Society Transactions*. Under the first two names (to *c.* 1880) it published many passionate – even vitriolic – articles and letters advocating a return to 'Christian design' (i.e. Gothic) as against 'pagan' (i.e. Classical) in cathedral 'restoration'. This attitude, coinciding with the Oxford Movement for more dignity and ceremony in services, helps explain the often wholesale eviction from Greater Churches of all postmedieval furniture and fittings, however fine.

It is also well worth consulting *The Builder*, *The Architect*, publications of the Society of Antiquaries (*Archaeologia*, etc.), the journals of the Archaeological Institute of Great Britain and the British Archaeological Association, and of local architectural and archaeological societies. Lastly, and very importantly, cathedral archives and municipal libraries generally contain authoritative records and original drawings, rare prints and often old photographs, all of the greatest value in tracing the many changes in our Greater Churches.

Notes

1 The fact that a fair number of monastic naves survived the Dissolution, while the rest of the great church was demolished or left to go to ruin, was due to their allowed use as parish churches. These continued to exist as such and sometimes the whole converted church was purchased by the parishioners – or the nave exchanged for the monks' choir – see Appendix II.

2 Mostly in Dugdale, *Monasticon*, III (1673).

3 See G. Cobb, article on King, *Antiquaries Journal* 1975, LIV, pt II, 299.

4 See article by Rowland Pearce, *Antiquaries Journal* 1963.

5 Unless they had been altered in Decorated or Perpendicular times!

6 W. Sparrow Simpson, *Chapters in the History of Old St Paul's* (1881), 269.

7 A fee claimed by choir-boys from any person entering the church wearing spurs.

8 Sparrow Simpson, *op. cit.*, 238, 277–78.

9 *Ibid.*, 278–80.

10 *Topographical Excursion* (1634).

11 Sparrow Simpson, *op. cit.*, 278–80.

12 Rev. S. Shaw, *History and Antiquities of Staffordshire* (1798), I, 242–43.

13 Sparrow Simpson, *Gleanings from Old St Paul's* (1889), 282–83.

14 Hacket rebuilt the central spire and the great W window (removed 1869), and refurnished the choir. At Durham Cosin supplied remarkable new Gothic choirstalls and towering font canopy (and charming Classical font), and erected a splendid Classical organ-screen (on which, in 1683, was placed a magnificent organ to match).

15 See E. M. Below, *Our Churches* (1900), 67–73.

16 See article by R. A. Cordingley, 'Cathedral Innovations', *Ancient Monuments Society*, 1955, III, 39–44.

17 The case of St Albans and Lord Grimthorpe was exceptional – a newly constituted cathedral was without funds in a crisis and Grimthorpe got himself the job, *carte-blanche*, by offering to pay for the work out of his own pocket in return for complete freedom of action.

18 J. Perkins, *Westminster Abbey, Its Worship and Ornaments*, I 1938, 131–46, II 1940, III 1952.

19 J. Ralph, *Critical Review of the Public Buildings . . . of London and Westminster* (1734), 86.

20 Charles Ball, *Historical Account of Winchester with Descriptive Walks* (1818).

21 At Bristol Scott suggested clearing the E limb, bringing the choir forward and rebuilding the nave. But when, in pursuance of this advice the screen was removed, he disclaimed all responsibility for it.

22 But he has two things to his credit: he built the present Prebends Bridge (1770s) and added the effective parapet and pinnacles to the W towers.

23 Cordingley, *op. cit.*, 39, says he was chapter architect, and that Wyatt, apart from reporting the chapter house to be 'in a ruinous state' (denied by Carter), had nothing to do with its destruction.

24 *Ibid.*, 39; John R. Boyle, *Comprehensive Guide to the County of Durham* (1892), 209.

25 He scraped the east end and rebuilt the rose window – it is said, to his own design, but Nicholson's engraving of 1780 (fifteen years before Wyatt's arrival in Durham) shows the same design as at present, a Perpendicular rendering of a 13th-c. original (which must have been a twin of the western rose of Notre-Dame, Paris).

26 Boyle, *op. cit.*, 210.

27 See pl. in Storer.

28 *If* it was a Gothic church being 'restored' renovat

35 That is, as a work of art; from a religious point of view it was widely condemned as too ritualistic.

36 The Thistle chapel, by Sir R. Lorimer, is a fine example of modern intricate craftsmanship – architecture, carving, glass and enamel.

37 Of the late 17th or early 18th c.

38 A parallel example was the between-the-wars replacing of the remarkable 17th-c. wooden fan 'vault' over the nave of St Botolph's, Boston, by a flat ceiling – the more deplorable as the old roof was of course not destroyed by enemy action as at Llandaff.

39 They also demolished the cloister and chapter house. See Department of Environment Handbook, *Carlisle Castle* (1937), 9.

40 Assuming that the 'bishop's chapel' was originally the Lady chapel.

41 See pl. in Lyson, *Cambridgeshire* (1808), 216.

42 Drake, *The History and Antiquities of the City of York* (1736).

43 Ill. in Peach's Britton's *Bath Abbey* (1881), 66.

44 Ill. in *Sussex Archaeological Collection*, L, 184.

45 Other cathedrals which had nave sermons were Salisbury, Oxford, Hereford and Bristol – see plans in Browne Willis (1730).

46 Boyle, *op. cit.*, 255.

47 Corlette (Bell), 46; but Mackenzie Walcot, *Memorials of Chichester* (1865) says 1844.

48 At Chichester the library is now housed in the chapel of the N transept (the old chancel of St Peter's church).

49 Stubbs, 95.

15. Hereford: Scott's metalwork screen, now dismantled and stored in a museum.

Bath

THE IMMEDIATE predecessor of Bath Abbey was a great Norman church, begun in the 1090s by Bishop John de Villula of Tours (1088–1123) as his cathedral of the Somerset diocese. It was about four hundred feet long – nearly twice the length of the present church – but, probably in consequence of Bath's becoming subordinate to Wells, it fell into disrepair and by 1500 was quite ruinous.[1]

Bishop Oliver King (1495–1503), following a vision which he is reputed to have had in the palace at Bath, determined to rebuild the church but, for reasons of expense, on a very reduced scale. It covers only the nave of Villula's cathedral and has had a strangely chequered existence.

Left unfinished at the Dissolution of the monasteries, stripped of its roofing and of everything saleable, its carcass was eventually (1560) given to the Corporation of Bath for a parish church. Then followed a painfully slow process of repair, which eventually, at least as regards the cost, became a fine piece of team-work. (Very many contributions are fully recorded.) But although the choir was fitted up for divine service and reconsecrated some time after 1588,[2] the church was not fully roofed until the reign of James I. From the 17th to the early 19th centuries many changes were made in the fittings, but structurally it remained substantially unaltered.

In 1833, however, the Corporation began an extensive restoration of the church, costing over £10,000, which affected both interior and exterior, and included new pinnacles and flying buttresses. The architect was G. P. Manners. Even more drastic was Sir G. G. Scott's restoration under the Rev. Charles Kemble (1860–74), who himself contributed generously towards the cost[3] (see below).

The exterior

In the early 17th century the exterior was concealed by numerous houses, especially along the north side, built by the Corporation of Bath on the abbey precinct which it had bought after 1584. As Peach says:[4] 'Around the abbey they built houses, dens, shops, taverns, so closely that they hugged her as it were in a tight unholy embrace, which for 250 years polluted and disgraced her very life.' To a modern eye, these buildings look picturesque rather than otherwise. 'So completely did these buildings cover the ground that all egress to the Grove on the east from the Churchyard on the west was blocked' and the north aisle of the abbey, which had an entrance at each end, became a common thoroughfare to these places. This so disgusted Marshal Wade that he caused a passage to be made through the houses from east to west, called Wade's Alley – how this was effected is hard to imagine.

In 1816 the Rev. Francis Skurray preached a sermon in the abbey: 'How doth it offend the eye of taste when we consider [the abbey's] beautiful exterior screened from public view by crowded and incongruous deformities.' This aroused public concern and led to a clearance of the houses between 1824 and 1835.

The restoration of 1833 under Manners involved dramatic changes to the exterior. High and low pinnacles were erected along choir and nave, and hollow flying buttresses added to the latter! The turrets of the (hitherto unspired) tower and those of the west and east ends of the church were provided with tall crocketted spires, to receive which the eastern turrets were converted at the top from rectangular to octagonal. (These spires in fact replaced earlier short open-work ones which had formerly crowned both ends but had disappeared by 1816. Malton's and other old prints show slight open-work pinnacles at the transept fronts as well.) The restoration of the roofs of the choir-aisles is described by Peach in 1887:[5]

These aisles were covered with leaden roofs in 1520, and denuded thereof by Henry VIII about 1539; and

16. The west door after 1901. Scott restored the whole front substantially to its original appearance, but did not complete the canopies to the niches. These were finished in 1901, and a new statue of Henry VII by George Frampton added above the door.

supplied, in 1558, by Peter Chapman Esq., and others, with the late heavy parapet wall and stone and wood roofs in the shape of a V, having the aquaduct at the base of the V; one wing of which, leaning on the windows of the choir, caused them to be deprived of the glass to the height of five feet, and in lieu thereof to be built up with stone. . . . The other wing of the V rested against the ponderous parapet wall, which obscured the fine bases and proportions of the . . . flying buttresses. These heavy parapet walls are now [1833–34] being partly removed, the stone blocking up the windows taken out, and replaced with glass and the new sloping roof covered with lead, which is placed in the identical grooves of the lead roof of 1520.

He also mentions that the main roofs of the choir and transepts which had been raised about two feet above their original level of 1520, were also now lowered and covered with lead, again placed in the original grooves against the tower, thus matching Bishop Montague's unaltered, lower and lead covered, nave roof.[6]

16 The fine west front, unique in England with its symbolical decoration, had heavily carved doors which had been presented by Bishop Montague's kinsman Sir Henry Montague in 1617. These were now 'repaired and recarved at the expense of the Corporation' by a Mr James Jones.[7]

22
23 Scott, beginning in 1859, replaced Manners's hollow flying buttresses with solid ones (to support his intended fan vault) and substituted open-work battlemented parapets along the nave, transept and choir for the lower and simpler ones which had been there before (mostly pre-Manners). The new parapets were based on the original ones on the gable and choir-aisle ends (the latter formerly plain and horizontal).

Scott also restored the west front aisle parapets to what they had been before being altered by Manners, and commenced a general restoration of the west front which through lack of funds came to a halt – it seems, before he died in 1878. Among the other things he achieved was the replacement of Manners's spires on the turrets with lower, open-work ones as before 1816. He renewed the crocketted canopies over the Apostles each side of the ladders, the angels at the top of which had become unrecognizable through decay, and substituted blocks of stone to be carved later. He also removed three canopies by the west door, two large and one small, with a view to renewal. The two larger ones sheltered time-worn statues of Saints Peter and Paul. In the event, however, they had to
16 brave the weather for another twenty years, until 1895, when new canopies were added. Work on the

26 west front, including new angels, was completed by Sir T. G. Jackson (architect), George Frampton (sculptor) and Farmer and Brindley (carvers). Frampton also contributed two new figures – Christ above the great west window and Henry VII above the main door. Since then other items of sculpture have been renewed.

25 Early in the 20th century (c. 1908) the turrets of the east end and of the tower received new open
24 crocketted spires (those on the tower carrying vanes) in place of Manners's slightly taller solid ones. In 1923 a covered cloister designed by Jackson was erected along the south side of the nave as a war memorial to the 1914–18 War.

The interior

We have no views of the interior as it was originally. The first choir-screen (appearance unknown) was paid for by Thomas Bellot or Billet, steward and later executor of Lord Burleigh. He was conspicuous for his gifts, which also included £60 for the glazing of the east window with 'variegated coloured glass in mathematical but
30 picturesque manner, which he called "billet-
37 wise", being a play upon his own name'.[8] This remained until 1872.

Bishop James Montague (1608–16) contributed £1,000 for covering the nave and aisles with charming plaster ceilings and providing a fine
32, 41 stone pulpit. The bishop was buried in the nave
27 under a handsome monument. A description of the interior (evidently before 1725) says: 'The Quire is adorned with a good organ, but the pews and gallery are irregular and the altar is very mean.'[9]

The earliest views of the interior show it as it was from about 1725 to 1825. The choir-screen consisted of a low wooden partition with six Doric columns supporting a gallery on which was a fine organ by Abraham Jourdain, set up in 1708. (The space between was later glazed.) The organ and screen, with Bishop Montague's nave pulpit, are
27 well shown in Vertue's splendid engraving of 1750 which also depicts, through the screen, Wade's
28 Baroque altarpiece and magnificent altar-rails and the canopy of the choir pulpit and what look like stalls. Prior Bird's chantry chapel was filled with seats 'for noblemen and men of worshipp', and mutilated to receive monuments and what Warner called 'the clumsy mis-shapen wooden seat called the Bishop's Throne'[10] (appearance unknown). There were galleries in the choir, two on the south
31 and one on the north. Nattes' engraving of 1806 shows the handsome three-decker choir pulpit

with ogee-topped sounding board, also the blocked-up lower parts of the clerestory windows as described by Peach (see p. 26). The altarpiece by Samuel Trufnell, presented by Wade in 1725, was 'of costly marble, veined black, gold and purple' in the Rococo style of the period. The central compartment had a picture representing the Adoration of the Magi – by 'Mr Robinson of London'.[11] According to Hick,[12] Wade also presented velvet cushions and silk curtains for the choir in 1726.[13]

In 1825, at the instance of Bishop Law (1824–45), various improvements were effected to the interior, including 'a new gallery in front of the organ and a new Gothic screen designed by Manners[14] erected under the tower'.

Great changes were made by Manners in 1833 and later. Wade's altarpiece was sold in that year and, according to Hick,[15] removed to the palace at Wells, but Peach (1887) says 'it was sold some years ago and now forms one side of the hall at Grosvenor Villa'. It is still there, but partially dismembered. Also in 1833, the splendid wrought-iron communion-rail was disposed of to William Beckford, and for over a century it functioned as a balcony to his house in Lansdowne Place West. In 1959 it was returned to the abbey and arranged in two tiers as a grille under the present organ.

At the same time the spandrels at the top of the great square-headed east window were stopped up (on the inside), which must have been a decided improvement, for the square head accords ill with the two-centred arch of the fan vault; but they were opened up again in 1872. A photograph of about 1860 shows the exterior with 'billet' glass in the whole window, with sun and moon in spandrels, and engravings around 1850 show the interior *without spandrels*.

Up to 1834 both the walls and the pillars of the church were encrusted with monuments – over six hundred of them. Those on the pillars were then removed and eventually joined the wall monuments to make a continuous series of tablets beneath the aisle windows, forming an amazing collection of sculpture and inscriptions – pious, touching, fulsome, pompous, allegorical, historical, anecedotal, diverting or boring.

The old organ, after being extended farther towards the nave, was finally removed[16] and replaced by an enormous new instrument, whose Gothic case extended in front of and above the springing of the western tower arch, and with the screen below effectively blotted out all but a small glimpse of the choir vault.

Manners's doings were approved by Tunstall, who says:[17]

The irregular pews were removed and the present more appropriate ones substituted; the old galleries, with their boarded backs and glazed doors were condemned; the inappropriate organ loft was replaced by an elegant screen, designed by Mr Blore after the model of Prior Bird's oratory; the Roman fittings up behind the communion-table, with Marshal Wade's unsuitable altarpiece, were removed, and the whole choir now looks as it ought to do, strictly appropriate to the original style of the building.

When Bishop Montague's pulpit went is uncertain, but the bishop's throne was sold under Manners, and Prior Bird's chantry fully restored by Edward Davis, who published an illustrated monograph on it in 1834. In this he described its sorry condition before his repairs: 'its fronts defaced by monuments, its lower compartments ... blocked up, while those parts permitted to remain exposed were washed and rewashed with coats of different hues until all sharpness of the carving was lost'.

The clock, which was removed from the tower to the gable of the north transept, is described by Peach as follows:[18] 'The machinery connecting the clock and hands is extremely ingenious, and reflects great credit on Mr Lautier (a well-known clockmaker who lived for many years in Bridge Street). The rods which convey the power are seventy-five feet in length; the horizontal rod is the full length of the transept, and is supported on friction-rollers, so skilfully constructed as to counteract the action of heat or cold on metallic bodies.'

But within thirty years of Manners's improvements, so praised by Tunstall in 1847, taste had changed, and under Scott almost all Manners's furniture was thrown out and the interior opened out from end to end.

This complete clearance of Manners's furniture must have left the interior looking bare and empty. Only the screen of 1825 was spared: it was removed to the west end and re-formed, with traceried woodwork filling the arches, to act as an inner porch, but is now gone.[19] But the new Victorian stained glass contributed some colourful warmth. Bellot's glass in the east window was removed to the north clerestory around 1872, to be replaced by a splendid window by Clayton and Bell.[20]

Scott's new furniture included an ineffective stone reredos (originally containing the Decalogue,

Lord's Prayer and Creed), elaborate altar-rails, almost suggesting Art Nouveau, and finely carved stalls and pulpit by Farmer and Brindley. Especially striking were the intricate metal gasoliers of fifteen lights by Skidmore of Coventry. These are now converted to electricity. But both the great central burner of 120 lights, painted and gilt, and the two standard candelabra of 107 lights, also by Skidmore,[21] are now gone.

Lastly, Scott removed Bishop Montague's attractive plaster ceilings over nave and aisles – a great pity – and erected stone fan vaults identical to those in the choir.[22]

Between 1930 and 1939 the interior was enriched by additions each side of the east window, containing four statues carved by F. Brook Hitch from designs by A. G. Walker; they represent St Alphege, St Dunstan, John de Villula and Bishop Oliver King. At the same time Scott's reredos was modified by the removal of the Decalogue.[23]

During World War II the glass of the east window was badly damaged (1942), but it was repaired in 1955 by M. C. Farrer Bell, great-grandson of the designer. The shields in the fourth window of the north aisle were taken from the clerestorys after the bombing of 1942.

Bibliography

Carter, 1798. John Carter, *Some account of the Abbey Church of Bath*. 10 architectural engraved drawings including fine plan.

Warner, 1801, 1811. Rev. R. Warner, *History of Bath*. 2 vols, 2nd smaller and clearer.

* Britton, 1825. John Britton, *The History and Antiquities of Bath Abbey Church*. 10 fine engravings including fine plan.

Tunstall, 1847. James Tunstall, MD, *Rambles About Bath and Its Neighbourhood*. 3rd edn 1856.

Peach's Britton, 1887. R. E. M. Peach, Britton's work (1825) reprinted and continued to the present with additional notes.

Peach, 1888. R. E. M. Peach, *Bath, Old and New – a Handy Guide and a History*. 2nd edn. 1891.

* Perkins (Bell), 1901. Rev. T. Perkins, MA, *Bath, Malmsbury and Bradford-on-Avon*, Bell's Cathedral Series.

* see also bibliography to the Introduction.

17. View from the south-east, by Malton, c. 1790. The central tower has no pinnacles, and those of the east end and south transept are of open-work design.

Hick, 1913. E. M. Hick, *The Cathedral Church of SS Peter and Paul ... commonly called Bath Abbey*, Homeland Handbooks. Very useful.

Original Bath Guide, 1762. This edn 1917.

Home and Foord, 1925. G. Home and E. Foord, *Bristol, Bath and Malmsbury*, Cathedrals, Abbeys and Famous Churches Series. Interesting on monuments.

Brakspear, n.d. Sir Harold Brakspear, *The Cathedral Church of St Peter and St Paul at Bath*. 11th edn after 1955, revised and extended by E. M. Hick.

* Wright (Pitkin), 1962. Reginald W. M. Wright, *Bath Abbey*, Pitkin Pictorial, 2nd edn 1973.

Notes

1 *The Itinerary of John Leland* (c. 1535–43), speaking of John de Villula's tomb in the presbytery at Bath, says: 'who's image I saw lying there an nine years sins, at the which tyme al the Chirch that he made lay to wast, and was onrofid, and wedes grew about this John of Tours sepulchre'.
2 Britton, 56.
3 It cost between £32,000 and £48,000. See Hick, 95.
4 Peach's Britton (1887), p. xv.
5 Peach's Britton (1887), 43, apparently quoting from Mainwaring's *Annals in the Record for 1833*.
6 Indications remained (see Malton's and other early prints) to show that flying buttresses were originally intended but, as at York, the eventual wooden ceiling rendered them unnecessary, and hence Manners's hollow flyers are for show only. In *Gentleman's Magazine*, Feb. 1834, pp. 213–15, an interesting article

18. The east end in 1816 (Storer). The pinnacles have been removed. Note the fine 17th-century house abutting the church.

19. View from the north-east in 1829. The 17th-century house has been demolished, but some gabled houses mark the entrance to Wade's Alley.

shows that the pinnacles were erected after much advice against them: 'Mr Garbett, the eminent architect of Winchester' won the day for pinnacles (Peach's Britton, 1887, 44 note). *Gentleman's Magazine*, Feb. 1834, p. 215, sheds light on the hollow flyers: 'Mr Hooking subsequently suggested that if the strength of the wooden roof was suspected, the flying buttresses to the nave might be managed in artificial stone, or in Bath-stone blocks, bored to lighten them'. It is curious that the whole of this passage is practically identical with that in *Gentleman's Magazine*, Feb. 1834, p. 213 (where the V is stupidly put upside down!)

7 See Peach's Britton (1887), 96, for report of the restoration. The work was done 'in a manner most creditable to that able sculptor and a brass plate commemorating these circumstances has been placed behind one of the shields'. It may be assumed that 'recarved' means 'recarved in parts'.

8 Peach's Britton (1887), 69.

9 *Magna Britannia et Hibernia, Antiqua et Nova* (1727), IV, 734.

10 Richard Warner, *The History of Bath* (1801), 250.

11 Information obtained from Bath Reference Library.

12 Hick, 84.

13 Of this 18th-c. interior, Carter writes: it is 'so filled with mortuary lie-traps, theatric galleries and boxes for fashion, folly and religious inattention, that the head and heart of an antiquary are distracted and torn' (*Gentleman's Magazine*, 1802, p. 517). J. Storer, *History and Antiquities of Cathedral Churches of Great Britain* (1814–19), says: 'Prayers are read in it twice every day; but should good sense and sound policy ever unite with a little rational piety, the city will either establish the usual cathedral service here, or resign its patronage to those who would introduce that impressive . . . worship to console the minds and spirits of the numerous invalids who annually visit Bath.' But, visually, the old interior

must have been attractive.

14 But Tunstall, 23, says it was designed by Blore.

15 Hick, 84.

16 The organ-case of 1708 appears to have survived until the early 19th c., being shown in three engravings: Vertue (1750), Storer, *op. cit.* (1814) and Britton (1825), but Coney's large etching of 1817 (8 vol. edn of W. Dugdale's *Monasticon Anglicanum*) shows, unaccountably, a quite different case, although the screen below seems largely unaltered. Peach's Britton (1887), 59, says: 'In 1835 . . . the fine old organ was discarded and is now doing duty at Yatton'; but Hick, 38, says: 'This old organ was removed in 1838 to the Chapel of the Bishop's Palace, Wells. Later it was placed in a west gallery at Yatton church. Of its case nothing remains except two figures last heard of at a furniture dealer at Bristol.' Whether this is so or not, these figures were still at Yatton in 1955 (N. Pevsner, *Buildings of England: North Somerset*, 1958, p. 353). They were of Sts Peter and Paul, and with that of King David, still in Bath Abbey, they topped the organ of 1708.

17 Tunstall, 23.

18 Peach's Britton (1887), 43, quoting *Mainwaring's Annals in the Record for 1833*.

19 Brakspear, 20.

20 Clayton and Bell were also responsible for the glass in the great west window and in the south transept.

21 Peach's Britton (1887), 60.

22 To see what the old ceilings of the nave aisles looked like, one should obtain permission to scan the ceiling of the vestry (between the S choir aisle and S transept) which is of the same date and similar design to those Scott so wantonly destroyed (ill. in Wright, Pitkin).

23 Apparently the woodwork was movable: the frontispiece to Perkins (Bell) shows the side arches open to reveal the monuments to Col. Champion and Herman Katencamp each side of the west doorway.

Bath: the exterior

20. The west front in 1797 (*European Magazine*). Note especially the absence of flying buttresses, the open-work pinnacles and the triangular pattern of the aisle parapets. The house on the left marks the west end of Wade's Alley.

21. The west front about 1806 (Coney). The pinnacles have been removed. Here one sees clearly the embryonic flying buttresses of the original building.

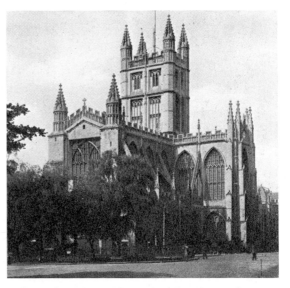

24. View from the north-east, *c.* 1867, with the tall pinnacles designed by Manners.

25. View from the north-east, *c.* 1920. Manners's pinnacles were replaced about 1908 by open-work ones like these given by Scott to the west front.

22. The west front in the 1850s, showing Manners's alterations. Flying buttresses have been built on the model of those supporting the choir; open-work pinnacles are replaced by solid, given also to the central tower, and an upright pattern replaces the triangular on the aisle parapets.

23. The west front, *c.* 1890. Scott has restored the pinnacles and parapets to their original appearance. But the angels at the top of the ladders are still blocks of uncarved stone and the canopies flanking the door are missing.

Right
26. The west front after 1901, once more close to its appearance in 1797 (pl. 20) but with the addition of the flying buttresses intended by the original builders.

Bath: the interior 1750–1850

27. The choir in 1750, a print by George Vertue. Through the splendid Georgian choir-screen, surmounted by the organ, can be seen Wade's altarpiece and choir pulpit. The pulpit in the foreground is Bishop Montague's. Note too the roundels of the sun and moon in the corners of the east window.

28, 29. Wade's altarpiece and altar-rails (Vertue). When the altar was dismantled, the rails were reused on a balcony in Lansdowne Place (*below*). They are now back in the abbey.

30. The choir looking east, *c.* 1850. Manners has removed the old screen and altar, replacing the latter with a Gothic reredos, three-decker pulpit, etc. of his own.

32. The nave looking east, 1817 (Storer): the same screen and organ seen from the other side. The plaster ceiling is of the early 17th century and the nave piers still have their clusters of monuments.

31. Nattes' aquatint of the choir looking west, c. 1806. The screen, organ and pulpit, the latter now three-decker, are those of pl. 27, but the stalls do not appear and galleries have been built in the aisles.

33. Nave and choir screen, c. 1817 (Coney), showing a new organ-case and screen doors.

34. The new Gothic screen and organ installed by Manners between 1825 and 1834.

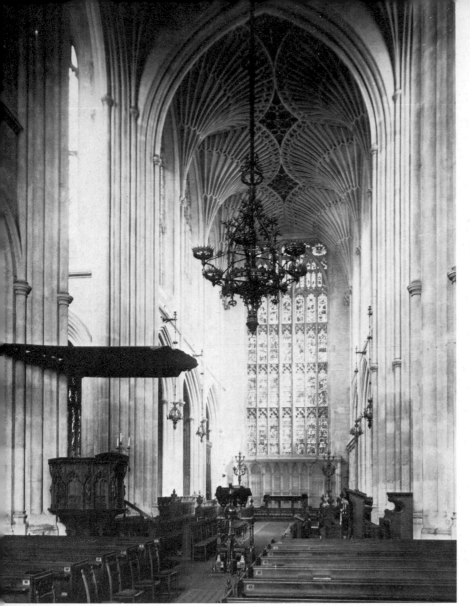

35. Looking east from the nave after Scott's restoration of the 1860s. Almost all the features introduced by Manners have been removed: screen and organ have gone entirely and there is a new pulpit and reredos and new glass in the east window.

36. The east window in 1935, with new niches and statues on either side.

Bath: the interior after 1850

37. The east end in 1851, showing the corners of the windows blocked, an aesthetic improvement. The 'billet glass' and furnishings are the same as in pl. 30.

38. Exterior of the east end before 1872, showing the 'billet glass' installed in the 17th century, and the corners with roundels of sun and moon blocked and invisible from inside.

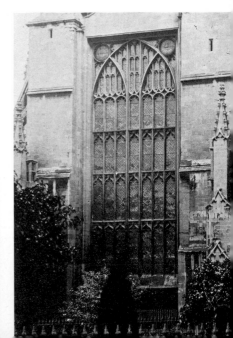

39. Britton's engraving looking across the nave in 1825: a vivid impression of the monuments placed against the pillars, and of the old aisle ceilings, replaced by Scott with fan vaults.

40. When Manners's screen was taken down in 1865, parts of it were reused to make an inner porch at the west end, later removed in its turn. This photograph also shows the new nave vault by Scott, to be compared with that in pl. 32.

41. Plan of Bath Abbey by Carter, showing the old vaulting patterns. Scott covered the nave and its aisles with fan vaults copied from those of the east end. Only the vestry, off the south transept, retains its original ceiling.

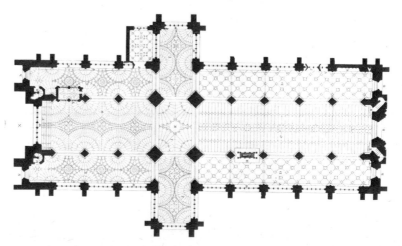

Bristol

THE HISTORY of Bristol Cathedral, in common with that of the nearby Bath Abbey, concerns a partly ruinous church and its subsequent reinstatement – at Bath in the 16th and early 17th centuries, at Bristol in Victorian times.

St Augustine's abbey church, Bristol, founded in 1140,[1] and served by Augustinian canons, was made a cathedral in 1542 by Henry VIII. The following extracts from its sadly depleted records (many destroyed in the Civil War and the riots of 1831), will give a human touch to some of the vicissitudes of the cathedral and its one-time close in the last four hundred years.

The relations between the dean and chapter and the city Corporation were not always cordial. In 1557 the Privy Council wrote to the mayor and aldermen, requiring them 'not to absent themselves' from attending the cathedral church until 'the dean and chapter should wait upon them, or fetch them out of the city with their cross and procession, being the same is very unseemly'.[2] And in 1606 we hear of a gallery near the pulpit made by the Corporation by leave of the dean and chapter. The bishop objected and complained to the archbishop that it made the church look like a playhouse, and he ordered its demolition, but was ordered by the king to restore it. The bishop yielded a grudging obedience, but erected the gallery only three feet from the ground and removed the pulpit too far away to be heard from the new erection! In consequence the Corporation forsook the cathedral and for some years went to St Mary Redcliffe to hear the sermon.[3]

In 1634 three Tourists from Norwich[4] came to Bristol and tell us that 'in [the cathedral] are rich organs, lately beautified; and indifferent good Quiresters'. This organ was destroyed in the Civil War. In 1645, on the surrender of the city to Fairfax, the lead roof of the bishop's palace was stripped off, in wet weather, while Bishop Howell was still there, and his wife in child-bed! She died from exposure while the bishop and his eight children were turned out into the street. He himself died a year later, and the citizens of Bristol undertook the education of his children 'in grateful memory of their most worthy father'. He was buried in the eastern Lady chapel under a stone bearing the one word 'Expergiscar' (I shall awake). Sadly, this stone is now lost.[5]

It is also said that under the Protectorate, the mayor, Walter Deyos, had 'lead stripped from the roofs of the Cathedral and the Cloisters, but that further destruction was prevented by other members of the Corporation'.[6] Barrett[7] says the soldiers 'made the Palace a malthouse . . . and there they grouned at a mill erected there as well as made their malt for several years – and they had it in design to put up a furnace for brewing at the east end of the choir in the place of the altar'.

In Dean Towgood's time (1667–83), a difference broke out between the Corporation and the dean and chapter, first with regard to the bidding prayer, and then as to whether the state sword might be carried erect into the cathedral before the mayor and Corporation. This quarrel lasted some four years, fomented in its origin by Bishop Guy Carleton (1671–78). That hardy campaigner – he had hastened to fight in the royal army though he had already held two livings – fell foul of the chapter for what he considered its lack of spirit, and publicly abused Prebendary Crossman, the leader of the opposition, 'a perjured and saucy fellow who ought to have his gown pulled off his back'.[8] And in 1682 'Mr Heath, the organist, was expelled for keeping a disorderly ale house, in which the death of a tippler had occurred'.[9] The late 17th century was, on the whole, a rather dim period in Bristol.

But things improved in the new century: Brown Willis[10] records that the cathedral 'is truly no elegant structure, being reputed one of the meanest

42, 43. Bristol Cathedral from the north, about 1760 (West and Toms) and in 1938. In the top view houses occupy the site of the present nave; in the foreground is the medieval market cross and on the left the now-demolished church of St Augustine the Less. The later view shows Street's completed nave and west front; the market cross is not the original (removed to Stourhead in the 1760s) but a replica made in 1850; a century later it and the trees were cut down.

Cathedrals in the Kingdom;[11] however, by the generosity and zeal of the present set of members, it is so well adorned that it wants for no cost or art to render it beautiful, and is daily improving, and may be said to be kept in as good repair as any church whatsoever'.

Sadly, things deteriorated again towards the end of the 18th century and the following extract from a newspaper shows that as late as the 1840s philistinism was by no means dead. Latimer quotes a letter in the *Bristol Journal*, 5 April 1845, which states that 'a cast-iron stove with an immense black vertical flue, passing through the beautiful groined roof', had just been placed in the choir of the cathedral!

In 1831, during the riots in support of the Reform Bill, the cathedral was, it seems, nearer to destruction than at any time in its history. The bishop had spoken against the Bill in Parliament, and late at night on 30 October the mob stormed the palace, broke up the bishop's furniture and fired the building. They then broke open the chapter house where the dean and chapter's records were housed, and these were handed out of a window and hurled into a bonfire or the palace flames. The 'reformers' then turned to the cathedral which they attempted to enter 'but were with difficulty induced to abandon' its destruction 'by the tactful cajolery of a private citizen, Mr B. Ralph, who told their drunken leader that no reformer would destroy the people's property'. Bishop Grey had escaped from Bristol that afternoon disguised in a servant's clothes![12]

Of College Green (originally the cemetery of the abbey) the Norwich Tourists of 1634 say: 'neere the Cathedral is a fayre and large College Yard, beautify'd with many shady trees and most delightful walks, about which stands many stately buildings (besides the Bishops Pallace, the Deanes, the Chancellors, and the Prebends Houses),[13] wherein many Gentlemen and Gentlewomen of note doe Live'. In 1709 it is noted that College Green was newly railed, the old trees cut down and new ones planted, and in 1733 that further expenditure was incurred on 'the walks in the College Green'.[14] Fifty-six years later Barrett[15] calls it 'the resort of the gay, the beaux and belles of Bristol to walk in, as in the Mall in London'.

In 1733 the high cross was removed from its original position at the centre of the old city and, after long neglect, erected on the green; but in the 1760s it was again taken down – as an obstruction to the promenaders! It long lay unclaimed and was eventually given by Dean Barton (1763–79) to

Henry Hoare, Esq., of Stourton, Wilts., by whom it was at last appreciated. He erected it at the expense of £300 in the grounds of his seat, Stourhead,[16] where it may still be seen. Curiously, in 1850 a new Civic Cross was erected on the green (architect John Norton) but it too was demolished,[17] on the spoliation of the green in 1950, when all the surrounding trees were uprooted and hundreds of tons of earth removed to make it a windswept sunken lawn.

Thus, with the burning of the bishop's palace in 1831,[18] the demolition of the old deanery (north wing in 1865, the rest before 1906),[19] and the minster house (prior's lodging) in 1882–84, the virtual destruction of the cathedral close was accomplished.

The interior

At the time of the cathedral's foundation by Henry VIII in 1542, the church consisted of only a choir and transepts. It seems that the Norman nave of the abbey church had been ruinous since the 14th century, and so it remained until Abbot Newland (1481–1515) began to rebuild it 'to the soiles of the wyndos of the north side and the west end'. But nothing more was done, and after the Dissolution of the monasteries it appears that the remains, old and new, were cleared away, except for foundations and some fragments adjoining the tower.[20]

The western arches of the tower and transepts were then walled up. In 1629 a window was made in the blocking wall under the tower.[21] Houses were built on the site of the nave. In 1835 these were demolished, but it was not until 1868–88 that a new nave and west front were built to the designs of G. E. Street (see below).

The choir

In 1542 the ancient arrangements seem to have been as follows:

a choirscreen [or pulpitum] where the present screen stands and a rood-screen on the west of the crossing . . . the stalls, dating from *c*. 1520 and the High Altar where they have now been restored. Then in 1542, the old High Altar, steps and reredos and the rood-screen were entirely removed and the Altar of the Eastern Lady Chapel with its 14th century reredos . . . became the principal altar. The ancient Choir Screen was also removed, but a worthy successor, acquired from the dissolved House of the White Friars, was bequeathed to the Cathedral in 1542 by one Thomas White and was erected at the second bay eastwards of the crossing with the stalls immediately east of it. In the ante-chapel thus formed, a pulpit was erected and, in time, pews for hearing of sermons.[22]

43

69

74

71–73

42

A watercolour of 1830[23] depicts this screen. It was 'some five feet thick from east to west, and contained stone stairs to the top from either side of the choir entrance' and was elaborately decorated with heraldic emblems. 'Over the quire door on an oval shield were the words *Vigilate et orate*, and immediately over the doorway on the inside was an old painting of the Last Judgment. On the east side of the pulpitum were the arms of Abbot Elyot [1515–26] on the side of the Dean's stall, and the arms of Berkeley with mermaids as supporters over the stall of the canon in residence. The place of honour on the quire side was occupied by a Tudor rose.'[24] The central feature of the pulpitum (illustrated in Lyson's *Collection of Gloucestershire Antiquaries*, 1804) consisted of a Tudor arch under a square head with elaborate cresting. On the spandrels were sculptured two splendid Tudor roses, the arms of Henry VIII and Prince Edward (later Edward VI) and shields with the device and monogram of Thomas White, the donor of the screen. Several of these details have been saved and incorporated in side screens to the chancel.

In 1561 the dean and chapter were sent a letter from the commissioners for demolition of roods, images and other ornaments of Popish worship, which Britton quotes:[25]

Whereas we are credibly informed that there are divers Tabernacles for Images, as well in the fronture of the Roodloft of the Cath. Church of Bristol, as also in the frontures back and ends of the Walles wheare the Comm Table standeth we . . . require you to cause the said Tabernacles to be defaced, hewen down and . . . to be made a playne walle with morter plaster or otherwise and some scriptures to be written in the places [and upon the east wall of the choir] the commandments to be painted in large characters with convenient speed . . . from London, XXI December 1561.

It is curious that objection should be taken in this letter to 'Tabernacles for Images' if, as the wording seems to imply, they were empty.

Between 1622 and 1632 payments are recorded to a certain John Clarke 'for preparing stone and carving the four Evangelists [which] have been sett upp before the quire door though the work was hindered' and for 'making the arch over the quire door, new stoone stayers up to the organ and preparing the arches for the twelve prophates before the quire doore'.[26] In 1683 a new organ by Renatus Harris was installed on top of this pulpitum.

The 1830 watercolour shows the 'prophates' painted flat on the filled-up niches; they had been plastered over in the Civil War and seemingly forgotten until 1804 when they were uncovered and remained visible until 1860.[27] There is no sign of the stone figures of the four Evangelists, but four tall panelled pedestals may have been intended for them. The organ of 1683 overhung the screen, especially in the centre where it was supported on two huge carved corbels.[28]

When the Lady chapel altar became the high altar of the cathedral in 1542, the reredos probably remained intact until the orders of 1561 just mentioned. Even if the carvings were defaced and plastered over as was instructed, the side panels were later opened out and found to be uninjured, as they remain today. Of the few references to the altarpiece before 1800, I know of two that speak of it as 'gilded and repaired by Deans Towgood and Levett' (1677–83, 1685–93)[29] and as 'embellished with costly painting and gilding'.[30] But a writer of 1727 tells us that 'the altar is very neat and hath an ascent to it of black and white marble steps; and on each side, on a pannel of the wainscot, the painting seems to continue an aisle of the church';[31] while another visitor, in 1753, says that on either side of the altarpiece 'are two painted Galleries on a flat canvass, infinitely superior to anything of the sort I ever saw. Nobody could tell of what master they are, but I take them to be of Serjeant Streater. . . . I have seen some good things in way of him.'[32] Can these paintings be the same as those on the 'pannels of the wainscot' just mentioned? Both postulate a central altarpiece which was then, probably, so usual an object in churches that description was deemed superfluous.

Can the first two of the above extracts refer to the two outer arches of the medieval reredos?[33] If so, this is confirmed by J. Peller Malcolm in 1813 when he says: 'The altarpiece, elevated on fine steps of marble, is almost as the architect of the choir left it. One alteration indeed has occurred. . . . Three magnificent arches, separated by buttresses of three gradations, enriched with crockets and finials filled the space from the pavement to the base of the east window. Two of these are perfect, but the centre is covered by a modern altarpiece of four Corinthian columns enclosing an arch painted with a nimbus (Glory?) by Van Somers [1576–1621] supporting an entablature and circular divided pediment.'[34] This is the only actual description of this Classical reredos that I know of (see note 37).

In the Bristol Museum and Art Gallery there is an unfinished drawing (artist unknown, early 19th century?) which, in its careful delineation of a most handsome altarpiece, confirms and exceeds this description. The altar itself is, amazingly, modelled on a foreign baroque sarcophagus![35] On the back of the drawing is the following curious inscription: 'The minster church of Bristol. Proposed altarpiece from designs projected by Mr Inigo Jones.' A well-known architectural historian confirmed that the design in the drawing could well have been by Jones or his office, and suggested that its general outline was similar to the famous south porch of St Mary's, Oxford, often attributed to Jones. But he knows of no such design for a reredos among Jones's drawings.

This drawing also shows an anachronism hard to explain. 18th-century plans of the cathedral show only one pulpit, the stone one in the ante-choir or nave, given in 1627 by Bishop Wright. Plans after about 1800 show another pulpit, on the north side of the choir, immediately east of the stalls and opposite the bishop's throne. (In the 18th-century plans, this site is marked Arch-deacon of Dorset's stall'.) However, the 'Inigo Jones' drawing shows a fine Wren-period pulpit on the *south* side of the choir and *west* of the stalls, but no throne beyond them; and as the stalls, in all plans before Scott, show them continued to and returned across the east face of the pulpitum, there was no place in the choir in line with the stalls for such a, or any other, pulpit. So the drawing, though so convincingly executed, remains in this particular a mystery.

However, since writing the above, I have discovered the following from Liversage (1853):[36] 'Formerly the sermons were preached from the [1627] pulpit – the congregation, at the conclusion of the Nicene Creed, leaving the choir and ranging themselves on benches about this pulpit; but, in 1821, this inconvenient plan was put an end to; a movable pulpit was placed in the choir, but ultimately, the present pulpit was erected on the spot where the stall of the Archdeacon of Dorset stood; the stall [up to] now occupied by the canon in residence, being appropriated to the Arch-deacon.' If the date '1821' was a misprint for 1801, this passage could well account for the appearance of the wooden pulpit in the 'Inigo Jones' drawing, and would reduce the mystery of why the artist had ended the stalls abruptly each side instead of continuing them out of the picture. Perhaps he thought the pulpit and its ogee tester would not show up against their canopies?

Returning to the altarpiece, from 1800 to Victorian times the numerous, although slight, references to this fine piece of woodwork confirm that it was generally held in abhorrence.[37] It was removed in 1839[38] – a great loss – and disappoint-ingly the central panel of the medieval reredos behind it was found to be quite defaced. This was then restored as the side panels, following a paper reconstruction by Britton.[39]

'In point of taste', Fletcher writes,[40] 'the Chapter of AD 1800 were no better than their con-temporaries. Dreadful work was done at the opening of the new century upon the altarpiece', but he does not say what! He does say that c. 1839[41] 'the east end of the cathedral was restored at a cost limited to £60, and the Grecian altarpiece of 1802 was removed'. What do these statements mean? Was a new reredos made in 1802 from 'Jones's' projected design? Or was an authentic 17th-century one brought from elsewhere and, if so, where could it have come from? These questions give more point to the words 'proposed altarpiece' in the endorsement on the art gallery drawing. But also, why '*Mr* Inigo Jones' 150 years after his death? A second mystery! Fletcher[42] also tells us that at about this time the eagle lectern given to the cathedral in 1683 by George Williamson, sub-dean, was disused and later disposed of. It was purchased for St Mary-le-Port church, Bristol – did it survive that church's destruction in the war?

Victorian restorations

In 1859 G. G. Scott and J. S. Pope were consulted by Dean Elliott and the chapter, and a report was made by Scott recommending opening up the whole cathedral, curtailing the choir by its west bay and making a 'nave' of the three western bays. The result, for which Scott disclaimed all re-sponsibility, was that the pulpitum was thrown out and for many years the dismembered stonework was allowed to decay in the churchyard.[43] The stalls, erected by Bishop Bush (1542–54), were moved one bay eastwards, apparently suffering in the process, and some poor new work was inserted. In 1860 an Early English stone and marble screen was built under the eastern arch of the tower, but was not connected with the stalls by side screens. *The Ecclesiologist* commented that it reminded one 'of a gate to a field with the hedges taken away'.[44] As for the new paving, the writer says that 'the sanctuary alone has been repaved; the pattern and materials are such as would disgrace a railway station', and 'the *one* step across the entrance to the sanctuary is laid with plain white, yellow, brown and blue or green tiles, in mere draughtboard arrangement, and without pattern tiles'. He also condemns gas standards on huge stone bases as 'of hideous and ridiculous design'.

Street left the old choir more or less alone, but

after his death in 1881 J. L. Pearson, appointed architect to the cathedral, rearranged and enlarged the choir, bringing it forward three bays westward to its old position before 1542, demolishing the screen of 1860. The stalls he purged of the 'poor' work of 1860 and very considerably altered their design (c. 1895); and he placed the altar in its medieval position, two bays from the east end, which thus again became the Lady chapel. The reredos was erected in 1899 (after Pearson's death) followed by the present choir-screen in 1904.

In the early 1860s there was a public subscription to rebuild the nave. Street was appointed: the foundation stone was laid in 1868 and it was complete, except for the west towers, by October 1877. While generally adhering to the unique design of Abbot Knowle's choir (no triforium or clerestory and remarkable aisle vaults), Street, quite properly, varied the details of his nave – for instance the capitals to the main piers and the design of the aisle vaults.

The central tower, showing weaknesses, was underpinned by Scott in 1865, and ten years later, on Street's advice, its parapet and pinnacles were removed. New ones were not added until 1893 when the whole tower, except for the turret pinnacle, was refaced[45] following the old design. At about the same time the old north entrance was removed, and the great window above it – a poor late work – was replaced by a more 'correct' Geometrical design.

There was great controversy over four statues by Redfern of the Latin Fathers (St Ambrose, St Augustine of Hippo, St Jerome and St Gregory) on the new north porch, at which some extreme Protestants took umbrage as being papistical, and after much ill feeling, the dean ordered their removal. The offending effigies were later transferred to the tower of Street's East Heslerton church, Yorkshire. Their places on the porch were eventually filled by statues of the four Evangelists.

Street's squat west front is perhaps less successful than his nave. It was finished by Pearson after 1880. An illustration in *The Building News* (29 Oct. 1876) shows the towers with pyramidal lead-covered roofs – never built. Pearson also 'restored' the abbey gateway, replacing bay windows destroyed in the 18th century, and needlessly demolished two medieval houses west of the west front.

Bibliography

* *Browne Willis, 1727*. 2nd edn 1742.

Barrett, 1789. William Barrett, FSA, *History and Antiquities of the City of Bristol.*

The Beauties of England and Wales, XIII, 1813, by Rev. J. Nightingale.

* *Britton, 1830*. John Britton, *The History and Antiquities of . . . the Abbey and Cathedral of Bristol.*

Cursory Observations on the Churches of Bristol, 1843. 'By an occasional writer.'

Recollections and Reflections . . . in Bristol Cathedral, 1849. By L. W. G.

Pryce, 1853. George Pryce, *Notes on the Ecclesiastical and Monumental Architecture and Sculpture of the Middle Ages in Bristol.*

Liversage, 1853. Peter Liversage, *A History of Bristol Cathedral.*

Nicholls and Taylor, 1881. J. F. Nicholls & J. Taylor, *Bristol Past and Present*, II.

Latimer, 1887–1902. John Latimer, *Annals of Bristol*, III.6 vols.

* *Massé (Bell), 1901.* H. J. L. J. Massé, *Bristol, The Cathedral and See*, Bell's Cathedral Series.

Fletcher, 1932. Canon R. J. Fletcher, *A History of Bristol Cathedral, from Documents in the Possession of the Dean and Chapter.*

Fitzgerald, 1936. Canon Maurice Fitzgerald, *The Story of Bristol Cathedral.*

* *Harrison (Pitkin), 1975.* Dean Harrison, *Bristol Cathedral*, Pitkin Pictorial.

Notes

1 Fitzgerald, 2, appendix.
2 Fletcher, 22.
3 Fletcher, 27; Fitzgerald, 48–49.
4 *Topographical Excursion* (1634). For details see bibliography to Introduction; see also under Ely, Lichfield and Winchester.
5 Fitzgerald, 51.
6 Fitzgerald, 52.
7 Barrett, 330.
8 Fitzgerald, 53.
9 Fletcher, 36.
10 Browne Willis (2nd edn 1742), III, 762.

* see also bibliography to the Introduction.

11 This lack of appreciation of medieval architecture was further exemplified in the action of the dean and chapter in 1714 when the chapter house was repaired and sash windows inserted into its splendidly panelled Norman interior (commemorated by a Latin inscription).

12 Fletcher, 54; Fitzgerald, 60–62.

13 Most of these houses were originally part of the domestic buildings of the abbey. A petition of 1668 lists and names these monastic remains as at that date. See Fletcher, 34.

14 Fletcher, 38, 40.

15 Barrett, 294.

16 Barrett, 475.

17 And broken up. Its upper part survives, set up in Berkeley Square, Queens Rd.

18 The ruins were not cleared away until 1963 (see Reece Winstone, *Bristol As It Was, 1866–70*, 1967, ill. 59).

19 When the central library was built on its site.

20 Fletcher, 13, 15.

21 *Accompt Book of Bishop Wright, 1622–32*: 'Paid to John Clarke, freemason, for making the great window in the west end of the church, finding stone and beating down the old wall, £40:0:0.' It was rebuilt to a poor design in 1710.

22 Fletcher, 19.

23 By J. H. Clarke, in the Braickenridge Collection in the Bristol Art Gallery. Reproduced in A. Vallance, *Greater English Church Screens*. (1947), pl. 90.

24 Vallance, *op. cit.*, 95.

25 Britton, 52.

26 *Accompt Book of Bishop Wright, 1622–32*. Clarke was paid £5 for the first job, which seems rather inadequate, and £7.5s for the second. The niches referred to are those ordered to be walled up in 1561.

27 Masse (Bell), 54.

28 These corbels were described in 1899 as being in the cloister. They are now in the cathedral and newly painted. Both are sculptured, the one originally on the north having the arms of Bishop Wright impaling those of the see of Bristol, and of Dean Chetwynd (a chevron between three mullets) impaling Bristol and a royal crown with the cypher CR and the Berkeley shield; and the other having the arms of the City of Bristol, the Merchant Venturers and the Berkeley Arms.

29 Barrett, 291.

30 Browne Willis (2nd edn 1742), 762.

31 *Magna Brittania et Hibernia, Antiqua et Nova* (1727), IV (Somerset), 747.

32 I am indebted to Mr Arthur Sabin, late Hon. Archivist to the dean and chapter of Bristol for this quotation from a letter of Sir Edward Littleton to a Mr Edward Marco, dated 3 Apr. 1753.

33 Perhaps the writer was shortsighted as his 'painted wainscot' was, of course, carved stone.

34 J. P. Malcolm, FSA, *Excursions in Kent, Gloucester, Hereford, Monmouth and Somerset in the years 1802, 1803 and 1805* (1813), 180.

35 Compare Thomas Allen, *History and Antiquities of London: Westminster and Southwark* (1828), III, 758, describing the German Catholic Church, Great Trinity Lane: 'The altar is richly decorated, it is of a sarcophagus form painted in imitation of marble.'

36 Liversage, 47.

37 Barrett, 291, does not mention the wooden altarpiece.

W. Matthew's *New History of Bristol, Guide and Directory* (1794), 58: 'At the altar is a circle surrounded by cherubs, done by Vansomers.'

The Beauties of England and Wales, XIII (1813), 666: 'The altar has an emblematic painting of the triune Deity, being a triangle in a circle surrounded by cherubs, done by Vansomeren [sic].' In a note he contrasts this 'triangle in a circle surrounded by chubby-faced boys' with the silver image 'of a decrepit old man with a beard down to his knees, and a triple crown on his head . . . which the Lady Mary Wortley Montagu saw in Ratisbon'.

J. Storer, *History and Antiquities of Cathedral Churches of Great Britain* (1814–19), merely repeats re the circular picture of the Trinity, etc.

Britton, 55, refers to the central compartment of the medieval altar-screen as 'now covered by a modern altarpiece' but does not describe it. Later he says it is 'shamefully defaced by the tasteless operations of some house-painter'; and (note 9): 'Few things can be more displeasing to the eye and annoying to the feelings than . . . painting over a fine and interesting stone screen to imitate a piece of theatrical scenery which is the climax of bad taste.' Was it just whitewashed or gaudily coloured?

B. Winkles, *Illustrations of the Cathedral Churches of England and Wales* (2nd edn 1838) does not mention it.

Murray's *Handbook* (1864), 151, calls it 'a frightful Corinthian structure of wood'.

Liversage says of the 'Altar Screen, Lower Part': 'The central recess is quite modern, and for the following account we are indebted to an eye witness. When the Corinthian wooden reredos, which so disfigured the church was removed in 1839, contrary to all expectation, no central recess was found. The surface of the wall behind it was rough, showing clearly that an altar-screen, very different to the modern one, had once existed. On excavating the central recess a low pointed doorway was discovered, evidently communicating from the exterior, but of this no trace now remained. The arch and the niches on either side, with the corbel heads and shields of arms above it, date from this restoration.'

38 Latimer, 250, says the wooden altarpiece 'was purchased by the Irvingites for their church on the Quay' – now the Roman Catholic 'St Mary on the Quay'. But a recent visit of mine failed to locate any remains. (Fletcher, 59, says the altarpiece 'was given to the church of St Leonard Shoreditch' – almost certainly a mistake.)

39 Britton, pl. VII.

40 Fletcher, 51.

41 Fletcher, 59.

42 Fletcher, 50.

43 Massé (Bell), 55; Vallance, *op. cit.*, 96.

44 *The Ecclesiologist*, XXII, 1861, p. 217.

45 Massé (Bell), 25, says it was *rebuilt*, with some original stones incorporated.

44. The medieval pulpitum, removed from the White Friary, Bristol, at the Dissolution and erected in the cathedral in 1542: a drawing by J. H. Clarke of 1830 looking across the church from the north-west. The organ was set up in 1683, the figures of prophets in the niches painted 1622–32. The pulpit was given in 1527 by Bishop Wright.

45. The central doorway of the old pulpitum, a drawing published in 1804 (Lyson).

46. One of the surviving fragments of the old pulpitum.

Bristol: the screen and pulpit

48. The choir looking west, showing the other side of the same pulpitum, unaltered 16th-century stalls and bishop's throne, and the new pulpit opposite with tall canopied tester.

47. View east from the crossing, 1836 (Winkles). The pulpitum, placed half way down the present choir, created a 'nave' of two bays.

50. Street's new nave, soon after completion. The screen is that erected in 1860.

Opposite
51. The same view after 1904, showing the new screen designed by Pearson.

49. The choir looking west after the completion of Street's nave. The screen of 1860, which replaced the pulpitum, is two bays further west, under the eastern arch of the tower.

52, 53. Bishop Wright's pulpit (see pl. 44) had an elaborate tester and heraldic panels. By 1850 (*right*) it had been shorn of both, and is now gone altogether.

Bristol: Lady chapel

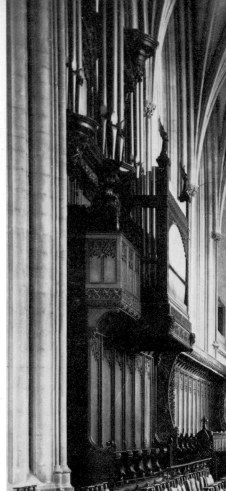

54. The Lady chapel looking east, a drawing made before 1839. It is the only record of the Classical reredos attributed to Inigo Jones. The medieval reredos can be seen behind it. Note too the pulpit with ogee tester. No bishop's throne: could that shown in pl. 48 have been made afterwards?

Centre
55. The same view after Pearson's restoration. The Classical reredos has disappeared, and the medieval one uncovered, repaired and used as the high altar.

57, 58, 59. Photographs of *c*. 1850, 1899, and 1940 showing the successive small changes made to the upper part of the Lady chapel reredos. The early photograph shows the present line of shields and lozenges with its frilly upper cornice on a high step above the reredos cornice. Then the parapet was lowered and placed in front of the lozenges and shields, and finally the two parts were united and lowered directly on to the reredos cornice and the whole altarpiece gaily coloured and gilt. Between 1850 and 1899 the side windows received a new parapet of quatrefoils, later replaced by a zig-zag pattern, and the sedilia on the right were restored by removing the tomb placed against them and rebuilding the missing parts (see pl. 3, contents page).

56. Pearson's huge new reredos, erected in 1899, effectively cut off the Lady chapel from the choir, which he moved two bays west to its medieval position.

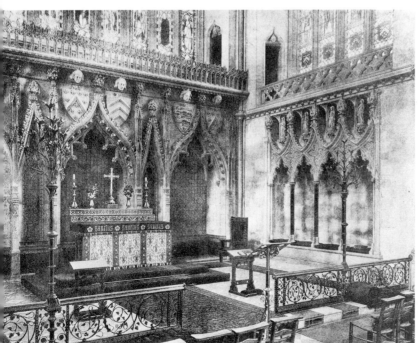

Bristol: screens and porches

60. North choir aisle, looking east (Winkles, 1836), showing the medieval wooden screen.

61. The same aisle, c. 1860. The screen has been removed and at the end the 'Nell Gwynn' window inserted.

62. Corresponding view of the south aisle showing a similar screen and old glass, now destroyed.

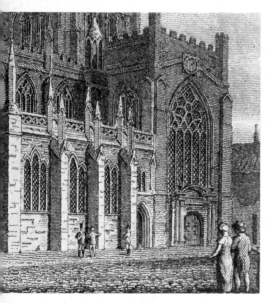

63. The north transept about 1800 showing the Classical doorway built against it in the 18th century (Storer).

64. Inside the same doorway, with its interior porch (Coney). Note the 'debased' 18th-century tracery of the window and the 17th-century font.

65. The same window and doorway about 1870, the latter denuded of pillars and pediment. Note the ironwork over the entrance to the green.

66, 67. Street's north porch with its original statues – St Ambrose, St Augustine of Hippo, St Jerome and St Gregory. These were regarded as too papist and after a public outcry the dean ordered their removal. They were replaced (*right*) by the Four Evangelists, and the originals found a new home in another Street church in Yorkshire.

Bristol: the building of the nave

68. View from the north-west, 1817 (Storer). The space west of the crossing is occupied by a medley of houses.

69. By about 1865 the houses have been demolished, but work on the nave has not yet begun.

71. In a photograph taken soon after pl. 69, looking south-west, scaffolding for the new nave has begun to be erected.

72. In the 1870s the nave and lower storeys of the towers are complete. The crossing tower has been shorn of its old pinnacles.

70. The cloister, in the angle of the south transept and the (unbuilt) nave, portrayed by Lyson in 1804. To accommodate Street's nave, the north alley was demolished and rebuilt a little south, between the buttresses. Note the crude rebuilding of some of the tracery.

74, 75. Views from the south-west, taken in 1860 and 1912. Street's nave and west front replace the jumble of old houses, some of them partly medieval.

73. View from the north-east, c. 1890, with the west towers now built to their full height and the crossing tower refaced with new pinnacles.

Beverley

ACCORDING to Daniel King's poor etching of 1656, this superb collegiate church of St John had, over the crossing, a small Perpendicular lantern, seemingly octagonal, with dwarf spire. But this disappeared before or during the extensive repair and refurnishing of the early 18th century.

Laxity in the upkeep of churches in the early 17th century is remarked on by Lord Clarendon: 'People took so little care [of churches] and parsons of their chancels . . . that instead of beautifying or adorning them in any degree, they rarely provided against the falling of many, and suffered them at least to be kept so indecently and slovenly that they would not have endured it in the offices of their own houses, the wind and rain being suffered to infest them.'[1]

By 1716 the minster 'had become so much delapidated . . . that its restoration was despaired of. The windows were shattered, the roof decayed, the gutters, battlements and other parts perishing and the whole [north] transept was an absolute ruin. The north gable had fallen away from the building, as it appeared, irretrievably; for the upper part overhung at least three feet and a half.' For this repair, permission was obtained to take suitable stone from St Mary's Abbey at York[2] – robbing Mary to pay John! The work of rescue was fostered by interest and subscriptions from the MPs for Beverley, John Moyser, Esq., Sir Charles Hotham and later Sir Michael Wharton. Nicholas Hawksmoor was called in to report on the condition of the minster and issued an appeal for its restoration with a plan and elevation of the west front, which he estimated would cost £3,500.[3]

What part he had, if any, in the repair that followed (c. 1716–40) is not clear, but the north transept front was amazingly returned to the perpendicular by a builder and carpenter from York named Thornton, who constructed a huge contrivance of wood to cover the front which, by means of screws, was gradually forced back to the upright – a remarkable achievement indeed![4] Before 1730 the stump of a tower was erected over the crossing, bearing an ogee dome, said by John Coates to have been designed by Lord Burlington.[5] Gent[6] mentions this cupola:

'Tis certainly pleasant to view this Fabrick at a Distance on a Summer's Day, with its beautiful Dome, and a Ball, gilt with Gold, glittering in the refulgent Beams of the Sun. The following [woodcut on opposite page] is but a small Representation of the church; a copy of which was given me by the same Person, who has lately obliged the Public with a large one, done from a Copper-plate, worthy to adorn a Parlour. This North Prospect I present . . . to show my distant Readers the magnificent Form of this venerable Structure.

The dome was, sadly, removed in 1824 – a great pity, as it gave just the right emphasis to the crossing that the (restored) flèches achieve at the twin western-towered churches of Notre-Dame, Paris, or St Gudule, Brussels. Now Beverley Minster shares with Westminster Abbey the painfully unfinished appearance that their central stumps produce.

The interior

In the Middle Ages Beverley had at least three parish churches besides the minster: St Mary's, at the opposite end of the town, St Martin's, apparently united to St John's (the Minster) under Henry VIII,[7] and St Nicholas, said to have been destroyed in the Civil War. Being without a meeting-place, the parishioners of these parishes petitioned the mayor and governors as trustees of St John's for accommodation in the nave of the minster for all three congregations. This was granted, 'pews and galleries were soon erected, and early in . . . 1660, a corporation order was made that "Mr Ward, Mr Stancliffe, Mr Acklom and Mr Hunter, together with the ministers and churchwardens of St Martin's and St John's parishes, should be empowered to sell all and every the pews which are newly built in the minster, and to give an account of their actings therein to this chamber".'[8] How long these fittings remained in the nave does not appear, but in the great repair

76. Beverley Minster from the west, before 1897, virtually as it is today except that soon afterwards the niches were filled with statues.

53

from about 1716 to 1740, new pews and galleries were erected and the interior of the church was lavishly adorned with new furniture, described by Gent as follows.[9] After relating the reinterment of the relics of St John, on 25 March 1726, during the laying of the new chequered pavement, he says:

To describe all its present Beauties: The aforesaid pavement in the Body of the Church, Margin'd with black Marble: That in the Choir, still more exquisitely fine, of four different Colours, in form of an Hexagon or Cube: the altar, built after the *Corinthian* Order (up to which is an Ascent of 6 steps, and curiously arched above, with the emblem of *St John* behind) the Table being of fine white marble, presented to the Church by *John Moyser* Esq.; the lesser Cross on each side; that Part, on the South, now a Place to transact Parish Affairs; and some of the North, made a Vestry: The Place call'd *Sanctum Sanctorum*, handsomely paved with Stones of two Colours; The Skreen on the Back of (and ancient decay'd Spire-Work like Canopies over) the Stalls, artfully mended, and Supplyd: the carved Skreen of fine white *Roche-Abbey* Stone, dividing the Choir from the Western Part of the church, done after the old *Gothick* order: the new Pulpit, Desk and Cover of the Font of Aggate Stone: which was remov'd from the West End to the South Wall: the nicely contrived Seats, and neat Galleries for the Parishioners in the Side Aisles, of the *Dorick Order* (resembling those of *St Alban's* at *Rome*) supported by Pillars of Wood, without any Damage to those of stone, which uphold the Church: the large Effigies of the Four Evangelists . . . with their proper Emblems beneath, which adorn the Inner Side of the Great West Door; up to which, on the Outer, are new and handsome, round Steps of fair and white Stone: To tell how wonderfully the late Mr *Thornton* of *York*, contrived an Engine to skrew up perpendicular the Wall aforesaid, that hung over 3 feet and a half: How a great part of the Large Cross [transept] (from whence the painted Window of *St Martin* had been taken) was nobly rebuilt, and the Outside, and Towers, especially from the West End of the South Side, to the Door, repair'd: Truly, to give all these just Encomiums would swell my Volume to a greater Degree, than design'd.

What happened to the 'handsome round steps'?

There are other interesting descriptions of the choir fittings. No proper drawing of the altarpiece is known, only a partial side view in Gough's plate of the Percy Shrine. It seems to have been finer than one would gather from Gent – a splendid design comparable to that in Trinity College chapel, Cambridge. In 1829 Scaum[10] describes it as 'a gorgeous wooden composition having eight Corinthian pillars supporting a triumphal arch surmounted by a gilded Eagle', and in the same year Oliver writes:[11]

Everything was formed on Grecian Models; the galleries were supported by doric pillars and a dome with doric triglyphs. Before the old altar screen was placed a wooden one of Grecian work on which stood eight beautiful corinthian pillars supporting a splendid triumphal arch, surmounted by a magnificent Eagle: the pulpit, the reading-desk, the cover for the font, all made at the same time, were all in the same taste; and by way of climax of absurdity, an entrance screen into the choir was erected, in which the Grecian and pointed styles were mixed together, and a kind of non-descript monster was produced referable to no species of architecture.

But later in the book he says:[12] 'The organ screen is a beautiful specimen of the Grecian style of architecture with English decorations; but lamentably misplaced amidst such a profusion of pure English ornament.'

Sir Stephen Glynne's description (1829) of this choir-screen will show still more how taste had changed in a hundred years. He says it had 'a very good effect when viewed at a distance, but on approaching it, the horrid mixture of Italian work with "Gothic", of festoons of flowers, canopied niches, figures with harps, arches both pointed and semi-circular, etc., becomes too evident, and at once stamps this gorgeous screen the production of corrupt taste and a false idea of magnificence'.[13]

A correspondent (unnamed) to *The Builder* in 1848 writes:[14]

Not long ago I visited Beverley. . . . A gem it is . . . were it not for two sad inconsistencies . . . the absence of the central tower and the barbarous treatment of the interior by erecting a hideous rood-screen, of the very worst taste . . . and filling up the lofty and beautiful chancel arch with *red-cloth*, as the clerk informed me – *to keep the place warm*. He, however, told me that it was proposed to remove it, and fill the arch with *glass* instead. Now, the miserable effect of this vandalism, every ecclesiologist knows in Lichfield Cathedral, where the taste of Mr Wyatt introduced it.

Eleven years later (9 April 1859) 'a lover of Good Taste' writes in the same journal: 'The interior of Beverley Minster . . . is daubed almost throughout with the brush and the whitewash.' He urges the authorities 'to set to work in good earnest and let all the vile coating be removed . . . another eyesore in the building is the organ-screen, one of the vilest erections, I should think, extant, in a church of any pretensions'.

About this time a large folio of lithographs of Beverley Minster appeared, with ten outline views drawn by J. Johnson and lithographed by A. Newman. Those of the nave and transept showed 'The Proposed New Choir Screen' of three finely moulded Decorated arches (the central larger and higher than the others) with four carved angels above and an elaborate crested summit. It was never built.

82
83 From old photographs the choir-screen seems to have been a delightful rococo-Gothick design, and Scott's removal of it in the 1870s is much to be deplored.[15] It sustained a fine organ by Snetzler set
85 up in 1767[16] and in the niches on either side of the centre archway are lead figures of St John of Beverley and King Athelston, the work of W. Collins of Driffield in 1731.[17]

The nave fittings

In a manuscript transcript in my possession, of a diary kept by two architects, Edward Cresy (1792–1858) and Geo Ledwell Taylor (1780–1873), during a tour in 1816 through England to record details of cathedrals and other churches, Taylor says:

the nave is fitted up for the Service, the design, I apprehend, was Mr Hawksmoor's and has claim to some invention. . . . Galleries are formed over the side aisles, supported on two [Doric] columns between each pillar, with entablatures in front; these are returned at the outer perpendicular of the columns and continued round behind the Pillars without touching them; there are other columns opposite the front ones near the outer wall, but not touching it – they are ascended by flights of steps from the Transepts – close pews under the Galleries. The centre has only open Pews, besides the Pulpit and Reading-Desk.

Cresy adds that 'there is great merit in the Carpenter not attaching any of this cumbrous work to the building. The sixth arch to the tenth, both inclusively are thus filled up, and public worship is held here on Sundays.' Of the dome, he says that 'the interesting tower or lantern is modern and principally built of brick with an ugly domical lead covering on which is a ball and cross'.

95 In the library of the Society of Antiquaries there is a fine photograph of a splendid baroque pulpit, simply inscribed at the back 'from Beverley Minster'. This movable piece of furniture is outstanding in its wealth and variety of beautiful detail, but the design as a whole is rather confused, its elegant back legs, triangular base, hexagonal body and circular tester – the latter unfinished – crying out for some pyramidal ornament on top. Unfortunately the whereabouts of this remarkable pulpit is unknown as is, apparently, any old description of it. Did it leave the minster before interest in these fittings was revived by the restoration of 1826? And in any case where has it been hiding (and perhaps still hides!) all this time?

Of all this 18th-century work there still remain the fine statues and gates from the choir-screen, the
83 wonderful font cover, and the remarkable west and other inner door-facings. Besides some grotesque
93 corbels on the west end of the south aisle,[18] a
92 number of small figures in the base of the canopies of the choir-stalls,[19] several oak settles of good design and some fragments of the former organ-case.[20]

Opinions have changed about the font cover.
96 Scaum says:[21] 'The cover . . . is a remaining specimen of the absurd taste which characterized the period.' Oliver[22] is more civilized, describing it as 'of richly carved oak, highly decorated with a combination of figures and flowers tastefully disposed in wreaths and festoons'. Hyatt[23] merely describes it as 'an inappropriate canopy of elaborately-carved oak'. Pevsner, however, writes of it as having 'eight elaborate scrolls and a dove on top. A magnificent piece of metropolitan quality.'

The nineteenth and twentieth centuries

'In 1824 the nave fittings were demolished (not without opposition)[24] and the choir reredos taken down, exposing the mutilated medieval altar-screen plastered over and showing traces of painted commandments, Lord's Prayer and Creed.'[25] 'Mr Comins who had been bred up in the cathedral works at York . . . under Mr Shute'[26] was in charge and in 1825 he 'restored' the screen, or rather rebuilt it, as described by Scaum:[27] Comins 'carefully examined the mutilated work of the original, took casts of the ornaments and mouldings and carved an entirely new pinnacle of exquisite beauty'. Everyone was so pleased that it was decided to restore the whole; the first stone of the
88 new screen was laid in March 1825 and the work
90 completed in February 1826 (complete with grotesques!) Scaum says that 'a range of stone altar-rails, quite in character with the screen has since been added'. It is interesting to note that very similar communion-rails were set up in York Minster after the fire of 1829. Both sets disappeared in Scott's time, those of York reappearing in the Lady chapel there about the turn of the century but now gone. Old photographs show these rails to have been very handsome – far better than their Victorian successors.[28]

Of the ancient choir-stalls, we read in Oliver in 1829:[29]

Till very lately a back ran behind the whole length of the tabernacle-work, and a canopy, extending in one

continued line from east to west, overhung the pinnacles. They were both original parts of the work. In the
progress of the alterations now going on the removal of
the former became necessary [why?]; and the effect has
been very good, in exhibiting more clearly the elegant
and delicate tabernacle work. Something, however, is
still wanting to relieve the back part of the work, which
was never intended for exposure; and some persons,
perhaps, will be disposed to regret the canopy, as an
ornament not common in such a situation, and giving to
the choir a peculiar and distinctive character.

The canopy was removed, but when? Does 'regret
the canopy' mean 'regret its being there' or 'regret
its removal'? But the implication of 'the removal of
the former [the back] became necessary' is that the
canopy was not removed then.

Comins also opened up and restored 'two arches
adjoining the centre tower, which had dropped
when the north transept gave way and were at that
time bricked up from the ground'.[30]

Oliver[31] tells us that in 1826 'a new pulpit
designed and executed by Mr Fowler of Winterton
has been recently introduced. It is disposed at
present at the east end of the centre aisle' and had a
canopy. It was later moved to the north side of the
choir (without tester), and later still to the nave (as
old photographs show).

In 1866 Scott was called in. He removed the
altar-rails and pulpit of 1826, demolished the choir-
screen and organ, and designed an elaborate
wooden screen which was constructed after his
death in 1878 and carved by James Elwell of
Beverley.[32] Finished in 1882, it cost £3,300; and
choir-gates designed by Oldrid Scott and made by
W. Walton of Beverley were added in 1890. Later
the screen was surmounted by a splendid organ
incorporating parts of its Snetzler predecessor in a
handsome case designed by Canon Nolloth in
conjunction with Messrs Hill of London. Nolloth
was also responsible for filling the upper panels of
the reredos and those immediately over the altar
with *opus sectile* mosaics of angels, saints and
figures of the twelve Apostles and so on, and the
lower niches with stone effigies by Mr Hitch of
Vauxhall. The mosaics were by Messrs Powell, all
under the superintendence of J. L. Pearson.[33]

Between 1897 and 1901, to mark Queen
Victoria's Diamond Jubilee, the niches of the west
front were filled by sixty-nine statues, including
one of the queen (north side of the north tower).
The Builder[34] speaks of 'cheap statues for Beverley
Minster – £35 a pair – what sort of statues for such a
price? Are they mason's work or perhaps made by
machinery?' No sculptor or architect is named
there, but in the correspondence files of the Society

56

for the Protection of Ancient Buildings there is a
letter from Thackeray Turner which names a Mr
Robert Baker of Beverley as responsible. Perhaps,
being a Beverley man, Baker loyally charged only a
nominal price? Between 1911 and 1914 this same
Mr Baker carved the many oak figures that now fill
the upper niches of the splendid choir-stalls.[35]

Lastly, a circular one-legged movable nave
'altar' (hard to recognize as such), together with
straight communion-rails, and candlesticks, were
presented by the Friends of the Minster in 1970 and
placed in the centre of the main crossing.[36]

Bibliography

Gent, 1733. Thomas Gent, *The Ancient and Modern
History of the Loyal Town of Rippon.* 'Diversion on
Beverley', 73–100, on St Mary's and the minster. Useful
information on repairs and refurnishing of St John's
just completed.

Oliver, 1829. George Oliver, *The History and Antiquities
of the Town and Minster of Beverley.*

Scaum, 1829. George Scaum, ed? G. Poulson, *Beverlac; or
the Antiquities and History of the Town of Beverlac*, 2 vols.
Interesting on Comins's 'restoration' then in progress.
(Only cover of book says 'Compiled by G. Poulson'.)

* *Hyatt (Bell), 1898.* Charles Hyatt, *Beverley*, Bell's
Cathedral Series.

Wigfall, n.d. Rev. W. E. Wigfall, *A Small Guide for
Visitors to Beverley Minster*, c. 1937?

Forster, 1945. J. R. Forster, *Beverley Minster – A Brief
Guide*, many edns 1945–55.

* *Macmahon (Pitkin), 1967.* K. A. Macmahon, *Beverley
Minster*, Pitkin Pictorial, 2nd edn 1975.

Notes

1 Scaum, 677–78. Such laxity was not unknown as late
as the end of the 18th c. Oliver, 344, says of the Percy
chapel and tomb: 'After a long succession of unaccountable and indecent ravages . . . the sepulchre itself was
violated so recently as the year 1793' and (note 80): 'In
the above year, the sexton, assisted by other persons,
had the audacity to open and ransack this sacred vault,
together with that of the lady Idonea Percy, in the hope,
doubtless, of finding a hoard of concealed treasure. Being
disappointed in their expectations, they scattered the
contents with savage rudeness, and wantonly bowled
the skulls along the floor. It is even said that one man . . .
obtained a finger joint from Earl Percy's hand, which he

* see also bibliography to the Introduction.

procured to be tipped with silver and used for a tobacco stopper'!

2 Oliver, 239–40.

3 Hawksmoor's description of the minster in this appeal is delightful: 'not built all at a time, or of the same style, but of an admirable tast and performance after the Monastick Order; But especially the West Front, which is most stupendously magnificent, Beautiful and Durable'.

4 Thornton died at York and was buried in St Olave's church. His epitaph reads: 'Near this place lies the body of William Thornton, joiner and architect who departed this life September 23, 1721, aged 51 years.'

5 *Gentleman's Magazine*, 1799, pt 1, 93, 94.

6 Gent, 88.

7 Scaum, 714.

8 Oliver, 229–30.

9 Gent, 91.

10 Scaum, 679.

11 Oliver, 242.

12 Oliver, 326.

13 Quoted by Aymer Vallance, *Greater English Church Screens* (1947), 134.

14 *The Builder*, 1 Mar. 1848, p. 118.

15 Forster (4th edn 1956) says: 'A mixed style screen was erected, remains of which can be seen in a garden at Cleethorpes.' Is it there now?

16 Vallance, *op. cit.*, 133–34.

17 Rupert Gunnis, *Dictionary of British Sculptors, 1660–1851* (1953) and Richard H. Whiting, *Georgian Restorations of Beverley Minster* (n.d.) give 1731, but Vallance says 1781 – a misreading of the date on the back of the figures?

18 Whiting, *op. cit.*, 5, says: 'Immediately behind the font and ajoining the south door of the nave . . . stood the parish church of St Martin, built over a crypt, at sometime used as a charnel house, of which traces can be seen outside. The 18th-century restorers moved its windows – four hundred years older – inwards to light the south aisle, and built a wall arcade under them to match, more or less, the existing arcade farther east, but the stone is different and the mock Gothic figures in the newer piece . . . have heads and faces, which betray the secret of their age.' Rather than accepting that the '400 year old windows' were moved from St Martin's (and as the present seem exactly similar to those further east), it appears more probable that they are 18th-c. copies – the closeness of the Georgian wall arcading (except for the busts and heads) is proof of ability to imitate the windows just as well.

There is little information about St Martin's, but it is said to have been attached to the W end of the S aisle and united to St John's at some time (Scaum suggests time of Henry VIII), and that it survived until the late 17th c. seems confirmed by Oliver (229, 230): 'The church of St Nicholas, it is said, was destroyed in the Civil War. . . . But the tower or steeple . . . was left standing, for we find amongst the corporation records a licence which was granted in 1693, to the mayor and alderman . . . of Beverley by John Archbishop of York, to take down the old steeple of Holme Church St Nicholas, and dispose of the materials in repairing the . . . churches of St Martin and St Mary in Beverley as occasion should require.' Daniel King's etching of 1656 shows no trace of St Martin's (but only a blank window) – this is true. But look at his transept front – no doorway! (His propensity to omit important features is conspicuous in his north view of Rochester Cathedral where there is no Gundulph's Tower – partly demolished *c.* 1800, lower part remains.)

19 Hyatt (Bell), 82, says: 'Some of the peculiar carved heads in the canopies representing divines in wigs and bands, were obviously added in Georgian times.'

20 Whiting, *op. cit.*

21 Scaum, 686.

22 Oliver, 321.

23 Hyatt (Bell), 116.

24 We learn from Scaum (682–83) that in 1822 the trustees suggested removing the pews and galleries in the nave and fitting up the choir for Divine Service. Opposition delayed the carrying out of this plan (by Messrs Rickman and Hutchinson) until 1824. The seating that was removed occupied five bays of the nave and included, according to Taylor, 'galleries, close and open pews, pulpit and reading desk' (no mention of communion table), so that it is fairly clear that the choir must have been long deserted, perhaps since the pewing of 1660. Oliver (332–40) provides a description of the new choir fittings in 1829; they included a new pulpit by 'Mr Fowler of Winterton' and the old altar-table presented to the church by John Moyser in 1717.

25 Hyatt (Bell), 90.

26 Scaum, 679.

27 Scaum, 682.

28 G. Cobb, 'Fashions in Fitments', *Ancient Monuments Society*, N.S. III, 1955.

29 Oliver, 332, quoting Coltman, *Short History*, 51.

30 Scaum, 684, note 1.

31 Oliver, 333.

32 This was apparently Scott's only *choir*-screen carrying an organ (that at Chester Cathedral is placed in the N transept arch).

33 Hyatt (Bell), 90–91.

34 *The Builder*, 26 Mar. 1898.

35 Forster (3rd edn 1955).

36 See frontispiece to Macmahon (Pitkin), 1975.

92

77. Detail from Daniel King's etching of 1656, the only record of the old lantern over the crossing.

78. Tayleur's view from the south-west in 1817, showing the ogee dome over the crossing, erected in the 1720s and demolished in 1824.

80. Pivoted scaffolding devised by William Thornton of York with which he forced back the north transept front into an upright position; drawing published in 1739.

81. Inside the west front. The doors show work of about 1730 (see pl. 93), the statues around it are of mid 20th-century date.

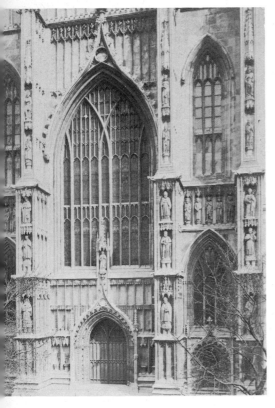

79. Centre of the west front, with the new statues added in honour of Queen Victoria's Diamond Jubilee.

Beverley: the nave and crossing

82, 83. Looking east down the nave before the removal of the 1767 organ and loft, and (*right*) a close-up of the Rococo-Gothick screen with its splendid wrought-iron gates. These gates are now in the north choir aisle, while the statues are in the south nave aisle.

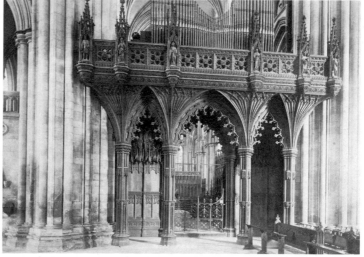

84. The screen designed by Scott to replace that shown above, and erected after his death. It now sustains a fine organ.

Beverley: the choir

85. The choir looking west, showing the other side of the 1730 screen with its organ. The stalls are medieval.

86. The same view after the erection of Scott's screen but before the addition of the organ. Organ pipes can be seen not only above the screen but also at the sides.

87. The same view after the construction of the present organ, and showing the new gates designed by Oldrid Scott, the whole rivalling its predecessor.

88, 89. The choir looking east (*above*), showing the reredos as left by Comins in 1826. At first the niches were left blank, to be filled later with rather fussy decoration (*right*).

90. Finally, at the end of the 19th century, the niches were filled with statues and the upper panels with mosaics representing angels, saints and apostles. Note, at the bottom, Comins's grotesque carvings.

Beverley: the Georgian contribution

91, 92. Two sections of the blind arcading of the south aisle, the upper one genuinely medieval, the lower one a very convincing imitation by 18th-century craftsmen.

93. The great west doors, added in the 18th century, full of lively design though often eccentric in detail (e.g., the 'kissing' faces).

94. The south choir aisle in the 1860s, showing the back of seating placed behind the stalls, like those facing them across the choir.

96. The splendid Baroque font cover; like the 1730 organ-screen it was regarded as an 'absurdity' in the 19th century.

95. An 18th-century pulpit photographed probably about seventy years ago and captioned 'From Beverley Minster'. No clue exists as to its present whereabouts.

63

Selby

AFTER the Dissolution of the monasteries, the Abbey of Selby was granted to Sir Ralph Sadler in 1541 for £736 and a yearly rent of £3-10s-8d. He sold it the same year and the abbey changed hands three times by 1711, when it was acquired by Lord Petre of Writtle.[1]

Before the Reformation Selby parish church 'had its situation on what is now called Church Hill . . . but with the advent of new religious influences under the Scottish king, there came a disposition to make use of the nobler edifice; and James I granted letters patent, dated March 20th, 1618, making it the Parish Church'.[2] What caused the abbey church to remain unmolested and unused for eighty years is not clear. Possibly the quick exchange of ownership, indicating no great interest in the property, ensured its survival, and that, probably by 1618, decay had rendered the old parish church untenable.

Selby Abbey church, now the only complete one in Yorkshire, had, according to Daniel King's poor etching of 1655,[3] a fine tower, apparently of transitional Norman character, half of which fell down on 30 March 1690, carrying with it the south transept, which was not rebuilt until early this century. The tower lay in ruins until 1701. In the repairs which followed, costing under £100,[4] it was given a plain sturdy upper storey, with beautiful tall baluster-like pinnacles. The western bay of the choir lost its wooden 'vault' in the fall and three windows (clerestory and aisle) were destroyed, their gothic tracery being replaced by debased fenestration. These defects remained until 1889.

The west front, with its unfinished towers, had no gable until 1873, when Sir G. G. Scott raised the nave roof, carried it forward to the west end and provided the present Early English gable.

By the end of the 19th century the central tower was held in abhorrence: about 1890, the pinnacles were taken off, followed, in 1902,[5] by the whole upper storey.[6] Oldrid Scott, who had issued a report on the insecurity of much of the church, especially the north transept,[7] produced his designs for the present tower and the south

transept, but these could not be built until the essential repairs had been carried out. Then in 1906 the building suffered a grievous fire: an appeal was launched and £43,000 was collected. In the restoration that followed, the tower was at last erected and the church rededicated in 1909, the transept following in 1912 – at the sole charge of William Liversidge, J. P.[8] Oldrid Scott, who died that year, left designs for heightening the west towers, which, however, was not done until 1935 – by his son C. M. Oldrid Scott – the six old pinnacles being reused and two new ones added. Thus the appearance of the exterior between 1890 and 1935, a mere forty-five years, was more drastically changed than that of any other Greater Church in the country in a comparable period.[9]

The interior

This had meanwhile undergone three successive restorations. Morrell says:[10]

Chiefly owing to the energy of the . . . Rev. J. W. Harper [1850–89] a successful effort for restoration of the church was commenced in . . . 1852, to improve accommodation . . . in the choir . . . Mr G. G. Scott being the architect. The whole of the internal walls . . . were cleansed of numerous coats of yellow-wash, four side galleries were taken down, and all pews, pulpit and reading desk were removed. It is to be regretted that the low wall which divided the chancel [from its] aisles, and which carried the canopies over the stalls,[11] should also have been removed. The ground of the choir to the depth of two feet, was dug up, and concrete laid down, to prevent damp. A new flooring was put down of stone and wood, and the choir fitted up with substantial and chaste oaken seats designed by Mr Scott, and admirably executed under his instructions, by Mr Richard Hardisty, of Selby. In 1857 an oaken pulpit elaborately designed by Mr Scott, to harmonize with the decorated Gothic of the choir was placed therein, the cost being paid out of the church rate. The restorations begun in

---

97, 98. The west front of Selby in 1867 (*top*) and as it is today (*bottom*). Central tower, upper parts of the west towers and gable have all been built since 1872.

1852 were done at a cost of £1500 defrayed by a special subscription for the purpose.

In 1865, by the exertions and under the superintendence of Mr. Wm Liversidge, junr., the churchwarden of the year, considerable improvements were effected. . . . The choir was fitted up with three of Gurney's stoves and piping etc. at a cost of £160 . . . thirteen of the clerestory windows of the choir, and also the upper East window [in the gable] which had been filled up with brickwork . . . were thoroughly restored, at the sole expense of the Right Hon. Lord Londesborough, with new stone-work and re-glazing at a cost of £250.

All this by 1867, the date of Morrell's book.

115 Up to this time the nave was cut off from the choir by a wooden screen reaching from floor to ceiling (pierced by a doorway and four glazed Perpendicular windows) against the east side of which the organ was placed in 1824.[12] This screen
116 was removed around 1869 by Scott and the interior laid open from end to end. And as the extremely decayed remains of the Jesse glass in the main part of the east window had been taken out before 1864 for repair, the interior presented a very dreary sight, until 1889, when the glass was made good
119 and replaced, the choir decently restored with stalls, side screens and fine altarpiece by Oldrid Scott, and the sedilia 'restored' with tall spires to the canopies.[13]

This new woodwork was all destroyed in the
120 fire of 1906, and new furniture, including a reredos similar in outline to the one burnt, but larger, and
121 an elaborate wooden choir-screen, were installed. This screen was executed by R. Bridgeman of Lichfield and the carved crucifixion on the reredos was by Peter Rendl, the Oberammergau 'Christus'. Sadly, a splendid 15th-century aumbery or relics cupboard on the north side of the sanctuary and other old woodwork were destroyed and the north transept badly calcined, but the tall wooden cover of the font escaped damage.[14]

The glass of the east window was said to be not greatly damaged in the fire, and was again repaired, by Ward and Hughes of Soho, at Mr Liversidge's expense for the second time, and very splendid it now looks. But it seems that, after long neglect and two restorations, only about a third of the figures of the Jesse Tree are ancient, although the Last Judgment in the tracery of the window may be more authentic.

The glass of the east window

The story of this glass is a dreary one – at least until modern times. A note in Morrell reads:[15]

The late Mr Bernard Clarkson, banker, of Selby, who had contemplated publishing a History of Selby, caused to be prepared eight elaborate engravings, by Fowler of Lincoln, in 1820, of the details of this famous window then remaining. The few copies that were struck off, passed into the possession (with other of Mr. Clarkson's MSS) of the late Edward Parker, Esq., of Alkincoats and Selby. . . . Considerable efforts [were] made to find Mr. Clarkson's MSS, though without success . . .

What a pity!

In 1831 Samuel Lewis writes:[16] 'In the last century, this window contained the Genealogy of Christ, but only a few scattered fragments remain', and Morrell[17] tells us that 'the erection of a gallery in the Lady Chapel at the Musical Festival of 1827 resulted in serious damage to the noble East window, and a severe hail-storm about twenty years ago completed its destruction, some fragments of which were recently inserted in one of the windows of the vestry.'

In view of these statements one would infer that very little indeed of the glass had survived. But Morrell[18] also says that

a considerable portion of the ancient glass of the East window is in the possession of the church-wardens and in . . . 1864 it underwent an examination by Mr. Wailes, of Newcastle, who reported that sufficient remained to enable him to effect . . . a genuine restoration of the ancient design . . . at a cost of £600. The tracery work of the upper part is nearly entire and exhibits the Day of Judgment [surrounding][19] . . . the crucifixion. There are also figures of St John and St Jerome. The remains now in the window are sufficient to indicate the design; figures of Kings, priests and warriors may be seen issuing from tombs, and grotesque representations of good and evil angels bearing the sentences from right and left hand of the judge to the gates of heaven and to the flames of hell.

According to Scott:[20]

Half a century ago the window was found to be decaying at a very rapid rate; therefore all but the tracery lights were taken down and stored away. In 1871 and 1878 Mr William Liversidge drew attention to the . . . important possession that the church had in the fragments . . . yet remaining; and to his munificence we owe . . . that the window has been replaced in the magnificent form in which it may be seen today. Messrs Ward and Hughes of London have done the work. . . . The beautiful backgrounds and borders[21] fragmentary though they were, lent a clue to the position of many of these figures, while the fact that the topmost panels in all seven lights have been handed down intact explains how . . . the restorer has solved the problem as to the arrangement of the 'tree'.

From a diagram in Moody[22] it appears that only twenty-four panels are marked as 'old' out of the

99, 100. In 1906 a disastrous fire destroyed most of the interior. *Top*: the nave and choir immediately after the fire. *Bottom*: the choir during rebuilding.

seventy in the seven lights of the window. But at the back of the diagrams we read: 'Since writing the foregoing [appendix on the window] we regret to say the window has been found to be more seriously damaged that at first imagined.' They thought the remains might go into the South Kensington Museum (now the Victoria and Albert). But as we have seen, they have happily been retained in situ.

Sad story of a monument

In Moody we read of 'a once magnificent, but now sadly mutilated monument, rich in heraldry and ornate carving commemorating John, Lord D'Arcy Meinell, who died . . . 1411. This, the only altar-tomb in the church, formerly stood in the third arch from the east on the south side of the choir. For some reason or other it was removed in 1857 to a place under the east window, when portions were either lost or destroyed. In 1890, it was removed, receiving new injuries. So far, it has not been re-erected!' Liversidge (1912) tells us:[23] 'Mr. C. Hodges, in some readable notes on the monuments, complained that this fine tomb had received most ignoble treatment. Of twelve shields on angels' breasts around the sides, only seven remain; and on the upper slab, the head, trunk and part of one leg exist, and these in dilapidated condition.'

Church sittings

Morrell says:[24] 'In 1824, as stated in a notice in front of the choir, the accommodation in the church was enlarged by the addition of 422 sittings, 298 of which were free, 91 being reserved to increase the income of the benefice. These were declared free by the Rev. J. W. Harper on his appointment to the living [1850], on the ground of the illegality of seat-letting in parish churches.'

Changes of use

Morrell,[25] speaking of the north porch, writes: 'Above is a chamber or parvice, which was used as an armory for the volunteers in 1803'. And in the 'chapter house' (sacristy), 'the upper storey . . . is now used as the Blue Coat School'.[26] In 1894 it was 'a parish room'.[27]

Bibliography

Morrell, 1867. William Wilberforce Morrell, *History and Antiquities of Selby Abbey*. Valuable for information and stuck-in photographs.

Scott, 1894. Herbert Scott, *The Story of Selby Abbey, From Rise to Restoration*. 'By the author of "Old Time Stories".'

Moody, 1908. Charles H. Moody, *Selby Abbey – a Resumé*.

Liversidge, 1912. William Liversidge, ed. H. Scott, *Story of Selby Abbey*.

* *Kent (Pitkin), 1977.* John Kent, *Selby Abbey*, Pitkin Pictorial.

Notes

1 Scott, 37–38. He continues: 'It was from . . . the Petres that Lord Londesborough, father of the present Earl, purchased the manor of Selby in the year 1854. The Hon. Edward Petre, we are told, liberally surrendered property, valued at £1,500, to open up an uninterrupted approach to the west front of the church, and he was . . . a generous supporter of the work undertaken . . . to improve the interior of the building . . . the same be said of the present Lord of the manor.'

2 Scott, 37.

3 Daniel King, *The Cathedral and Conventual Churches of England and Wales* . . . (1656). These prints were first pub. the previous year, in W. Dugdale's *Monasticon Anglicanum*, I.

4 From the church-wardens' accounts – quoted in Morrell, 205 (with list of subscribers) and 335. He adds that such an amount 'could scarcely be believed on any other evidence'.

5 Date given in Moody, 75.

---

* see also bibliography to the Introduction.

6 Photographs show that a fine pierced square clock-face succeeded a round one on the truncated tower (*c.* 1904–05), but disappeared after the fire of 1906 – why wasn't it retained?

7 Scott, 44, says of this transept: 'the great window not long ago was taken down and rebuilt owing to its dangerous condition' and was filled with glass 'showing every factor legend that was ever attached to [the Abbey's patron saint] St Germain'.

8 William Liversidge was Selby's great benefactor after becoming church-warden in 1865, and paid for most of the fittings of the post-fire choir. See Liversidge, ch. VIII.

9 St Albans Abbey as left by Lord Grimthorpe runs it pretty close – and that in only about twenty-one years!

10 Morrell, 209–10.

11 These canopied stalls sound interesting, but I know of no view of them. Were they 17th-c? What happened to them? Photographs of 1869–89 show many stalls but all uncanopied.

12 Date given in Scott, 41.

13 For details of the 1889 restoration, see Scott, ch. VI.

14 For details of the fire and post-fire restorations, see Moody and Liversidge.

15 Morrell, 201.

16 S. Lewis, *Topographical Dictionary of England* (1831), IV, 35.

17 Morrell, 202.

18 Morrell, 201.

19 The text has 'surrounded with', obviously a mistake for 'surrounding' or 'surmounting'.

20 Scott, appendix, 49–50.

21 Morrell, 201, mentions borders of crowns, lions passant, squirrels upon filbert branches, and chalices of gold.

22 Moody, 104–05.

23 Liversidge, 74.

24 Morrell, 209.

25 Morrell, 196.

26 Morrell, 203.

27 Scott, 44.

101. View from the south-west, c. 1860, before any restoration had taken place.

102. The same view after 1873, showing Scott's gable and new 'Norman' window south of the portal.

103. Part of the south side of the choir before 1889, showing the 'debased' tracery inserted after the fall of the tower in 1690.

104. View from the south, c. 1890, showing new tracery replacing that in pl. 103, and a section of the south choir aisle dismantled for rebuilding.

105. View from the south-east after 1912, showing Oldrid Scott's new central tower and south transept.

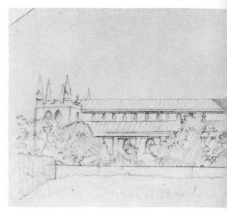

106. View from the north, 1655, by Daniel King, the only view of the old 12th-century (?) tower.

107. Reconstruction drawing of the church from the south, c. 1860. The tower has been

109. Between 1890 and 1902 the fine Georgian pinnacles were removed from the central tower.

110. Between 1902 and 1905 the tower lost its whole upper storey.

112. By 1909 the roof had been repaired and Oldrid Scott had completed the new central tower; the south transept, however, is still to be built.

113. The same view about 1912, with the new transept completed.

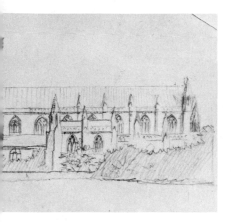

replaced by a Georgian one, built
in 1701, but the south transept
remains a ruin.

108. The south side, *c.* 1880: Scott has raised the nave
roof and built a gable at the west end.

111. The same view after the fire of 1906, nave and
choir roofless.

114. The same view after 1935, showing the church's
heightened west towers.

115. The nave looking west, c. 1867; a wooden screen with traceried windows blocks off the east crossing arch.

116. About 1871 the wall was demolished, opening up the whole choir to the west of the church.

117. Looking west from the choir before 1889. The western bay of the choir still has the flat plaster ceiling going back to the fall of the tower in 1690.

118. The same view after 1889, showing the restored wooden vault.

Selby: the interior

119. The choir looking east after Oldrid Scott's restoration of 1889.

120. The choir looking east after the restoration that followed the fire of 1906 (Oldrid Scott again). The crucifixion is by an Oberammergau sculptor, Peter Rendl.

121. Looking east from the nave, with the screen installed after the fire.

Ely

THE GREAT CATHEDRAL church of Ely, like that of Peterborough, suffered savage damage as a result of the Reformation. In 1541, at the beginning of the Puritan period of influence under Bishop Goodrich (1534–54), an edict ordered that 'all Relics, Images, Table Monuments of Miracles and Shrines be demolished'.[1] Peterborough was devastated at the end of that period, but Ely was shut up by Cromwell, as Governor of the Isle of Ely, and so saved from further damage. Apart from the confiscation of treasures and destruction of St Etheldreda's shrine, a fate common to all such centres of pilgrimage at the Dissolution of the monasteries, Ely suffered badly in two areas only. First, in the Lady chapel, with its truly unrivalled sculptured wall arcading depicting the life and legends of the Virgin, in which almost every one of the hundreds of figures was decapitated. Second, in the chantry of Bishop West (1515–34), which was deprived of its sculpture, not merely by mutilation but, in some cases, by chiselling all away. Stubbs[2] says this was 'probably in consequence of an order in Council made AD 1547–8'.

Ely Cathedral, on its slight eminence above the surrounding flat lands, with its unique silhouette which so delights us today, was, in the neglectful days of the 18th century, with its diminutive 'city', 'much on the decline . . . the adjoining lowlands having been several years under water . . . and the public roads . . . in so bad a state as not to be travelled in safety'.[3] In fact, back in 1635, a Lieutenant Hammond of the Military Company of Norwich who visited Ely, as recorded in his diary, found nothing to admire:[4] 'Most of [Ely's] inhabitants have such a turfy scent and fenny posture about them, which smell I did not relish at all with any content.' The palace, the writer added, was 'ruinated, decayed and drooping for very age', and the cathedral was 'in deplorable condition'. Nearly a century later, Daniel Defoe[5] says of the minster itself: 'The most remarkable thing I could hear [was that] some of it is so ancient, totters so much with every gust of wind, looks so like decay . . . that whensoever it does fall' it will be wondered why it did not do so 'one hundred years sooner.'

Decay and insecurity still persist yet mercifully it stands. Apparently this insecurity is mainly in the later parts of the church – the original building 'was in a much harder stone than was commonly used in the Norman age'.[6]

The seventeenth century

In the Civil War the cathedral suffered little, thanks to Oliver Cromwell. According to Carlyle's *Cromwell*,[7] he required the minister 'to forbear altogether the choir service, so unedifying and offensive, lest the soldiers should in any tumultuary or disorderly way, attempt the reformation of the Cathedral Church'.[8] During these seventeen years Bishop Matthew Wren (uncle of Sir Christopher) was confined in the Tower of London, where he wrote a large folio volume of Theological Meditations.[9] He was reinstated with the return of the king and died in 1667.

From medieval times, there was often a parish church attached to, or very near, the great church – as at Old St Paul's (two of them), Westminster Abbey, Rochester, St Albans, Sherborne and Worcester. At Ely one such, St Cross, was built against or near the north side of the nave in the 14th century. But by 1566 it was so delapidated that it was demolished,[10] although traces of it remained until 1662, when the north wall of the nave was refaced (see Daniel King's etching of 1656).

At the Dissolution of the monasteries, there were two belfries in the cathedral, with six bells in the west tower and six 'great and small' in the lantern over the old choir.[11] 'In the chapter accounts for . . . 1669 there are records of money spent for "Workmanship and materials in the reparation of the steeple and plumb house [south-west transept] . . . in the south side of it, and removing the bells out of the lantern into the said steeple, and building new belfries in the said

---

122. The west front, *c.* 1730 (Browne Willis). The engraving shows the spire (now removed), differently filled belfry windows and original west door.

The West Prospect of Ely Cathedral, the North Side of which is Ruined

T. Harris del: et Sculp.

steeple''.'[12] Were the two rings together in the tower for any time? If so, no wonder the tower was in a bad way! But Browne Willis says:[13] 'Here are now . . . only five small bells, which hang in the West steeple: they were cast in Dean Wilford's time [1662–67][14] who is reported to have melted down two very large Bells . . . and to have removed them from the Lantern Steeple where (as Fuller tells us) they hung in his time.' According to Fuller:[15] 'when the bells ring (in the bell-tower of the lantern) the wood thereof shaketh and gapeth (no defect but perfection of structure) and exactly choketh into the joynts again.' It is also recorded[16] that, during the repairs under Scott, Dean Goodwin (later Bishop of Carlisle) was shown grooves in one of the vertical beams on the south side of the lantern which proved that the bells were rung from the base of the eastern column of the arch into the south transept, where the ropes would just clear the stall-canopies.

In 1699 the north-west corner of the north transept fell down and was rebuilt by Mr Grumbold of Cambridge, whose work was approved by, among others, Christopher Wren. The remarkable hollow rusticated doorway in the rebuilt portion (practically identical with the old entrance to the College of Arms, London)[17] was, one may safely infer, from Wren's design.

The following comments on Ely and its cathedral in the 1690s are interesting. They are taken from the diary of Celia Fiennes, *Through England on a Side-Saddle in the time of William and Mary 1689–1702 (1888)*:[8]

The Bishop does not care to live long in this place, not being good for his health; he is Lord of all the island, has the command and the jurisdiction. . . . There is a good palace for the Bishop built, but it was unfurnished. There are two churches. Ely Minster is a curious pile of building, all of stone, the outside full of carvings and great arches, and fine pillars in the front, and the inside has the greatest variety and neatness in the works. There are two Chapples, most exactly carv'd in stone, all sorts of figures Cherubins Gilt, and painted in some parts. The Roofe of one Chappel was One Entire stone most delicately carv'd and hung down in great poynts all about the Church. The pillars are carv'd and painted with the history of the bible, especially the new testament and description of Christ's miracles. The Lanthorn in the quire are vastly high and delicately painted, and fine carv'd work all of wood. In it the bells used to be hung (five); the demention of the biggest was so much that when they rung them it shooke the quire so, and the carv'd worke, that it was thought unsafe; therefore they were taken down. There is one Chappel for confession, with a Roome and Chaire of State for the

priest to set to hear the people on their knees confess into his Eare through a hole in the wall. This Church has the most popish remaines of any I have seen. There still remains a Cross over the altar; the candlesticks are 3 quarters of a yard high, massy silver gilt, very heavy. The ffont is one entire piece of white marble, stemm and foote; the Cover was Carv'd Wood, with the image of Christ's being baptised by John, and the holy Dove descending on him, all finely Carv'd white wood, without any paint or varnish.[19]

She also complained Ely was 'the dirtyest place I ever saw – a perfect quagmire'.

According to James Essex (see below), the diocese of Ely in the mid 18th century was known as 'the Dead See'; 'children were sent to play in [the cathedral] on wet days, coal carts were taken along the nave floor because traction was easier there than in the city streets, a Farrier's forge occupied the Baptistery and pigeons were bred and shot in the Cathedral'.[20]

James Essex

Thus, although deteriorating both spiritually and structurally, the exterior of the cathedral continued visually unchanged until the middle of the 18th century, when its condition became alarming. James Essex, the Cambridge architect (1722–84), was called in to report and, in the great works under Bishop Mawson (1754–78), he strengthened the upper part of the east front, which was by then leaning outward by nearly two feet, and renewed the roofs over the whole of the eastern part of the church,[21] besides reinforcing the walls. Essex also largely reconstructed the octagon, but unfortunately drastically altered it – he removed the upper flying buttresses, made sharply pointed pinnacles rising from graduated buttresses in place of the square-on-section battlemented turrets of the lantern and, to replace the decorated windows in the latter, introduced plain 'church-warden Gothick', openings.

In the first edition of Bentham there are plates[22] showing the cathedral in 1756 (copied and improved from Browne Willis, 1730) and in 1765. These are from drawings by Essex, and those of the later date show the alterations as executed by him, except that the pinnacles are crocketted, and also show pinnacles on the lower octagon, which were not in fact built until Victorian times. But curiously, in spite of these published illustrations, very few seem to have noticed, at least not in print, Essex's deviations from the original design. The records usually just say 'he repaired (or saved) the

124

125

octagon'[23] (and this, long after Scott's restoration). But Scott saw the differences and he carefully reconstructed the original design and restored the flying buttreses in 1863.

Essex, although generally considered less lethal as a 'restorer' of ancient churches than Wyatt, certainly ran him close. For not only did he spoil the central octagon and perhaps destroy the 12th-century pulpitum (see Note 37), but he also recommended the entire demolition of the Galilee and condemned the needle spire on the west tower.[24] (The removal of the choir to the east end was, of course, the concern of the dean and chapter.) Yet, on the credit side, he at least saved the octagon from collapse, reroofed the eastern arm of the church and stabilized the east front – no mean achievement!

But later in the century the great church still seems to have been sadly neglected, as the following extract from the diary of the Hon. John Byng, later Viscount Farrington, 5 July 1790, shows: 'I think it a shabby, ill-kept edifice, I mean the inside, for the outside is very lofty and fine . . . the chapels are dawb'd over with whiting; and the stalls and altar are in a paltry taste.'[25]

James Wyatt

The next alteration to the exterior was in 1801,[26] when the spire on the west tower was taken down – not without protest from the townsmen.[27] This was done at the recommendation of Wyatt, who had been called in to make a report on the state of the fabric in 1796 under Bishop Yorke (1787–1808). In fact, the removal of the spire was probably necessary: the great tower had been a severe hazard to the cathedral ever since the erection of its crowning octagon around 1400,[28] and has continued so to this day. (I once heard, to my horror, a consulting architect say he would dearly love to demolish the octagon!) Other recommendations by Wyatt included 'the selling of the lead on the roof . . . and reducing of the number of bells from five to one', after which 'the roof of the Galilee was removed and the lancets . . . blocked up. Mr Bernasconi's contract, in 1801, for the repair of the west end, amounting to £232-14s.-6d., probably covered . . . this.'[29] Bernasconi also repaired the inner and outer portals of the Galilee and substituted radiating tracery (which still remains on the outer doorway) for the original tympana (the outer of which was a cusped, sunk vesica – see Browne Willis's west view of the cathedral). Although executed in Roman cement, Bernasconi's work is as sound today as when first executed.

Wyatt also lowered the ground round the Galilee so 'that instead of a descent at the entrance of three or four steps . . . there is now an ascent . . . of one step'.[30]

The unroofing of the Galilee was a shameful episode and was followed by the insertion of mullions and tracery in the hitherto open arch at its east end, looking into the tower (i.e. above the inner doorway to the church). As Dean Stubbs writes:[31]

Above the vaulting of the Galilee porch there is a large, lofty, almost forgotten chamber, from which originally a grand unobstructed view of the whole length of the Cathedral could be obtained through . . . the Western Tower arch. This chamber must indeed have formed a lofty gallery over the West door, and its three great lancet windows, forty feet further West than the ugly modern tracery which has stupidly been intruded into the tower arch, must for centuries have flooded the long Nave with the golden light of the setting sun.

The west tower and south-west transept

In 1801 the interior of the west tower, hitherto shut out from the nave, 'was much improved and beautified. . . . The old belfry floors with spars and beams for the bell ropes, which then disgraced it, were removed; and the noble and lofty arch by which it communicated with the nave was laid open to view'; 'a plain, vaulted roof somewhat above the points of the arches' was erected, but only in 'a soft plaster, by no means safe from accidental injury or designed mischief'.[32] Essex describes the south-west transept[33] in his report of 1757 as 'in a worse condition than any part of the church' although 'a great deal of work, both of wood and iron [had] been bestowed upon it, but with little judgment and as little service to the building'.[34] But what he did to strengthen the transept is not revealed.

This great building with its wealth of Norman and transitional arcading had been, from at least the late 17th century, boarded up with stud and plaster from the tower. Known as the 'Plumb House' and later as the 'Workshop', it was cluttered up with carpenters' benches, materials for repair and other lumber. It remained like this until the 1840s (see below).

The choir

Before the fall of the central tower in 1322, the monastic choir was under the crossing (as still at Winchester, Gloucester and St David's). Its wes-

77

tern limit was closed by a 12th-century pulpitum (carrying the organ), the west wall of which escaped the general destruction of the choir, and was retained when Alan of Walsingham's octagon arose above the new choir. Built on the old site within new (or repaired) north and south stone walls, this spanned the great octagonal space from west to east, as on Browne Willis's plan.

134

As far back as the 17th century this arrangement was considered unsatisfactory. Bishop Gunning (1675–84) had intended to remove the choir to the east end 'which if he had done, and left the Cross Isle and Lantern open into the Western Part, like St Paul's Cathedral, London, it would have added vastly to the Beauty of the Church'.[35] But it was not until 1770 that the choir, with its 14th-century stalls, was removed and placed in the presbytery – the six eastern bays of the cathedral. But to do this, many fine memorials scattered over the presbytery floor (shown in Browne Willis's plan) were removed and placed in the aisles – not without some suffering in the process (e.g. Bishop Hotham's sumptuous monument lost its effigy and the fine canopy its spired summit). Moving the choir brought other losses. On the outside face of the north wall of the old choir there was a painted row of seven Decorated canopied niches over as many cusped, obviously Early English, arches. Could not this difference of style – the later over the earlier – be due to the survival of much of the lower part of the wall, with its painting still visible, after the crash of 1322, and the rebuilding of the upper part with its consequently new decoration in the style of that day? These painted niches contained 'portraits' of six Saxon bishops and Duke Brithnoth (slain 991) and, on the demolition of the wall in 1771, seven cells containing their respective bones were found. These remains were carefully collected into as many cases and placed under Bishop West's tomb in his chantry chapel.[36] Lastly, the uniquely surviving Norman pulpitum was utterly destroyed.[37] Essex made a few sketches, not of the whole screen, but of details only, and these lay forgotten in the British Museum until 1909 when they were seen by W. H. St John Hope, who reconstructed the design from them.[38]

123

133

The new choir was enclosed to the west by an attractive 'Gothick' organ-screen and to the east by a modest reredos in the same style under the great east window. Bishop Mawson contributed £1,000 to the cost and commissioned an artist to fill the great lancets with 'modern stained glass', but his death in 1770 prevented its execution.[39] It is interesting to note the enthusiasm with which this transfer-

135
141

ence of the choir was regarded at the time. Bentham[40] says: 'it is allowed by the best judges to be one of the most useful and ornamental improvements that could have been effected; the Design was worthy of that taste and spirit of improvement which so eminently distinguishes this age and Country'. The organ and voices could be heard better, the view of the octagon was greatly improved, and the east end of the cathedral, formerly 'an useless encumbrance', now became 'the most useful part of the church'.

The custom of hearing the Sunday sermon in the naves of cathedrals (the 'sermon place'), to which the congregation migrated from the choir services, seems to have been widely established from the 16th to the earlier 19th centuries. At Ely, Browne Willis's plan shows a pulpit in the nave near the pulpitum (called variously rood-loft or organ loft) and he says:[41] 'the Bishop, Dean, Prebendaries and others of the Church sit before the Organ Loft to hear sermons, which are preach'd in the Pulpit . . . in the body of the church, with forms round it for the Inhabitants of the Town'.[42]

136

134

After the removal of the choir to the east end, the sermon place moved with it to the octagon and the two bays east of it, as mentioned by Stubbs:[43] 'Previous to the last removal [1852], the custom was that only one sermon was preached in the morning to the parishioners of the Cathedral Precincts and of the Parishes of St Mary and Holy Trinity, who assembled together and occupied seats provided by themselves in the Octagon and the two bays east of it [in front of the organ-screen]. The sermons were usually preached by the Canon in residence.' Bishop Harvey Goodwin in his *Ely Gossip* says:[44]

136

The worshippers from the Parish churches, as I was told, usually arrived in the Cathedral before 'College Prayers' were finished and walked about the Nave until the time for the Sermon came. The notabilities of Ely had their own recognized courses in the nave, into which others did not intrude. I gathered that the custom was a very social one and that the news and gossip of the day were freely discussed while the Church ambulant was waiting for its spiritual food.

As a result of this practice, 'a stranger will no doubt feel some disgust, at finding the greater part of this [south] transept lumbered with benches, which are removed, against Sundays and Holidays, into the space between the Octagon and the choir, where sermons are preached'.[45]

There were numerous gifts to the cathedral in Wyatt's time. A painting of St Peter released from prison by an angel was given by Bishop Yorke and placed on Essex's altarpiece in 1801. 'It is the work of Joseppe de Ribera, who was called the Spanish Titian, and flourished about the middle of the 17th century.'[46] And 'the mean pulpit, which formerly blemished this part of the Cathedral, has been removed to its proper place, a village church. The persevering munificence of Bishop Yorke substituted for it one of carved English oak, of an octagonal form, on Norman columns and arches with their characteristic mouldings, beautifully and correctly executed under the direction of Mr Groves, an architect of considerable repute'.[47] Then, in 1807, Bishop Yorke paid for the new window in the west tower to be made and beautified with painted glass, as Millers[48] says, 'at his Lordship's sole and great expense; and he enriched it with two very beautiful paintings on glass, one representing Pilate washing his hands, and the other Christ bearing his Cross. Two other paintings on glass were afterwards added by Dr Waddington. They were some of those numerous spoils of foreign churches ... brought into this country [and] dispersed in different parts of it.' These have certainly been transferred to a place fully worthy of them.[49]

The transepts

The eastern aisles, north and south, were originally divided into chapels and parted from the central space by wooden screens.[50] Those in the south transept were taken down in 1814, the chapels thrown into one to enlarge the library (formerly in the south chapel only) and the whole aisle boarded or walled up from the transept. (The southern bay is now opened up again as a chapel.) The opposite, west aisle seems always to have been walled up, 'so closely that the columns are almost hidden',[51] as Smart's view shows.[52] The upper part of this closing wall, just above the dado of intersecting arches, was removed in 1850 so as to show the capitals and arches of the arcade.[53] In 1849 'the Dean and Chapter have been compelled ... to undertake ... a very expensive and costly repair of the south Transept ... the principal timbers of the roof of which were found to be rotten. ... It is intended to replace entirely the mutilated sculpture of the timber cornice' and 'the painting of the roof'.[54] The next year this was finished: 'The bright rich colours of the angels contrasting with the chocolate and white in which most of the remaining decoration is executed.'[55] In this south transept, 'the carved oak door ... to the Dean and Chapter's vestry in the western aisle deserves attention. It is not exactly known' where it came

123. Up to 1770 a row of painted niches with 'portraits' of Saxon bishops survived on the wall enclosing the old choir. The only visual record is that printed in Gough's *Sepulchral Monuments*.

from. The carving is nearly identical with that on the door of Bishop Alcock's chantry and was 'no doubt ... attached to some building erected by that prelate. It was found at Landbeach, and sent to the Cathedral by the Rev. H. Fardell, one of the Canons'.[56]

Lastly for this period, Sweeting[57] mentions a pamphlet of 1827, *Notes on the Cambridgeshire Churches*, which tells of Purbeck shafts painted yellow ochre, Walsingham's stalls painted,[58] and nave, octagon, lantern and transepts colour-washed,[59] all recently done. He adds: 'Within about twenty-five years what had been introduced as embellishment was removed as disfigurements, and the removal cost possibly as much as the introduction.' In March 1830 Cobbet visited Ely and 'walked round the beautiful Cathedral, that honour to our Catholic forefathers and that standing disgrace to our Protestant selves ... it is in a state of disgraceful irrepair and disfigurement. The great and magnificent windows to the east have been shortened at the bottom, and the space plastered up with brick and mortar ... for the purpose of saving the expense of restoring the glass in repair. Great numbers of the windows ... have been partly closed up in the same manner and others quite closed up'.[60]

In 1848 Hewett could write:[61]

Never was there a more ill-judged step than the removal of the choir to the east end. . . . To give it such stinted proportions, and for this purpose to displace some of the fine old monuments, and to hide others, to obscure the pillars, and, above all, to erect the miserable organ gallery which we now behold, may surely be pronounced most tasteless performances. . . . The restoration of the Choir to its ancient position under the octagon has already been advocated; one other reason for desiring it seems to be this, that if the stalls are re-erected in Bishop Hotham's choir, they will obscure its graceful pillars as they now obscure Bishop Northwold's, but if erected under the octagon they will hide nothing. Hotham's portion would thus form a very good Sacrarium, separated from its aisles by light parcloses of stone running from pillar to pillar.

Victorian restorations

Ely had one of the earliest of the great Victorian cathedral restorations, and Dean Peacock (1839–58) was the driving force behind it. The work commenced in 1843, when one of the first things done was the releading of the roofs. But this good beginning was clouded by an act of vandalism: the demolition of the fine 13th-century sextry barn, just north of the Lady chapel, 'on the ground that the repairs it required were too expensive'. Releading a great roof is always a formidable undertaking, and the prospect of further great expenses to be incurred on the cathedral probably influenced the dean and chapter against preserving the barn – which, from many accounts, was a noble building.[62]

The clearance of the west tower and south-west transept began in 1845. The vaulted roof in the tower, erected in 1801, was removed and the beautiful interior made visible from below. The painting of its ceiling, still extant, was by a talented amateur, Henry Styleman le Strange of Hunstanton Hall.[63] Around 1847 Scott made a further improvement to the tower: in the early 15th century piers and arches had been inserted in and under the original ground openings of the tower to resist the weight of the octagon added to its top in the late 14th century. Above them could just be seen the outer moulding only of the original openings.[64] Now the space between these was excavated so as to show as many as possible of the elaborate mouldings of the original arches and give us some idea of their former splendour when seen close up from the tower's interior gallery. Stewart comments on these alterations:[65] 'The plaster vault and

belfry have been cleared away, and the threatening signs of settlement and unsoundness which were alarming a few years back, have been so disguised and modified by recent changes as to excite comparatively little attention; and there are few who know how difficult it has been to keep the structure together during so many centuries' – a still continuing difficulty!

The south-west transept was cleared, cleaned, repaired and opened to the public. A new foursquare Early English font by Scott, of 1853, was placed here to form a baptistery.[66] In the transept east wall, the entrance arch to an apsidal chapel (formerly 'blocked up and propped by a huge brick pier') was opened and the chapel rebuilt in 1848. (It is now called St Catherine's chapel – not its ancient dedication.) The adjoining arch to the south nave aisle was also opened up.

It may be of interest here to quote from the *Handbook* (1852):[67]

The restorations, which have been for some years in progress, have been executed throughout with the most scrupulous care, preserving every portion of uninjured surface, and re-producing what is mutilated or destroyed as nearly as possible in exact conformity with the indications of the ancient work afforded by the parts which remain, and in the same material. They were at first carried out under the direction of the present Dean, assisted from time to time by Professor Willis and by the occasional advice of professional friends; but towards the end of . . . 1847, Mr G. Scott was appointed architect to the works, and under his direction the re-arrangement of the Choir and the other restorations still in progress are being carried on.

Scott lost no time in examining the whole building and issued a report upon the state of the fabric and the amount of restoration needed. But his first and chief task was to superintend the removal of the choir from the six eastern bays of the cathedral to the threshold of the octagon, lengthening it by one bay and leaving the two easternmost bays as a retrochoir – this was accomplished by 1851.[68] Also, of course, Scott substituted new and more 'correct' furniture for Essex's choir-screen, organ and reredos; and, eventually, the empty panels under the stall canopies were filled with carvings of scenes from the Old Testament (north side) and the New (south side). They were designed and carried out by 'Mr Abeloos of Louvain'[69] and cost about £18 each to individual subscribers.[70] The sub-stalls, mostly new, and statuettes of abbots and bishops, were done by John Philip and 'Mr Rattee of Cambridge'.

The form and peculiar position of the new organ

143

(in place by 1851) in the triforium, on the north side of the choir and projecting over the stalls, was probably inspired by the famous organ in Strasbourg Cathedral.[71] The carving was by Mr Rattee and the gilding and so on by 'Mr Castell of London'. In the aisle there is an elaborate pierced
142 circular stone staircase to the organ – possibly inspired by the form of the organ-staircase in St Maclou at Rouen and the piercing of the earlier library staircase in Rouen Cathedral.

The carving of the new choir-screen 'from the
139 designs by Mr G. G. Scott is probably not sur-
140 passed by anything of the kind in the kingdom. The figures and groups are the work partly of Mr Rattee and partly of Mr John Philip. The brass gates and scroll work in the lower panels, are by Hardman of Birmingham; the ornamental iron work by Potter of London, who has also supplied hot water apparatus for warming the stalls'.[72]

Stained glass by Wailes was inserted in the eastern lancets in 1857, and the following year the gorgeous reredos – the first and most elaborate of
145 Scott's altarpieces – was finished, having taken five years to produce. Its five compartments were filled with sculptures in alabaster – Entry into Jerusalem, Washing the Feet, Last Supper, Agony in the garden and Christ Carrying the Cross, and with figures of angels, prophets, Evangelists and doctors. It cost £4,000 and was the gift of John Dunn Gardner, Esq. of Chatteris, Cambridgeshire, as a memorial to his first wife.[73]

Scott's restoration of the octagon in the early 1860s (as mentioned) involved refashioning the
126 lantern and its windows, restoring its flying buttresses, and, about 1876–79, adding pinnacles
127 to the eight-angle buttresses of the lower octagon. The interior was relieved of its white and yellow wash in 1850, when remains of the old colouring were discovered everywhere. *The Ecclesiologist* (Oct. 1850)[74] says of these remains: 'the bosses and ribs were gilt, and the spaces between the latter covered with a continued pattern of [pointed] quatrefoils in white upon a green ground . . . the whole effect of this design is to suggest raised tracery work. All this is being literally reproduced.' This decoration is shown in a lithograph of 1852 by Edward H. Buckler (across the octagon, north-west to south-east), but only over the chancel arch. But in a similar view (south-west to north-east),[75] the pattern covers the whole of the 'vault', and very fine it looks. The whole restoration of the octagon and lantern was a memorial to Dean Peacock and subscriptions to it amounted to around £10,000.[76]

The last great work was begun in 1858, when the nave roof, hitherto open to the leads, was
137 ceiled; and a grand scheme of painted decoration
140 (based on that of the ceiling of St Michael's, Hildersheim, in Germany) was devised by Henry Styleman le Strange, 'and the six Western bays were designed and the chief parts executed by him and finished in 1861'.[77] Sadly he died the next year but his friend, 'J. Gambier Parry, Esq. of Highnam Court, Glos. undertook to finish the work . . . which took him until Christmas 1864'[78] – a remarkable example of a great work being successfully accomplished by non-professional artists, and without fee! The following extract from Murray's *Handbook* (1862),[79] while the nave ceiling was proceeding, will show the pride generally felt in this and indeed the whole of the great restoration:

When the nave roof has been completed there can be no doubt that Ely will be the most magnificently restored church in Europe, and will afford one of the most perfect examples of a great medieval cathedral in the height of its original splendour. The colour, as far as it has yet gone, is very satisfactory. All gloom and coldness of neglect and white-wash has disappeared; and eye rests contentedly on the rich glass of the windows, and on the golden diapers of roof and corbels, set forth and relieved as they are by the neutral tints of the oak choir-screen and stalls, the grey stone of the walls and the dark marble of the Purbeck shafts and capitals.

In the early 1870s the west tower, always in trouble, was braced with iron bands. In 1873 the twelve hundredth anniversary of the founding of the abbey (preceding the present cathedral) in 673, was celebrated by a five-day 'Bisexcentenary' of St Etheldreda. This included special services, with sermons by bishops, organ recitals, a festival of choirs in the cathedral with 676 singers, luncheons, and a lecture by Scott (read by his son George) on the history of the building and so on. The same year an interesting account was published by Dean Merevale which includes Scott's lecture.

In 1878 the panelled ceiling of the south-west transept was painted by Gambier Parry, and the floor laid with encaustic tiles of marble.[80] The floors of the choir, transepts and nave and its aisles have likewise been renewed, leaving the choir and presbytery aisles only to show old paving and interesting gravestones.[81]

Ely must be almost the only old cathedral with only a few fragments of medieval stained glass.[82] But, in quantity at least, it must exceed all others in Victorian examples of the art[83] – much of it very bad, but the great east window by Wailes is fine and impressive.

Many other items of repair and decoration continued to the end of the century and beyond. In 1904 Stubbs[84] records expenses from 1843–98, including personal gifts, to be over £70,000.

Fortunately, in this century there is not much to record. The organ, enlarged in 1867, was entirely reconstructed by Harrisons of Durham in 1908 and again enlarged. In 1938 the Lady chapel was returned to the cathedral (see below) and restored. The same year, Bishop West's chantry was repaired under J. N. Comper and reopened for divine service; while Bishop Alcock's chapel was restored by the college he founded – Jesus College, Cambridge.[85]

In the 1950s the lantern timbers, found to be infested by the death-watch beetle, were restored from the result of an appeal by Dean Hankey, and it was under him 'that the Octagon was surely at last, after a delay of six hundred years, put to its ideal use as a site for an altar', in 1973, with furniture designed by the late George Pace.[86]

Lastly, the west tower was in trouble again, and after a survey by the late Donovan Purcell another appeal was launched and very thorough strengthening operation was carried out from 1973–74, with the 'most up-to-date techniques available' and Professor Heyman as consultant. Executed by Messrs Rattee and Kett, the repair cost about £200,000[87] – may it prove a lasting one!

The Lady chapel

As mentioned at the beginning of this chapter, the Lady chapel, which had most probably already been mutilated, was in 1562 given to the parishioners of St Cross, as their original church, first built in the 14th century north of the cathedral nave, was by then decrepit.

The following extracts (c. 1770–1870) testify, by their mention of remains of painting and gilding and fragments of stained glass, to the original splendour of this sumptuously ornamented building. And they also show to what pitiable state three hundred years of parochial use had reduced it.

Bentham (c. 1770)[88] writes that 'the elegance of this building could not preserve it from being mangled by the ignorant rage of Fanaticks; and the large remains of its sculpture are now miserably clogged and obscured by whitewash'.

According to Millers,[89] 'it displays a rich profusion of every sort of ornament; long since covered with an execrable crust of whitewash, but once beautified with colouring and gilding of which some very faint traces were lately visible,

where the wash was scaled off . . . poor dim shadows of faded splendour.' He says[90] that the roof bosses 'represent the Nativity, the Crucifixion and parts of the history of the Virgin Mary; the figures . . . painted in many colours and gilded; scrolls are annexed to some of them, on which are inscribed fragments . . . of the *Magnificat* and *Ave Maria.*'

Cresy and Taylor, writing in 1817,[91] both say that the wall arcades are 'now mutilated and whitewashed. The few parts that are cleaned show the whole to have been coloured of different gaudy colours, which [according to Cresy] could not improve the effect' – though, interestingly enough, Taylor disagrees. Both say that 'at the Ends [of the Chapel] are very wide windows . . . the divisions are wide and the heads not elegant. The vaulting is very flat, intricate but not elegant.' These criticisms were very unusual at that time.

Hewett writes:[92]

The most conflicting feelings assail us on viewing this remarkable structure . . . of five ample severies, surrounded by canopied niches of unwonted elaboration, lit by windows of great size and beauty, covered by a roof of almost magick lightness, and everywhere displaying the traces of the most brilliant colour, it is, perhaps, nowhere to be surpassed, or even equalled in splendour. Its area filled with the most vile pewing, its carved work broken down, its windows – here robbed of their painted glass – there altogether blocked up, it presents an unusual picture of decay and desecration.[93] One cannot easily believe that it is still used as a place of worship; yet so it is. . . . It is said of a well-known popish architect of the present day, that he burst into tears on first beholding this chapel and exclaimed 'O God! What has England done to deserve this?'

After mentioning that there were fragments of stained glass in some of the windows, the *Handbook* (1852)[94] says: 'The ceiling was painted azure blue and studded with silver stars; the bosses . . . have been richly coloured and gilded but . . . long since defaced with whitewash. . . . A few modern monumental tablets . . . do not contribute much to its adornment.'

Stewart[95] writes in 1868 that 'the whole building was covered with conventional figures of roses, lilies and crosses, painted in prominent colours on . . . white. . . . The timber roof, which now protects the vault, is a modern one, constructed in 1762. The space between the roof and the vault is lighted with circular openings or "oes", but the tracery which they once possessed was worked in clunch, and is almost destroyed by exposure to the weather.'

Of the stalls of the wall arcading, Millers says:[96] 'At the east end were eight of the same sort, and a central one, higher and wider than the rest. But this and one on each side of it are covered most preposterously by four Corinthian columns and a pediment' – the reredos.[97] He adds that 'the unsightly pews and benches that long disgraced [the Chapel] were all removed . . . in 1806' and 'have been replaced by new but rather inconvenient ones on a regular plan, and at a very considerable expense'.

During Scott's restoration, 'in pursuance of the temporary devotion of the Lady chapel to the Cathedral service, the ancient altar-levels have been restored and paved with encaustic tiles. We are sorry to have to add that, instead of the stalls being properly placed as originally intended, they have been ranged along the east end, right and left of the altar. Besides the extreme impropriety of this arrangement, the practical disadvantage has ensued of one half of the choir not being able to hear the other sufficiently well to keep the time even'.[98]

I remember how depressing the interior looked just before 1938 (when the chapel was returned to the cathedral) with the great south windows encumbered by long and dingy curtains. But when the Lady chapel ceased to be parochial, a thorough restoration was undertaken at the expense of the 'Friends' aided by a public subscription, the chapter funds and the Pilgrim Trust. Under the supervision of H. C. Hughes, a Cambridge architect, it involved cleaning the carvings by vacuuming, stripping the interior of its inappropriate furnishings,[99] laying a new floor, erecting an ampler altar, and removing the monuments to less obvious situations.[100]

Bibliography

* Browne Willis, 1730. 2nd edn 1742.

Bentham, 1771. James Bentham, The History and Antiquities of the Conventual and Cathedral Church of Ely. 2nd edn 1812, with 49 fine engravings.

Stevenson, 1817. William Stevenson, FSA, A Supplement to the second edition of Mr Bentham's History and Antiquities of . . . Ely. 16 fine engravings.

Millers, 1807. George Millers, A Description of the Cathedral Church of Ely. 3rd edn 1834, with 18 fine engravings.

* see also bibliography to the Introduction.

Hewett, 1848. John W. Hewett, A Brief History and Description of the Conventual and Cathedral Church of the Holy Trinity, Ely.

* The Ecclesiologist. Articles on Ely Cathedral restoration: X, 1849 (N.S. VII); XI, 1850 (N.S. VIII); XII, 1851 (N.S. IX); XIV, 1853 (N.S. XI).

Handbook, 1852. Handbook to the Cathedral Church of Ely.

Stewart, 1868. Rev. D. J. Stewart, Architectural History of Ely Cathedral. With plans of city, monastery, cathedral church, etc.

* Sweeting (Bell), 1901. Rev. W. D. Sweeting, Ely, The Cathedral and See, Bell's Cathedral Series.

Stubbs, 1904. Charles W. Stubbs, Ely Cathedral Handbook, 21st edn.

Dorman, 1945. Bernard E. Dorman, The Story of Ely and its Cathedral.

* Carey (Pitkin), 1973. Dean Carey, Ely Cathedral, Pitkin Pictorial.

Notes

1 These facts and considerations make improbable the alternative suggestion that the damage at Ely was effected in the Civil War – but there appears to be no record of when it was actually done.
2 Stubbs, 181.
3 Bentham (2nd edn 1812), 213.
4 Topographical Excursion (1635). For details see bibliography to Introduction; see also Bristol, Lichfield and Winchester. The name of the diarist is revealed by one mention of the town clerk of New Malden, Essex, a Mr Hammond, as his namesake. Passage quoted in R. Birt, Glories of Ely Cathedral (1949).
5 Daniel Defoe, A Tour through the Whole Island of Great Britain (1724–26), quoted in Dorman, 52.
6 Millers, 101, cites the 'high state of preservation' of the remaining Norman windows and corbel tables, etc., in his time.
7 Quoted in Murray's Handbook (1862), 257–58.
8 Compare their 'reformation' at Peterborough in 1643!
9 Bentham, 201, note.
10 The parishioners were then given the cathedral Lady chapel as their church, renamed Holy Trinity.
11 Stewart, 119.
12 Stewart, 65.
13 Browne Willis, 335.
14 In view of the date '1669' in the above chapter accounts, are we to infer that there was a delay of two years in paying for the removal, etc?
15 Thomas Fuller (1608–61), The History of the Worthies of England (1662), quoted by Stubbs, 98.
16 Stubbs, 117, quoting Dean Howson's Cathedral Essays.

17 See pl. in L.C.C. monograph on the college; and *The Wren Society*, XIX, pl. XIV. The great keystone still remains in Godliman St.

18 Quoted in *Fenland Notes and Queries*, I, 291–93, and Sweeting (Bell), 30.

19 See note 66.

20 Quoted from Donovan Purcell (article in *Era – Journal of Eastern Region of the RIBA* – Dec. 1968, I, 21). Unfortunately he gives no refs.

21 Dorman, 54: 'The roof, which was then constructed exactly as the roof of the nave now appears, was what is known as a trussed rafter roof. . . . After getting the East Front back into the perpendicular by means of screws [compare Beverley N transept front] Mr Essex constructed a fresh roof to the choir and Presbytery in what is known as the queen-post system, with enormous tie-beams which stretch from one wall to the other.' (Unfortunately no refs.)

22 Bentham, pls I, XLII, XLIII.

23 The earliest adverse comments on Essex's lantern known to me are in a ms copy of two diaries of 1817 by E. Cresy and G. L. Taylor, in my possession. Cresy (pp. 188–89) calls it 'a miserable production'; Taylor (p. 242) says 'the pinnacles at the angles are very thin and flat – I never can believe it is the original design of Walsingham, 1323, as we are instructed in the book of Miller' (Millers, 1807) and he mentions the missing flying buttresses.

24 Of the Galilee he wrote: 'Beginning at the West End of the Cathedral, the first part that presents itself is the Porch, the roof of which is in so ruinous a state that it is absolutely necessary to take it down. But as the walls are in a bad condition, occasioned by the Wett which has long got to them thro' the gutters, and as this part is neither ornamental nor useful, but must be attended with great expense, if repaired as it ought to be, it will be better to take it down quite, than repair it, as it will be of more service to apply the materials to the use of other parts of the Church.' He also calls the spire 'neither useful nor ornamental' (Essex's report to the dean and chapter, 1757, quoted by Stewart, 54, 65).

25 Dorman, 56.

26 Date quoted in Sweeting (Bell), 32.

27 Millers (3rd edn 1834), 38.

28 Millers, 65, quotes Essex's report: 'The great octagon tower is a very slight building, but has been much assisted by . . . timber work and other ties of iron, without which it could hardly stand.'

29 Sweeting (Bell), 32.

30 *The Beauties of England and Wales*, II (1801), 162.

31 Stubbs, 30.

32 Millers (3rd edn 1834), 44.

33 The term 'Galilee' was formerly sometimes used for this transept plus porch (e.g. Cresy and Taylor, and some earlier writers). Very confusing and incorrect!

34 Stewart, 65.

35 Browne Willis, II, 334.

36 Bentham, 85, 285–86; R. Gough, *Sepulchral Monuments* (1786), I, clvi; Hewett, 18; Stewart, 113.

37 It is generally assumed that Essex destroyed the pulpitum – he died in 1784 (Stevenson, 138) and, in Bentham (2nd edn 1812), addenda, 1, is a description of the original plan of the cathedral, 'drawn by Mr Essex, written by Mr Bentham and enlarged upon by Mr Essex', presumably some time after the removal of the choir in 1770. Essex says: 'the front of [the pulpitum] was a solid wall, pierced by three doors and decorated with small pillars and feint arches, behind which was a low arcade which supported the rood loft, the walls or battlements of which *are composed* of open work of little pillars and circles. The way up to this gallery was by a stone staircase, on the north side *still remaining* at (d)' – on the plan, which shows part of the *circular wall*. Surely the words here in italics indicate that the screen, at least in part, must have been left standing by Essex. This is confirmed by a report on the state of the fabric by Wyatt (1797) which recommends the 'removal of the old rood loft'. Sweeting (Bell), 32, says 'the ancient rood loft in the nave was removed. As it had ceased to be the entrance to the choir, it was probably deemed useless.' If the above reasoning is correct, and Wyatt's report not a forgery, Essex stands relieved of much opprobrium!

38 W. H. St John Hope, 'Quire Screens in English Churches', *Archaeologia*, LXVIII, 1917, pls IX, X; 43, 44; desc. 87.

39 Millers, 76–77, preserves details of what was intended: 'The middle light of the [upper] five was to have contained a whole-length figure of St Etheldreda, and below it, the Royal Arms; the next light on the right . . . a whole length of St Peter, and below, the arms of the Bishop impaled with those of the see; that on the left . . . a whole length of St Paul, and below at the arms of the then dean, Dr Thomas; and the two side lights the arms of the prebendaries, four and four, according to their precedent in the choir. The middle light below was to have contained a picture of the Nativity, with angels descending in a stream of light; the two side-lights, figures of the Four Evangelists. Each compartment was to have had appropriate decorations. . . . The figure of St Peter, and some of the Arms were finished'. Stubbs says these are 'now placed in the easternmost window of the northern triforium of the nave. . . . The heads only of St Paul and St Etheldreda were completed' and placed in two windows at the deanery.

40 Bentham, 285.

41 Browne Willis, 337.

42 But a letter from Dr Tanner to Browne Willis (quoted in Hewett, 15, and Stewart, 43) reads: 'on which [the ancient stone screen], toward the east, is placed the organ and on the west part are seats for the Bishop'. 'On' or 'before' – which is correct?

43 Stubbs, 123.

44 Quoted in Stubbs, 123.

45 Millers, 62.

46 Millers, 78.

47 Millers, 70, 71.

48 Millers, 55.

49 This window is well shown in a fine engraving by R. W. Smart, 1847 (reproduced Dorman, pl. 8), but the

glass appears to represent four figures and not scenes with people.

50 Millers, 62, says these were 'of inferior workmanship' and 'much shattered and defaced'. A. Vallance, *Greater English Church Screens* (1947), 42, says that one wooden screen, said to have been in the S transept but, since 1898 at St Edmund's Chapel, was, when he visited in 1914, 'painted with a thick coat of graining' and excessively restored.

51 Millers, 61.

52 Mentioned in note 49.

53 *The Ecclesiologist* Oct. 1850, N.S. VIII, 159.

54 *The Ecclesiologist*, Aug. 1849, p. 18.

55 *The Ecclesiologist*, Oct. 1850, p. 159.

56 *Handbook* (1852), 31.

57 Sweeting (Bell), 34.

58 Sweeting (Bell), 83, says they were painted mahogany colour, while earlier (1817) memoranda on Cathedrals (ms), 218, says the stalls were all painted a dark stone colour.

59 Stubbs, 26, gives 1823 for these five items.

60 Quoted by Dorman, 60.

61 Hewett, 17, 18.

62 Sweeting (Bell), 34–35.

63 Murray's *Handbook* (1862), 178.

64 Millers, 48: 'Look above the arch of communication of the tower. The different colours of the courses of the masonry (which however, are a good deal affected by different states of weather), plainly show the outline of a higher and wider arch within which the present was built.' And p. 45: 'The outward face of the top of the Western arch still remains perfect in its original form, with the appropriate ornaments resting on corbels', but they could only be seen from the 'roof of the portico'. (An aerial view shows this must have meant after the upper roof was removed, i.e. from inside the former upper room.) What does 'resting on corbels' mean?

65 Stewart, 66.

66 The old font, which stood in the nave, was given to the cathedral by Dean Spencer 1693; of most unusual design, it was removed in 1866 and given to a Victorian church at Prickwillow near Ely, where it still is. Bentham (pl. XXXV) shows it with finely carved wooden cover with statuettes of cherubs and, at top, of St John baptizing Christ, beneath the Holy Dove on the pulley. It is described by N. Pevsner (*Buildings of England: Cambridgeshire*, 365) as standing 'in its exquisite white marble beauty . . . like a gilt goblet on a poor man's bare boards. The bowl is decorated with large shells and strings of pearls emanating from them and wound round the pretty necks of cherubs.'

67 *Handbook* (1852), 17, note.

68 Although the 14th-c. stalls were carefully re-erected, *The Ecclesiologist*, 1853, XIV, 2, says the space of Bishop Hotham's three bays was too small for all thirty stalls aside: 'the superfluous stalls are used, without (of course) their canopies, for the westernmost subsellae' – the rest of the latter being new. Birt, *op. cit.*, 39, says

'there is still a litter of old canopies, for which no place was found, in the north triforium of the nave and the south triforium of the choir'.

69 Except for one panel – The Nativity – by John Philip.

70 Dorman, 63.

71 This position for the organ was not unknown in England. Engravings show organs projecting from N choir triforiums at Canterbury (Dart, *The History and Antiquities of the Cathedral Church of Canterbury*, 1726) and Lincoln (Hollar), and the organ under the N choir arcade is shown in Hollar's view of Old St Paul's choir.

72 *Handbook* (1852), 35.

73 Murray, 205.

74 *The Ecclesiologist*, Oct. 1850, N.S. VIII, 158.

75 Murray's *Handbook* (1862), pl. III.

76 Stubbs, 115–16.

77 Stubbs, 77.

78 *Our National Cathedrals*, anon. (188), II, 23.

79 Murray's *Handbook* (1862), 197.

80 Stubbs, 71.

81 The centre part of the octagon floor has a simple pattern of black squares arranged in saltires, of uncertain date – it appears in Turner's watercolour, but not in Bentham (pl. XLI) which clearly shows the previous design. This consisted of 'paths' of stone from nave, transepts and choir meeting to form a cross at an octagon of diminishing 'rings' of stones in the centre, and the angles of the cross are filled with stones radiating from them.

82 Carey (Pitkin), 16, 18: 'the West window is beautiful. Most of the glass is 16th-century French, with some very skilful adaptation dating from 1853.'

83 By 1866 about seventy windows had been so filled! See Sweeting (Bell), 36, for Dean Goodwin's progress report.

84 Stubbs, appendix II.

85 Birt, *op. cit.*, 40.

86 Carey (Pitkin), 18.

87 Carey (Pitkin), 20.

88 Bentham (2nd edn 1812), 286.

89 Millers (3rd edn 1834), 96.

90 Millers (3rd edn 1834), 97.

91 Edward Cresy and G. L. Taylor, ms account of cathedral visit (1817), 66–67 (Cresy), 224–46 (Taylor).

92 Hewett, 22.

93 Confirming this, the tracery of many of the windows etc. are in a state of rapid decomposition (Archaeological Institute, 'Ecclesiological and Architectural Topography of England', 1852, item 100).

94 *Handbook* (1852), 46–47.

95 Stewart, 141, 144.

96 Millers, 98–99.

97 The only description of the altarpiece I have met with. Whether it dated from before or after the repewing of 1806 does not appear.

98 *The Ecclesiologist*, Oct. 1850, N.S. VIII, 160.

99 Birt, *op. cit.*, 40.

100 Dorman, 70.

Ely: octagon and Galilee

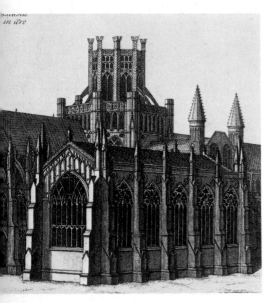

124. The cathedral from the north-east, before 1730 (Browne Willis). Scott based his restoration of the octagon on this engraving.

125. Essex's octagon, a photograph taken before 1863.

126. The octagon after Scott's restoration but before the pinnacles had been added to the lower stage.

127. The octagon after 1879, with Scott's pinnacles on the lower stage.

128–30. The Galilee outer portal. *Left*: detail of pl. 122, the only record of its original form, though marred by a later insertion. *Centre*: Bernasconi's work of 1801, which still remains. *Right*: Scott's design for a new outer portal, never carried out (*The Archaeological Journal*, 1879).

131. The Galilee inner portal: Bernasconi reconstruction of 1801 (Winkles) The original form is unknown.

132. Galilee inner portal after Scott's restoration. Note the new marble pillars. A design for the ironwork is temporarily painted on the new door.

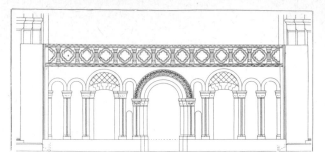

133. The Romanesque pulpitum was perhaps destroyed by Essex, but from his sketches W. H. St John Hope was able to make this reconstruction.

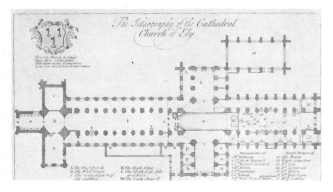

134. Plan of the cathedral in the early 18th century (Browne Willis), showing the choir in its old position under the octagon. The pulpitum, marked G, is one bay to the west.

Ely: choir-screen and nave ceiling

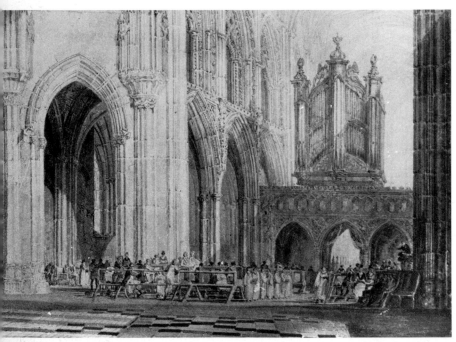

135. Wild's engraving of the central area after Essex's restoration, with Essex's new screen two bays east of the eastern arch.

136. Detail from Turner's painting looking across the octagon. Essex's screen and organ are the same as in pl. 135, but the pavement is new. The congregation is about to hear a 'nave sermon'.

Opposite
139. The choir looking west, *c.* 1858. Restoration of the choir is finished, but the new nave ceiling has only just been begun and there is scaffolding towards the west.

140. The same view after the completion of the ceiling. Note Scott's gasoliers and the organ suggested by that of Strasbourg Cathedral.

137. The nave looking east (Winkles, 1836), showing the open timber roof, later boarded and painted as it is today.

138. Looking east across the octagon towards the choir, after the completion of Scott's work. The new screen is two bays west of Essex's. Note the as-yet-unspoiled tracery between the eastern arch of the octagon and the choir vault.

142. Stair to the organ-loft,
designed by Scott – a
combination of two staircases in
Rouen churches.

141. Winkles's view of the choir
looking east after Essex's
restoration. The painting above
the altar was attributed to Ribera.

143. The choir looking east, as
left by Scott; the reredos has
been moved forward, creating a
retrochoir behind.

90

144. Font made for Ely Cathedral in 1693 (Bentham), now, sans cover, in Prickwillow church nearby.

Baptisterium Ecclœ Cath. Elien legavit ejusdem Ecclœ Decanus, et Collegii

Iohannes Spencer S.T.P. Corp. Christi Cantab. Prœpositus. 1693.

145. Altar and reredos installed by Scott in 1858. The five scenes above the altar are the Entry into Jerusalem, Washing the Feet, the Last Supper, the Agony in the Garden and Carrying the Cross. In the trefoil at the top: the Annunciation.

Peterborough

THE GREAT ABBEY CHURCH of St Peter at Peterborough was raised to the status of a cathedral by Henry VIII in 1541 – one of six monastic churches he so advanced – and it seems to have retained very largely its medieval splendour until the Civil War.

The Tudor cathedral

Until as late as the 18th century, Peterborough, in common with Canterbury, retained both the screens between nave and choir that were usual in a great monastic church – the stone pulpitum or organ-screen and, in front of it, the lighter rood-screen. At Peterborough engravings show the latter screen to be of wood, stretching across nave and aisles,[1] while at Canterbury Dart's plate shows its rood-screen to have been of iron.

Many details of the cathedral and its fittings before 1643 are preserved for us in Gunton, edited and published by Dean Patrick in 1686.[2] He describes several monuments in the nave, beginning with the picture of 'Old Scarlett', the verger who 'interr'd two Queens within this place' and died in 1594, aged ninety-eight;[3] and he mentions the 'comely font', which Bridges's plate of the 'Inward View of the Nave' shows to have been hidden in a pillar-box-like enclosure.[4] He goes on:

The Quire presents nothing legible in the pavement . . . only the wooden sides did very lately retain some memorial of their ancient ornaments, both paintings and writings, though their defect be now supplied with the gilded ceiling of the Ladies Chappel [taken down c. 1662][5] It was . . . in the time of Abbot W. of Watervile, near five hundred years since, ordered as we have lately known it, and the fashion of both Pictures and Letters, might plead such antiquity. For the paintings, they were not to be commended, neither here, nor in other places of the Church, for it hath long since been found fault with, that in *Peterborough Minster* you may see Saint *Peter* painted, his head very near, or altogether as big as his middle. Their subject was stories, and underneath Latin Distichs,[6] some whereof (though somewhat different) were written in the windows of the Cathedral church of Canterbury as the surveyor thereof Somner hath left Recorded.[7]

. . . Both sides of the Quire were adorned after an old

decent manner, with hangings of tapestry, but in the year 1643, they were taken away and dispersed.

But the greatest ornament of the Quire (and indeed of the whole church) was the High Altar, a structure of stone most exquisitely carved and beautified with gilding and painting; it was ascended unto by about a dozen steps, and from its basis reared after the manner of a comely wall some six feet high, upon which were several curious Pilasters supporting a fair arched Roof whereon were three goodly spires reaching almost to the top of the church, the whole frame dilating itself to each side, also gilded and painted, saving some void places, which were anciently filled up with Plates of Silver, as hath been mentioned in the Inventory.[8] I wish I could present the Reader with the effigies of it, as Mr Somner hath done in the Cathedral of Canterbury.[9]

The Altar or Table itself was a goodly free-stone, which was long since removed, and laid in the pavement adjoining, and a Table of wood set in its place, notwithstanding which change, the Abbots Chair of stone adjoining to the South end, suffered no alteration, but continued to our times.

Immediately over the altar on the flat ceiling of the apse was a painting of Our Lord seated in judgment with the four Evangelists and saints holding crowns. Ryves's *Mercurius Rusticus*[10] describes it as 'our Saviour pourtrayed coming in his glory with his holy Angels and at the four corners four Evangelists'.

'Beyond the Quire', Gunton continues, 'the most eastern part of the church, is the New Building, erected by abbot Robert Kirton. . . . The windows therein are fair, and lately beautifyed with painted glass, which contained no great matter worthy of recital, save only pictures of saints, largely expressed.' What became of these?[11] Gunton continues:

As you pass out of this building on the north side of the church, there was lately a passage into the now demolished Ladies Chappel, in which passage was a little Chappel, having on the right hand, archt over with

146. The west front about 1727 (Browne Willis), substantially as it is now but with a spire on the north-west tower.

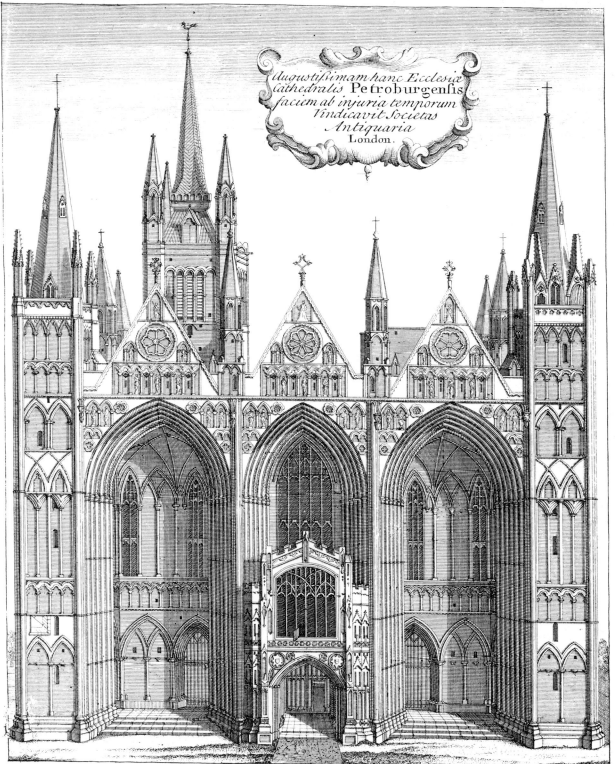

Augustissimam hanc Ecclesiæ
Cathedralis Petroburgensis
faciem ab injuria temporum
Vindicavit Societas
Antiquaria
London.

I. Harris fecit.

The West Prospect, or Front, of the Cathedral Church of Peterborough.

stone, having a fair East Window, and on the north side little windows looking into the Ladies Chappel. Overhead were two chambers, which common tradition hath told, to have been the habitation of a devout Lady called Agnes or Dame Agnes, out of whose Lodging-Chamber there was a hole made askew in the window walled up, having its prospect just upon the altar of the Ladies Chappel and no more.

It seems, she was devout in her generation, that she chose this place for her retirement and was desirous that her eyes, as well as ears, might wait upon her publick devotions.

I could never see any record to inform me who this dame Agnes was, and surely this church owes the world a better account of her than I can give, in regard she was a great Benefectoress to it, giving that, which at this day is commonly known by the name of Dame Agnes wood, not far from Peterborough.

Of the Lady chapel itself (built 1272–90) an inventory of 1539 records:[12]

Imprimis An image of our Lady with reddis Rissey[?], set in a tabernacle well gilt, upon wood, with twelve great images and four and thirty small images of the same work about the Chapel. *Item* a pair of organs, one desk and four seats, one tabernacle of the Trinity and one other of our Lady. . . .

The Eastern window of the Ladies Chappel was the fairest and goodliest in all the Church, scarce a fairer in any other Cathedral. It was adorned with painted glass, containing many stories, amongst the rest of Julian the Apostate with these two verses:

Cuspide Mecurii Julianus Apostata Caesus
Vincis ait, vincis hen, Nazerene potens.[13]

G. Ayliffe Poole[14] quotes an account, though without giving the source, in which the Lady chapel is said to have 'had fair glass windows with a figure of the blessed Virgin, together with her genealogy, which is called a Jesse [Tree]; and besides this there were figures of the Kings of England, from the first to the last, set in order around the walls, with their lives compendously inscribed beneath them'. It is not always easy to know whether in these extracts the words 'image' or 'figure' refer to a statue or a painting.

The only picture of this beautiful chapel known to me is included in Daniel King's 'North View of the Cathedral' (1656), which depicts the Lady chapel in front of the eastern arm of the great church. It shows five windows of three lights each, with as many cusped circles in the head. Very poorly drawn, they suggest plate tracery, but this is unlikely. The three windows of this pattern on the east side of the north and south transepts were probably identical with the side windows of the vanished chapel. The east window, to match these,

must have been a notable example of the Geometric style.[15] Gunton adds that there were in the chapel 'many fair gravestones'.

The Civil War

Gunton ends with a supplement, evidently by Dean Patrick, called 'A Short and True Narrative of the Rifling and Defacing of the Cathedral Church of Peterborough in the year 1643', from which the following extracts are taken:

Some soldiers of a Regiment of Horse under Colonel *Cromwell* . . . early in the morning . . . break open the Church doors, pull down Organs of which there were two Pair. The greater Pair that stood upon a high loft, over the entrance into the Quire, was thence thrown upon the ground, and there stamped and trampled on, and broke in pieces.

Then the soldiers enter the Quire, and there their first business was to tear in pieces all the Common Prayer Books, that could be found. The great Bible indeed, that lay upon a Brass Eagle for reading the Lessons, had the good hap to escape with the loss only of the Apocrypha.

Next day they break down all the seats, stalls and wainscot that was behind them, being adorn'd with several historical passages out of the Old and New Testament, a Latin Distich being in each seat to declare the Story.

There was also a great Brass Candlestick hanging in the middle of the Quire, containing about a dozen and half of Lights, with another Bow Candlestick about the Brass Eagle: these both were broke in pieces, and most of the Brass carried away and sold.

When they had thus defaced and spoiled the Quire, they march up next to the East end of the Church, and there break and cut in pieces, and afterwards burn the Rails that were about the Communion Table. The Table itself was thrown down, the Table-Cloth taken away with two fair books in Velvet Covers, the one a Bible, the other a Common Prayer Book, with a Silver Bason gilt, and a pair of Silver Candlesticks beside. But upon request made to Colonel Hubbert the Books, Bason and all else, Save the Candlesticks, were restored again.

Not long after, on 13 July 1643, Captain *Barton* and Captain *Hope*, two Martial Ministers of *Nottingham* or *Derbyshire*, coming to *Peterborough*, break open the Vestry and take away a fair Crimson satten Table Cloth and several other things, that had escaped the former soldiers' hands.

Now behind the Communion Table there stood a curious piece of Stone-work admired much by Strangers and Travellers; a stately screen it was, well wrought painted and gilt, which rose up as high almost as the Roof of the Church, in a Row of three lofty Spires, with other lesser Spires growing out of each of them, as it is represented in the annexed draught. This now had no Imagery work upon it, or anything else that might justly give offence, and yet, because it bore the name of the

High Altar, was pulled all down with Ropes, layd low and level with the ground.

Over this place in the Roof of the Church, in a large oval yet to be seen,[16] was the Picture of our Saviour seated on a Throne, one hand erected and holding a Globe in the other; attended with the four Evangelists and Saints on each side, with crowns in their hands; intended, I suppose, for a Representation of our Saviour's coming to judgment. Some of the company espying this, cry out and say, Lo this is the God these People bow and cringe unto; This is the Idol they worship and adore. Hereupon several Souldiers charge their muskets . . . and discharge them at it; and by the many Shots they made, at length do quite deface and spoil the Picture.

. . . Then they rob and rifle the Tombs, and violate the Monuments of the dead. And where should they first begin, but with those of the *two Queens*, who had been there interr'd: The one on the north side [Katherine], the other on the south side of the church [Queen of Scots], both near unto the Altar. First, then, they demolish Queen *Katherine's* tomb, *Henry* the Eighth's repudiated Wife.[17] They break down the Rails that enclosed the place, and take away the black Velvet Pall which covered the Herse: overthrow the Herse itself, displace the Gravestone that lay over her Body, and have left nothing now remaining of that Tomb, but only a Monument of their own shame and villany. The like they had certainly done to the Queen of Scots, but that her Herse and Pall were removed with her Body to *Westminster* by King *James* the first when He came to the Crown. But what did remain,[18] they served in like manner that is, her Royal Arms and Escutcheons which hung upon a pillar near the place where she had been interr'd, were most rudely pulled down, defaced and torn.

In the North Isle of the church, there was a stately Tomb in memory of Bishop *Dove*, who had been 30 years Bishop of the place. He lay there in Portraicture in his Episcopal Robes, on a large Bed under a fair Table of Black Marble, with a Library of Books about him. These men that were such Enemies to the name and Office of a Bishop, and much more to his Person, hack and hew the poor Innocent Statue in pieces, and soon destroy'd all the Tomb so that in a short space, all that fair and curious monument was buried in its own rubbish and Ruins.

In a Place then called the New Building, and since converted into a Library, there was a fair Monument, which Sir *Humphrey Orm*[19] (to save his Heir that charge and trouble) thought fit to erect in his own lifetime, where he and his Lady, his Son and Wife, and all their children were lively represented in statues, under which were certain English verses written:

> . . . Mistake not, Reader, I thee crave
> This is an Altar, not a Grave
> Where Fire rak't up in Ashes lies
> And Harts are made the Sacrifice
> Till time and truth, her worth and fame
> Revive her embers to a flame.

Which two words *Altar* and *Sacrifice* 'tis said, did so

provoke and kindle the zealots indignation, that they resolve to make the Tomb itself a Sacrifice: and with Axes, Poleaxes and Hammers, destroy and break down all that curious Monument, save only two Pilasters still remaining[20] which shew and testify the elegancy of the rest of the Work. Thus it happened, that the good old Knight who was a constant frequenter of God's public service, three times a day, and outlived his own Monument, and lived to see himself carried in Effigie on a Souldier's back, to the public market-place, there to be sported withall, a Crew of Souldiers going before in Procession, some in Suplices, some with Organ Pipes, to make up the solemnity.

When they had thus demolished the chief monuments, at length the very Gravestones and Marbles on the Floor did not escape their Sacrilegious hands. For where there was anything on them of Sculptures or Inscriptions in Brass, These they force and tear off. So that whereas there were many fair pieces of this kind before, as that of Abbot *William* of *Ramsey*, whose large Marble Gravestone was plated over with Brass, and several others the like, there is not any such now in all the Church, to be seen; though most of the Inscriptions that were upon them, are preserved in this Book.

Patrick then corrects a mistake made in *Mercurius Rusticus* – that the soldiers removed and sold the bell-clappers. He says they were taken out and hidden in the roof of the church by some of the inhabitants of the city to relieve them from the continual jangling of the bells by the soldiers that kept them awake at night. He goes on:

The windows in this Church were very fair, and had much curiosity of workmanship in them, being adorned and beautified with several Historical passages out of scripture and Ecclesiastical story; such were those in the Body of the Church in the Isles, in the new Building and elsewhere.

But the Cloister Windows were most famed of all, for their great art and pleasing variety. *One* side of the Quadrangle containing the History of the Old Testament, *another* that of the New; a *third* the Founding and Founders of the Church; a *Fourth* all the Kings of England down from the first *Saxon* King. All which, notwithstanding, were most shamefully broken and destroyed.

And amongst other things thus demolisht in the Windows, there was one thing Fame had made very remarkable; and that was the story of the Paschal Pickeril. The thing was this; Our Saviour was represented in two places, in the Cloister and in the great Western Window, sitting at his last Supper with his twelve Apostles; In one place there was a single Fish, in the other three Fishes in a Dish, set before him. This occasion'd that discourse, and common Talk, I remember, I have often heard, of the *Paschal Pickeril* of *Peterborough*.

Patrick says the reason for this was unknown but that one suggestion was that a 'devout and ignorant artist' supposing the Last Supper must have been in Lent and that Our Lord was a strict observer of it, took the liberty to substitute fish for the Paschal Lamb. He goes on to say that the 'particular piece of glass wherein the three fishes are portray'd' was preserved and was given to him by Gunton. Patrick proceeds:

the 'Reforming Rabble' . . . left nothing undemolisht, where either any Picture or Painted glass did appear; excepting only part of the great West Window . . . which still remains entire, being too high for them, and out of their reach. Yea to encourage them the more in this Trade of breaking and battering windows down, Cromwell himself (as 'twas reported) espying a little Crucifix in a Window aloft which none perhaps before had scarce observed, gets a ladder and breaks it down zealously with his own hand.

But before I conclude the Narrative I must not forget to tell, how they . . . broke open the Chapterhouse, ransack'd the Records, broke the Seals, tore the Writings in pieces, Specially such as had great Seals annexed unto them which they took or mistook . . . for the Pope's Bulls.

Patrick adds the soldiers were at Peterborough for about a fortnight, when they wrought all this havoc:

Thus in a short time, a fair and goodly structure was quite stript of all its ornamental Beauty and made a ruthful spectacle, a very Chaos of Desolation and Confusion, nothing scarce remaining but only bare walls, broken seats, and shatter'd Windows on every side.

. . . And thus the Church continued ruined and desolate and without divine offices for a time; till at length by the favour of a great Person[21] in the Neighbourhood, it was repaired and restored to some degrees of decency again; and out of the ashes of a late Cathedral, grew up into a new Parochial Church, in which way it was employed . . . until the King's happy Restoration.

Now the Town considering the largeness of the Building, and the greatness of the charge to repair it, which of themselves they were not able to defray, they all agree, to pull down the *Ladies Chappel*, as it was then called, (being then ruinous and ready to fall) and sell the materials . . . towards the Repair of the great Fabrick. . . . And this they did, mending the Leads, securing the Roof, Glazing several Windows, and then fitting up the Quire and making it pretty decent . . . by taking the Painted Boards that came off from the Roof of the Ladies Chappel, and placing them all along at the back of the Quire [stalls] in such manner, as they continue to this day.

1686 to 1822

153 The plates in Bridges (*c.* 1720) show the interior little changed since Dean Patrick's description of 1686. But in 1742 Browne Willis reports on the cathedral:[22]

I cannot but say that it is ill kept in Repair, and lies very slovenly in the inside, and several windows are stopped up with Bricks, and the glazing in others sadly broken; and the Boards of the Roof of the middle Isle or nave, which with the Cross-Isle is not archt with stone (but wainscotted with painted boards, as at *St Albans*) are several of them damaged and Broken, as is also the Pavement; insomuch that scarce any Cathedral in *England* is more neglected. However, as at the present, the Dean and Chapter have already set apart 700l and design to appropriate more on the Expiration of some Leases.

Sweeting[23] says that new seats were erected under Dean Lockier (1722–40) which were 'very plain and tasteless'. And he also tells us (1893) that 'until 1827 the choir . . . was composed of deal painted to resemble oak'. A new organ was also obtained. £1,500 was spent on these alterations.

Browne Willis's plan shows that in his time the choir was still in its original position under the crossing, but the Rev. Owen Davys[24] says it was removed to the eastern arm of the church in 1734; and apart from the actual date, the last plate in Storer[25] confirms this, with the organ-screen shown definitely between the eastern piers of the crossing.

Britton says:[26]

Considerable repairs and alterations were . . . required about 1780 at which time the mean gothic screen behind the altar, and the equally mean organ screen were erected. It is not generally known, and it will be scarcely believed, that the late Mr Carter was consulted, and gave designs for these subjects; for the style and ornaments are rather of the Batty Langley, than the Carter School; and it cannot but excite astonishment that an artist, who knew so much, and was so censorious of others could have given such designs. There seems no other way of accounting for it, but by supposing that he made some very slight drawings, and sent them to Peterborough where they were put into the hands of an ignorant and clumsy carpenter.

The only views of these screens that I know of are the organ-screen (sans organ) in Storer and the 154 altar-screen in Britton (pl. XIV: Elevation and 168 Section of the Transept). They certainly show how poor the designs were, although the organ-screen had a bizarre richness, with round, pointed and 'Tudor' arches, filled with designs resembling black lace. This screen was called by Rickman 'a barbarous piece of painted woodwork'. It was either sold or taken by the contractors as a perquisite, and ultimately found its way into a little garden at Woodston, just across the river, where it was transformed into an arbour, where I have often seen it. It was at last destroyed in a fire.[27]

According to Craddock,[28] Dean Tarrant (1764–91)

collected some fragments [of the old glass] that still remained, and formed the two central east windows with them. Four other windows in bad taste, consisting principally of shields and geometric figures, were afterwards added; so that the lights of the east end of the Cathedral are filled indeed with coloured glass, though of an unintelligible or uninteresting description. The central window in the New Building . . . is also filled with highly coloured glass in the taste of the last century.[29] These five windows belong to the worst period of English taste, when church architecture had lost all its vigour and church embellishment had degenerated into whitewash and deal pews, and the lion and unicorn. The Cathedral received no addition to its stained glass after these miserable insertions till 1856.

154 The flat ceiling of the apse had been decorated some time between the 1720s, the date of Bridges's plates, and 1812, when it was shown in a plate in Storer with six circular motifs like rose windows (Craddock[30] calls it 'a kind of floor cloth ceiling'), which remained until later than 1852 (shown in two lithographs of that date).[31]

150 About this time the exterior of the cathedral was altered for the worse. First, the bell-tower lost its lead-covered spire – early last century according to Sweeting (Bell). Of the central tower, Buckler says:[32] 'The ancient external roof of the Lantern was of an octagonal form, constructed of timber, and covered with lead, which was placed in a diagonal or *herringbone* manner. It appeared above the parapet of the tower, and terminated in battlements. This venerable and very curious object was destroyed in the year 1813, when angular turrets were built, which are not only too lofty, but assuredly inappropriate, being copied from those belonging to the Norman Transepts.'

152 These were nicknamed 'Dean Kipling's Chimneys' (Thomas Kipling, Dean 1798–1822). They remained until 1883.

The nineteenth and twentieth centuries

In 1822 James Henry Monk was appointed dean and was a highly civilized guardian of his cathedral and close, as Britton demonstrates.[33] Speaking of the 'great improvements now in progress', he says:

Every approach to the Cathedral, as well as the cemetery and courts around it, are laid out with the greatest attention to personal comforts and to pleasing effects. . . . The cemetery abounds with tomb-stones, it having been formerly the only burial place of the citizens. Another piece of ground is now provided at the western extremity of the city, and in this respect, as well as in the manner of laying out and embellishing the old 'church-yard', the dean and chapter have imitated one of the best practices of the Parisians. Here, as in 'Pere de Chaise' at Paris, the graves are planted and embellished with willows, laurels, pines and various trees, shrubs and flowers. Thus a scene, which heretofore, like most of the burial grounds of England, was filled with weeds, briars, and other offensive objects, is now pleasing to the eye of the observing stranger, and soothingly delightful to those whose affections and sorrows are associated with objects beneath its turf.

As for the cathedral itself, the dean and chapter first repaired defects on the exterior from their own resources. These repairs included 'new roofs to the transepts and bell-tower; columns, mouldings and ornaments in various parts of the church renewed; several windows, till then blocked up with rubble, opened and glazed . . . pinnacles, spires and shafts of the West Front carefully restored, two Norman doorways which had been obscured for ages, exposed to view'.[34]

In 1827 the dean and chapter commissioned Edward Blore to design completely new choir furniture; and an appeal to the public for funds to carry this out was launched, which brought in over £5000. 'The work in the choir included new stalls and seats, pulpit and throne; an altar-screen of clunch, filling up the lower part of the apse; and an organ-screen, also of clunch, with an open parapet and enriched with much diaper-work and many canopies and adorned with large [pointed] shields of arms, very brightly coloured,' and well designed – very unusual at that time (was Thomas Williment responsible?). 'These shields, which were of metal are now arranged on the walls of the Library [the room over the porch]. At first there were only four stalls on each side of the choir-entrance; others were added, in front of the Ladies' pews, when Honorary Canons were created in 1844.'[35] Britton[36] gives many details of Blore's choir, 'the whole fitting up [of which] is in the style of Edward the Third, more particularly in imitation of the Lady Chapel in Ely Cathedral'. Craddock[37] says that 'the whole of this woodwork was undertaken and admirably executed by a native carpenter, Mr Ruddle. The stonework was executed also by a native mason, Mr Thompson.' There are lithographs and numerous photographs of the choir thus fitted up, and these show a most curious thing. The canopy of the bishop's throne was originally upheld on four 'legs' as shown in photos of the 1860s and 1870s when the lantern was open to the church. But in later photographs, when the lantern was becoming unsafe and hidden by a

155

150

166

147. Up to the 1880s the south-east pier of the crossing was in so dangerous a state that it had been bound up with planks and iron bands (*The Builder*).

with planks and bound round with iron bands, which rendered it most unsightly.[39]

In 1882 J. L. Pearson pronounced the tower to be dangerous and the following year it was demolished, and rebuilt during the next three years. In 1884 a controversy arose as to the correct way of rebuilding the tower. Some people wanted the pointed east and west tower arches to be replaced by round Norman ones, while others suggested heightening the tower by one stage of work in the Norman style, using original stones (found during the rebuilding) where possible and placing the Decorated stage above it. This was the scheme advocated by the restoration committee and agreed to by the dean, but his chapter were unwilling to sanction any new work beyond actual restoration and they were backed by the bishop. Others wanted a lofty central spire to be added, for which Pearson made a splendid drawing. Long letters appeared in the papers on these various ideas, until at last the question was referred to the Archbishop of Canterbury[40] (Benson), who directed the tower

148. View from the choir during the rebuilding of the tower by Pearson, 1885.

temporary ceiling for safety, the canopy with its pierced and crocketted spire looks taller than before and, most surprising, is upheld by only two legs (at the back), the whole tester cantilevered out over the seat! Why this should have been done is a mystery – one would have understood if the reverse had been the case, with four 'legs' replacing a faulty cantilever! And why a scarcely different but taller spire and sans gable?

In 1873 a monstrous marble pulpit with stone balustraded steps was given to the cathedral. It was designed by Edward Barry in the Norman style, supposedly to match the 12th-century architecture.[38]

By the 1880s the condition of the central tower was giving great concern. For many years the south-east 'leg' of the tower had been strengthened

to be rebuilt exactly as before, except for 'Dean Kipling's Chimneys', which were not replaced. How different the cathedral would have looked if he had decided otherwise!

In 1887 the lantern tower decoration was completed. The ceiling is almost entirely the old one, only the painting being new (the work of Messrs Clayton and Bell). In 1886 the south transept ceiling was taken down for repair. All unsound wood was replaced by good oak. The diamond shapes are still to be seen but the black, white and brown patterns have disappeared – similar work in the north transept was undertaken later.[41]

To return to the exterior. In the 1890s the condition of the west front was causing concern. Pearson's examination revealed a state of insecurity necessitating partial rebuilding, which was agreed to by the dean and chapter and an appeal was made for £16,000. Immediately there arose a furious controversy between the 'conservationists', who opposed any rebuilding at all, and their opponents whom they dubbed 'vandals who wanted to destroy the front'. Mr Punch summed up the controversy (16 Jan. 1897) in this way:

An architectural settlement. *First man (eminent in painting, literature or science):* What a controversy about Peterborough Cathedral! Do you know anything about architecture? I don't. *Second man (ditto):* Nothing whatever. And I've never been within twenty miles of Peterborough. *First man:* Nor have I. Then let us go at once and sign a memorial to the Dean and Chapter asking them not to let anybody do anything *(Exeunt excitedly).*[42]

Fortunately the dean and chapter got their way and the front was repaired with the minimum of rebuilding: 'Of 2,006 stones taken down in the course of the rebuilding, no less than 1,836 were able to be replaced in the original positions, so that 170 only were found too decayed to be used again.'[43] Sweeting describes it further:[44] 'What had actually been done was this: the north gable has been taken down, and the outer orders of the moulding of the arch for some feet, and rebuilt; the innermost order has not been moved. Relieving arches have been put in at the back. The gable is now believed to be perfectly secure. The cross on the summit was replaced in its position on July 2nd 1897. This is what has been called "the destruction" of the west front.' But he adds:[45] 'In the following years the south-western gable was restored. This had never been in so dangerous a state as the other, nor so much out of the

perpendicular; but some of it had to be removed and replaced.'

After the conservative repair of the west front, with all the many statues preserved, it is sad to record that after the 1939–45 War these figures were found to be in a sorry state of decay.[46] A systematic replacement by new ones to the designs of Alan Durst was commenced under the cathedral architect Leslie Moore. Durst's work is described by the late George Pace,[47] in 1967, when cathedral architect: 'There could not have been a better choice. His approach to sculpture for churches is very much in the spirit of the Fletton church carvings, which are considered to have had such a marked influence on the 13th-century sculptures of Peterborough West Front, and yet Alan Durst's work could not have been done in any age other than the present.' From 1947 to 1949, the existing ties behind the gables being found defective, a scheme was carried out whereby the gables and spandrels of the main arches were tied back to the north-west and south-west towers.

The rebuilding of the lantern led to great changes in the interior. Blore's work was all cleared away, except for the screens round the apse, and the new choir enlarged to the west, with the screen and stalls placed west of the tower, and the bishop's throne, pulpit and altar to the east of it.

From 1890 to 1900 completely new furniture was introduced (including some few fragments of old work) which consisted of canopied stalls, bishop's throne and pulpit, all of finest oak, a new organ by Hill and Sons, a baldacchino (or altar-canopy as it was termed to avoid legal difficulties), and wondrous mosaic pavements – the last two items executed by Robert Davison of London – besides elaborate metal screens enclosing the eastern bays of the choir and the choir gates.[48] All these fine fittings were presumably designed or approved by Pearson. Pevsner[49] says the baldachino of 1894 was 'probably by J. L. Pearson', but Pace[50] says that 'Pearson was responsible for the new floor in the Presbytery and Quire, for the stalls, iron gates, Bishop's Throne, and the magnificent ciborium [baldacchino]. Sometimes Pearson's authorship is questioned, but there is no doubt. His drawings for the tower [and spire], the altar, and the marble floor, are in the R.I.B.A. Library.' Sweeting[51] reckons that all these repairs and refurbishings from 1883 to 1900, including the gifts by benefactors, would amount to about £58,000.

Lastly, about 1924 or 1925, the cathedral roofs were found to be infested by death-watch beetle, and the fan vault of the New Building to be

155
156
169

170

162

99

shattered. These were dealt with and saved by Moore. And at last the ugly front of the choir, with

157
163

the return stalls, was removed (a low panelled wall with carved tracery taking its place) to the immense improvement of the west to east vista.

170

Also, Blore's stone screens in the apse were demolished – a doubtful improvement.

Bibliography

Gunton, 1686. Simon Gunton, ed. and pub. Dean Simon Patrick, *History of the Church of Peterborough*. Very valuable.

Bridges, c. 1720. John Bridges, *The History and Antiquities of Northamptonshire*. Not pub. until 1791, by P. Whalley. Most valuable for engravings, esp. the 'Inward View of the Nave' and 'Inward View of the Choir'.

* *Browne Willis, 1730*. 2nd edn 1742.

* *Britton, 1828*. John Britton, *The History and Antiquities of the Abbey and Cathedral of Peterborough*. Superb engravings.

Davys, 1846. Canon Owen Davys, *An Historical and Architectural Guide to Peterborough Cathedral*.

Poole, 1855. G. Aycliffe Poole, 'The Abbey Church of Peterborough', Journal of the Architectural Society of Archdeaconry of Northampton and three other societies, vol. III.

Paley, 1849. F. A. Paley, *Remarks on the Architecture of Peterborough Cathedral*. 2nd edn 1859.

Craddock, 1864. Thomas Craddock, *Peterborough Cathedral: A General, Architectural and Monastic History*.

Sweeting, 1893. Rev. W. D. Sweeting, *The New Guide to Peterborough Cathedral*.

* *Sweeting (Bell), 1898*. Rev. W. D. Sweeting, *Peterborough, The Cathedral and See*, Bell's Cathedral Series. 2nd edn 1899.

Swan, 1932. Rev. E. G. Swan, *The Story of Peterborough Cathedral*.

* *Cartwright (Pitkin), 1975*. Canon J. L. Cartwright, FSA, *Peterborough Cathedral*, Pitkin Pictorial.

Notes

1 Craddock says this screen (he calls it the 'choir screen') was 'at present used to shut off the north transept aisle'

* see also bibliography to the Introduction.

The ills in B. Winkles, *Illustrations of the Cathedral Churches of England and Wales* (2nd edn 1838), II, 84, and Craddock, 120, confirm this when compared with the rood-screen in Bridges's 'Inward View of the Nave'. It is curious that A. Vallance, *Greater English Church Screens* (1947), seems not to be aware of Bridges's pl. which shows the rood-screen in situ (although he mentions the plan and the Inward View of the Choir – perhaps the nave pl. was missing from the copy of Bridges he consulted). And so, when discussing the present screen work in the N transept, he says it was 'moved hither, whence is a matter of conjecture'.

2 This account is here followed, as it gives more details, and seems, as regards the Cromwellian depredation, generally more reliable than that of Bruno Ryves, *Mercurius Rusticus* (1646), written during the dust of conflict.

3 The picture now in the cathedral is not the original, but a copy of 1747. Sweeting (Bell), 98.

4 Sweeting (Bell), 87, says this font was newly made in 1615 (it was destroyed in the Civil War) and that the present 13th-c. font was for many years used as a flower-pot in one of the prebendal gardens.

5 See Patrick's account, p. 96.

6 See Patrick's supplement (Gunton, 334), p. 94.

7 Many of these verses had perished by Gunton's time, but he recorded verses under the following pictures: the Prophet Isaias (S side); Gedeon's fleece; Nebuchadnezzar dreaming; Moses's Bush; Mary and Elizabeth; Aaron's rod budding; Boaz (N side); the fire descending upon the sacrifice; the Prophet Habakkuk (N side); David.

8 'Inprimis the High Altar, plated with silver, well gilt with one image of Christ's passion and a little shrine of copper, enameled, for the Sacrament' (Inventory dated 30 Nov. 1539, quoted by Gunton, 61).

9 Evidently, the poor engraving in the book (p. 64) was inserted by Dean Patrick – probably done from memory.

10 Ryves, *op. cit.*, 246.

11 Craddock and Murray describe their successors.

12 Gunton, 61.

13 Gunton, 100.

14 Poole, 212.

15 But Poole, after quoting the above verses on Julian the Apostate, says: 'I infer from the description of the glass, that a Perpendicular window had been inserted in place of the original one, the subject . . . being more in harmony with the fifteenth than with the thirteenth century. As I find Abbot Kirton, the founder of the New Building, enriched this also, in which he was buried in 1528, with much painting and gilding at the expense of 100*l*, I am disposed to attribute some such work to him.'

16 Shown in Bridges's 'Inward View of the Choir'.

17 The inventory of 1539 (Gunton, 61): 'Item two pair of organs, and two desks of latten, seven Basons hanging with four candlesticks, and Banners of silk above the Quire joyning to the tomb where Queen Katherine lieth buried.' Sweeting (1893) 31, says, 'a "hearse" was placed near the spot, probably between the two piers, some marks in the pillar may indicate where the supports

149. Daniel King's etching of 1656 contains many inaccuracies but is the only record of the old Lady chapel to the east of the north transept.

stood. This may have been something in the nature of a flat wooden frame, coloured and perhaps inscribed supporting some of the heraldic insignia used at the funeral. Some banners so used remained in the Cathedral in 1586.'

18 Sweeting (Bell), 32, says: 'The funeral took place on 1 Aug. 1587. A handsome hearse was erected between the two pillars; and judging from the plan in Browne Willis it must have been a sumptuous and elaborate structure. Remains of this were to be seen as lately as 1800.'

19 On p. 98 this is spelt 'Orme' and further details of the memorial given.

20 This is not true, as the marble background and outline of the monument with its arched recesses (that contained the statues) and carved spandrels are still to be seen.

21 Oliver St John, Chief Justice of the Common Pleas.

22 Browne Willis (2nd edn 1742), III, 504.

23 Sweeting (Bell), 2nd edn 1899, 29.

24 Davys, 68.

25 J. Storer, *History and Antiquities of Cathedral Churches of Great Britain* (1814–19). Unfortunately Storer's plan contradicts his plate, showing the choir under the crossing, and several authors (Winkles, Craddock and Sweeting) infer or state that Blore's choir was not on the former site (i.e. it was moved east of the tower). But if so, and in spite of the above 'several authors' and the contradiction in Storer, it seems incredible that such a careful draughtsman as Storer could have depicted the 18th-century screen in the *wrong position* – under the eastern arch of the tower and 55 feet east of the medieval site (Craddock, 157). The choir must, surely, have been moved earlier, as Davys says. Did Storer perhaps copy another plan by mistake?

26 Britton, 73.

27 Sweeting (Bell), 30.

28 Craddock, 202.

29 Murray's *Handbook* (1862), 83, tells us this glass was in 'wretched harlequin quarrels, than which the simplest white glass would be infinitely preferable'.

30 Craddock, 209.

31 Soon afterwards, in Dean Saunders's time (1853–78),

the chancel roof was repainted with gold and colours and the apse ceiling redecorated, as at present, from a design by Scott, with an emblematical representation of Christ as the Vine, the Disciples being half figures in medallions among the foliage (Sweeting, Bell, 64).

32 J. C. Buckler, *Views of Cathedral Churches of England and Wales* (1822).

33 Britton, 59–60.

34 Sweeting (Bell), 30. Craddock, 151, quoting Davys, says thirty-six windows were repaired, and that the Norman doorways had 'been hidden under mean depressed arches'.

35 Sweeting (Bell), 30.

36 Britton, 75–78.

37 Craddock, 120, note.

38 Sweeting (Bell), 83–84.

39 As early as 1593 the cathedral accounts record the sum of £47.4s.9p as spent on 'The great column near the choir repaired with iron and timber' (Sweeting, 1893, p. 73).

40 Rev. E. G. Swaine, *The Story of Peterborough Cathedral* (1932).

41 *Ibid.*, 74–75.

42 *Ibid.*, 80.

43 *Ibid.*, 80.

44 Sweeting (Bell), 2nd edn 1899, 35.

45 Sweeting (1893), 81.

46 As early as 1922 decay had commenced. Swaine (1932), 31, wrote: 'St Peter is a majestic figure in the central gable, and he held his keys until ten years ago, when they fell to the ground.'

47 G. Pace, Friends of Peterborough Cathedral *Annual Report* (1967), 9.

48 The short stone pillars supporting these gates were part of an unrealized design for a choir-screen and, together with the boarded backs of the return stalls, were an eyesore for thirty years.

49 N. Pevsner, *Buildings of England: Northamptonshire* (1961), 363.

50 Pace, *op. cit.*, 6.

51 Sweeting (1893), 82.

Peterborough: the tower and screen

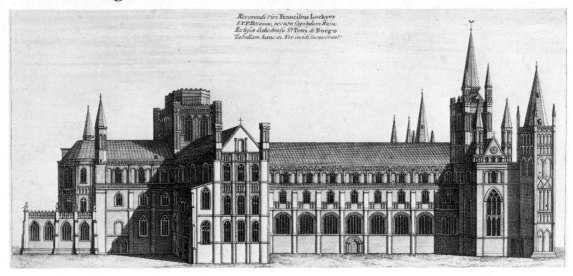

150. View from the north-east before 1730 (Browne Willis). The wooden octagon surmounting the central tower was removed in 1813.

151. View from the north-west, early 19th century. The turrets round the central tower seem to have been heightened and the north-west tower has lost its spire (Greenwood's map of Northamptonshire, 1830).

152. View from the north-east about 1860, showing the tall turrets to the central tower known as 'Dean Kipling's Chimneys'.

153. Up to the 18th century Peterborough retained both the pulpitum and choir-screen of the medieval abbey church, one behind the other, just west of the crossing. A view of 1720 (*above*, from Bridges) shows the pulpitum surmounted by the organ.

154. Crossing and choir about 1817 (Storer), showing Carter's screen. The organ has been omitted in order to expose the east end.

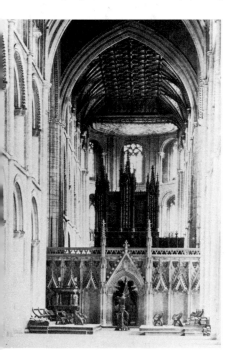

155. Crossing and choir, *c.* 1880, before the rebuilding of the crossing, with Blore's screen and organ.

156. The same view as it appeared from 1895 to 1935. Blore's screen has been removed and one simply sees the backs of the return stalls and two columns.

157. The same view today, with the whole vista opened up and a nave altar installed west of the choir.

158. The crossing from the south transept, some time between 1873 and 1884. The nearest pier is the one strengthened with iron clamps (see pl. 147).

159. The Norman pulpit, designed by Edward Barry in 1873.

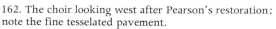

160, 161. The choir in 1720 (Bridges's 'Inward View'). Where the stalls cross the transepts, behind the plain Georgian furniture, is woodwork from the demolished Lady chapel (see pl. 149). *Inset*: the pre-Civil War reredos, with its three tall gables, recorded in Gunton's *History* of 1686.

162. The choir looking west after Pearson's restoration; note the fine tesselated pavement.

163. The same view after 1935, with the return stalls removed and the vista 'opened up'.

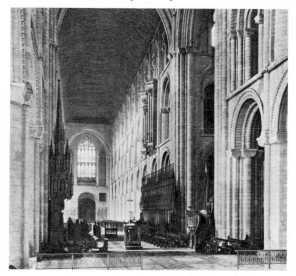

164. The choir looking west, c. 1850.

Peterborough: the choir

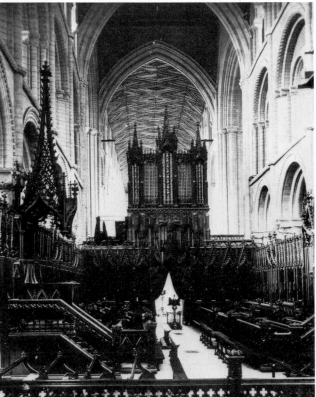

165. The same view, c. 1880.
On the right, the pulpit and
its steps have been moved east, to
be opposite the bishop's throne;
the throne has been given steps,
and (amazingly) the tester
changed from post to cantilever.

166, 167. Detail from a photograph of about 1860, showing Blore's bishop's throne with its original top supported on posts and (*right*) the whole choir, *c.* 1880: the throne with its new cantilevered top (sans gable), Blore's screens and reredos.

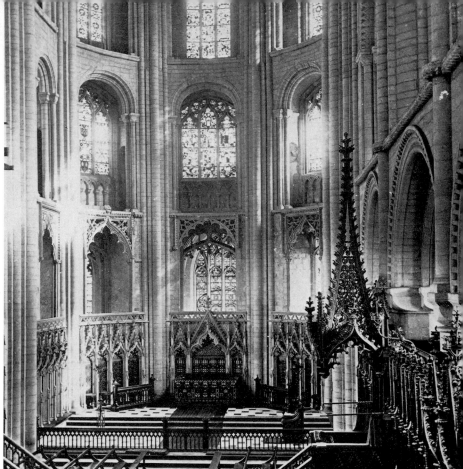

168. Britton's engraving of 1828 shows the panelling which surrounded the apse before Blore's restoration.

169. The apse after 1890, with panelling designed by Blore and Pearson's baldacchino over the altar.

170. The apse after the removal of Blore's panelling *c.* 1935.

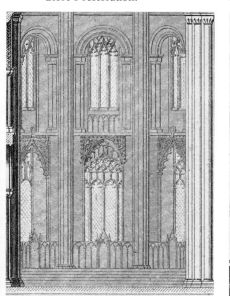

Salisbury

SALISBURY CATHEDRAL, with its finest of spires and unrivalled close, survived the Reformation structurally unharmed. In 1560 the spire was struck by lightning that occasioned a 'cleft all down for 20 feet'.[1] To repair this and other delapidations, regulations were made for contributions from the predendaries to a fabric fund.[2] That important repairs were executed at this time can be inferred from Wren's report of his survey of the cathedral, where, speaking of the roofs, he says: 'The south end of the greater crosse and halfe the maine body from the Tower to ye west hath been wholly made new, I suppose within 100 years.'

The great church escaped serious damage in the Civil War. Indeed, workmen were frequently seen engaged on repair rather than destruction; and on being asked who was paying for it, they replied: 'Those who employ us will pay us . . . they do not desire to have their names known.'[3] In fact, the benefactors seem to have been the Hyde family.[4]

There appears to be no description of the cathedral before Wren's survey of 1669, made at the request of Bishop Ward (1667–89), and it seems the necessary repairs urged by Wren were carried out by the bishop. The new roofing, mentioned above, is, according to Wren, 'of a better form than the old with principalls braces and purloynes, and the beams tucked up. A little more time will necessitate the continuance of this work till ye whole church be so covered, for most of the rafters of ye olde timbering are rotten at foot and ye Wall Plates decayed because the gutters be as high as ye Feet of ye rafters.'[5]

The exterior and precincts

It is interesting that Wren commends the 'many large bandes of iron within and without [the tower] keyed together with much industry and exactnesse . . . without which the spire would spread open the walls of the tower nor would it stand one minute'. Yet a few lines further on he condemns the use of iron in good architecture because of its tendency to rust and so on. He was evidently so impressed by the fineness of the Salisbury ironwork[6] that, in this case, he decided to use iron again – but with a proviso: 'because the artist at first hath much trusted in Iron, I should advise' its further use in the spire. He then describes the making of iron chains of eight 'links' to encircle the spire within and without, and adds: '*note*, these irons will be best wrought at some Port Towne where they worke Anchors and other large worke for shipps for I have found by experience that large worke cannot be wrought sounde with little fires and small bellows'.[7] Price tells us the timbers within the spire were substantially repaired in 1738[8] (the tradition of iron-banding was continued, two hundred years later, by Scott, as we shall see).

Defoe[9] has an interesting note on the exterior of the tower in the 18th century: 'The glass in the several windows, being very old, has contracted such a rust, that it is scarcely to be distinguished from the stone walls; consequently it appears as if there were no lights at all in the tower but only recesses in the stone', and he urges new glazing in squares.

The cathedral had a providential escape from destruction in 1741. On 26 June, at ten o'clock at night, the tower was struck by lightning, but it was not until the next morning that a floor within the tower was seen to be burning. It was soon put out, but only just in time.[10] Extraordinary that the fire should have spread so slowly!

Of the laxity of the times, Price tells us of a custom which had prevailed from time out of mind. In the Whitsun holidays, a fair was held within the close, at which people were allowed to ramble over the roofs and gutters of the church and even to go up on the spire, sometimes eight or ten at a time. According to him, 'The late bishop, dean and chapter, put a stop to these foolhardy practices', the danger of which to the participants and to the cathedral was increased by the fact that 'these people never went up, but when heated by liquor. . . . It seems they had certain sports in their passage up and down [the spire] viz. those who were the

171. Scott's metalwork screen for Salisbury, designed in the
1860s, made by Skidmore of Coventry and destroyed in 1959.

highest had the pleasure of discharging their urine on those below', and he enlarges upon the consequent damage to the lead and stonework.[11] In 1901 Gleeson White[12] says the steeple climbing had only ceased 'some sixty or seventy years ago'!

In about 1759, to save money, the dean and chapter demolished the southern part of the 15th-century library, over the eastern cloister – about 27·4 out of 44·1 metres (90 out of 145 ft).[13]

John Carter[14] writes in 1803:

The north cloister, by a peculiar circumstance unparalleled in all other Cathedrals, stands detached from the south wall of the nave, whereby an avenue is obtained . . . it is at present of much service in being made the rubbish repository of the religious pile. Here let the infatuated antiquaries, like me, pore out for broken painted glass, funeral trophies of helmets, gauntlets and banners; parts of rifled tombs, sculptured gravestones, enriched paving tiles, and all the off-scourings of professional improvers.

By the 1780s the churchyard was sadly neglected. As a visitor in 1782 says, it was 'like a cow-common, as dirty and as neglected, and through the centre stagnates a boggy ditch'.[15] According to Dodsworth:[16] 'The avenues were indifferent and after heavy rains difficult to pass; for the water . . . from the roofs ran along open gutters into a large ditch which transversed the churchyard, where in dry seasons it stagnated and became extremely offensive.' In 1789 James Wyatt was called in and it was perhaps to his sole credit that the close was cleared up. Dodsworth continues: 'A new circular underground drain was formed, three feet in diameter, which runs from the west to the east end; and receives all the water from the north side of the church. The ground itself was raised and levelled, and spacious gravel walks were made to the principal entrances. As this operation rendered it necessary to cover the graves, an exact plan of the churchyard, with the dates and a reference to each . . . interment, is now lodged in the muniment room. The area of the cloister has been since used as a cemetery.'

But now on the debit side. Wyatt's churchyard works were not an unmixed blessing, as we learn from *The Builder* in 1867:[17] 'A number of men are just now . . . exhuming a large portion of the Cathedral wall which has been literally buried . . . for nearly 80 years.' To cover Wyatt's drain, 'it was earthed over, thus necessarily covering some feet of the base of the Cathedral wall' which caused damp and decay in the stone.[18] The culvert, now useless, was removed and the base of the wall exposed.

Until 1790 Salisbury possessed a freestanding bell-tower to the north of the cathedral. Price tells us:[19] 'There is . . . in the centre of the belfry a single pillar of Purbeck marble laying in its natural bed; and this pillar supports the vast load of the floors, bell-frames and bells, as also the timber tower, and the spire above with its covering of lead.' He gives (in his pl. 10) 'a scheme for a domed roof when the spire stands in need of being repaired.' Gleeson White says:[20] 'The lantern storey was removed in 1757 by order of the Dean and Chapter.' By 'lantern storey' he must mean the octagonal third storey (actually not a lantern as it seems to have had no openings).

Alas, it was all destroyed by Wyatt. Dodsworth, of course, approved:[21] 'As it had been only partially applied to its original use since 1745, and as it greatly intercepted the most striking view of the Cathedral, it was taken down and the materials employed in making the repairs.'

Wyatt also removed two small porches – one on the south side of the retrochoir, which Colt-Hoare says[22] 'even the projectors of the innovations admitted to be beautiful, though in decay'; and the other 'at the northern termination of the principal transept, apparently built in the time of Edward III in a chaste . . . though not ornamental style.' In a note he adds: 'This latter porch was given to H. P. Wyndham, Esq., and re-erected [1791] in the grounds of the College.'[23] Dodsworth says:[24] 'When taken down, the parts that joined the transept were found to be finished in the same manner as those exposed to view.' (Did it originally cover a well?) He notes that Wyndham 'added a kind of spire and pinnacles'. These are shown in a woodcut of the exterior of the porch, in Rev. Peter Hall's *Picturesque Memorials of Salisbury* (1834).[25]

The choir and chapels before Wyatt

Of Bishop Ward's (1667–89) beautifying of the choir Pope says:[26] 'at his expense . . . the whole choir was laid with white and black squares of marble'. Dodsworth[27] attributes them to Wren, and says that 'the choir was enclosed with a wooden screen, ornamented with painted wreaths of flowers, which, though elegant in itself, was neither suited to the character of the building nor the solemnity of a place of worship. The expense was defrayed by a new contribution amounting to 340l, and the bishop's stall and parts adjoining were repaired at the charge of the prelate himself.'

Further descriptions of these decorations occur

174

177

181

180

in Defoe:[28] 'The painting in the choir is mean and more like the ordinary method of common Drawing Room or Tavern painting than that of a church.' In another edition he says: 'The choir resembles a theatre rather than a venerable choir of a church; it is painted white with the panels golden, and groups and garlands of roses and other flowers intertwined run round the top of the stalls; each stall hath the arms of its holder in gilt letters on blue writ on it, and the episcopal throne with Bishop Ward's arms upon it would make it fine theatrical decoration, being supported by gilt pillars and painted with flowers upon white all over.'

178
173   Of the chantry chapels[29] destroyed by Wyatt, one each side of the Lady chapel, the Beauchamp Chapel on the south was the more ornate, with a finely panelled ceiling and four tombs – an altar tomb of the founder Bishop Beauchamp (1450–81) in the centre, and canopied tombs at the sides to his father and mother and Sir John Cheyney. The
172   Hungerford Chapel, on the north side, was less ornate but lavishly painted. A small volume of 1719 describes it:[30]

This Chapel is kept in a very ill state, and ready to fall, though the Family has been Apprized of it. There have been several fine Pieces of Painting, particularly at the West End; St Christopher carrying Christ over the River; over the south door is the figure of a Doctor of Divinity in his academical (Oxford) habit. . . . Near the former, over the Figures of Death and a Traveller. . . . Then over the Figure of a Sceleton . . . on the south wall near the East End under an Angel.

The 'Traveller' in the above list is mentioned by Milner: 'I also bear in mind the curious figure, as large as life, of the *Gallaunt* or beare of the middle of the 15th century, with his high-crowned hat, his curled locks, his hand loaded with rings, and bearing a wand, his fashionable tawny-coloured jerkin, and his sharp-pointed shoes.'[31]

Before Wyatt, the Lady chapel 'was used for Early Prayers and crowded with seats, by which its beauties were in great measure concealed'.[32] At this time, under Bishop Hume (1766–82), Wren's stalls and screen

being then deemed too gaudy, the choir was enclosed by a new screen painted in imitation of oak. This . . . however, though much more appropriate than the former, scarcely deserved the name of an imitation of the pointed or gothic style.[33] Hitherto, also, the sermons were delivered in the nave, and the congregation were accustomed to remove from the choir to hear that part of the service. But at this period the pulpit and seats were taken away and the whole service has been performed in

the choir. In the course of the alterations the iron chapel erected by Walter Lord Hungerford [vulgarly called 'the Cage', and which Gough says was painted with blue, gold, green and vermilion] was removed [to the choir – opposite the Audley Chapel] at the expense of the Earl of Radnor [to be his family pew.] The [present] East Window of the choir was also decorated with stained glass, the Elevation of the Brazen Serpent, designed by Mortimer and executed by Pearson, at the expense of his lordship[34] [1781].

James Wyatt

Of Wyatt's fell doings at Salisbury, let Dr Milner[35] tell the tale:

First the altar-screen has been entirely taken away, in order to lengthen the choir by admitting into it the Lady Chapel and the other low aisles behind it. Secondly, two beautiful chapels, on each side of the Lady Chapel . . . which could not be brought in to form part of the choir have been destroyed, and their carved ornaments in the style of the 15th century, are stuck up in different parts of the church . . . the workmanship of the 13th century. Thirdly, a diminutive communion table, without rails or other fence,[36] is placed at the [extreme east end] where, so far from commanding respect, it is hardly perceptible.[37] Fourthly, to make these alterations it has been necessary to remove the monuments and disturb the ashes of an incredible number of [illustrious] personages.

Wyatt arranged these dispossessed memorials between the nave pillars in two long rows from east to west, often placing the effigies on the wrong tombs or slabs or on bases made up of fragments.[38] He also removed the screens enclosing ten chapels in the transepts,[39] besides demolishing the beautiful original 13th-century pulpitum (which he   185
partly re-erected in the north-east transept), the   189
magnificent organ by Renatus Harris, 12·1 metres (40 ft) high, set upon it in 1710, and the great rood-beam, slightly to the east of it, which had survived since the figures had been destroyed at the Reformation.[40]

In place of these furnishings so wantonly destroyed, a new stone Gothic choir-screen and   186
new organ by Samuel Green, the gift of George III   190
'as a Gentleman of Berkshire' (then in Salisbury's diocese) were erected – the organ-case partly new. Wyatt also designed a new bishop's throne and pulpit and added canopies to the stalls, with galleries at the back, 'stage-boxes' as Milner called them.[41] In the former Lady chapel a reredos was constructed from the destroyed Hungerford and   182
Beauchamp Chapels. 'The three central niches formed the original altarpiece of the Beauchamp Chapel [1486], whilst those on either side were

172, 173. The Hungerford and Beauchamp chapels, which originally flanked the east end of the cathedral and were demolished by Wyatt at the end of the 18th century (Gough's *Sepulchral Monuments*).

constructed from the entrances to that and the Hungerford Chapel [1470] . . . The canopies of the niches under the side-windows . . . were formed by a cornice from the Beauchamp chantry.'[42]

'The Communion-table is of stone . . . it is composed of the parts that remained of an old altar-piece that was discovered on the removal of that of the Lady's Chapel, at the commencement of the late improvements. The parts alluded to supported a range of Gothic niches of curious workmanship, greatly defaced, and, in point of finishing, were not unlike those lately discovered at the chapel of New College, Oxford.'[43]

Lastly, there was Wyatt's destruction of the stained glass. Some of the medieval glass in the cathedral is said to have been removed by Bishop Jewell (1560–71), but much remained until the early 18th century if Celia Fiennes is to be believed. She says in her diary that 'the windows of the church, but specifically of the Quire, are very finely painted and large [sic] of the history of the Bible'; and the same of the chapter house windows. But under Wyatt 'the most woeful destruction of painted glass' took place, as Winston describes it:[44] 'In the words of my informant, whole cartloads of glass, lead and other rubbish were removed from the nave and transepts, and shot into the town-ditch, then in course of being filled up.' Some of this glass was recovered and, with other pieces that survived the destruction, collected by 'Mr Ranger,

who since 1819 has been employed in placing the greater part of the stained glass in its present position'.[45] To show the utter disregard for such old glass, the following letter is interesting:

John Berry, Glazier, of Salisbury, to Mr Lloyd of Conduit St, London, 1788 – Sir, I have this day sent you a Box, full of old Stained and Painted glass, as you desired me to due, which I hope will sute your Purpose. It is the best that I can get at Present. But I expect to Beate to Peceais a great deal very sune, as it is of now use to me, and we do it for the lead. If you want more of the same sorts you may have what thear is . . . your Omble servant, John Berry.[46]

At the time, Wyatt's vandalisms were generally approved, even by the Society of Antiquaries, and Britton was only mildly critical.[47] Horace Walpole, Richard Gough (of *Sepulchral Monuments* fame), Sir Henry Englefield and, especially, the Rev. John Milner and John Carter were almost the only voices raised against his doings – to little effect, except at Durham, where Carter's insistence saved the Galilee.[48]

Typical of the favourable view are the following panegyrics, both of 1818: 'The Bishop's Throne is supposed to be the first piece of its kind, forming altogether a perfect piece of Gothic architecture, which is imagined at this time not to be equalled for richness of stile or correctness of design',[49] and

The vulgar Grecian screens introduced by Sir Christopher Wren have been removed, the Lady Chapel thrown into the chancel, the altar carried to the east end of the building, and fitted up with some of the finely-sculptured Gothic niches found in the chapels; the episcopal throne, prebendal stalls and choir, are equal in elegance and delicacy of Gothic ornament to anything in the kingdom. The screen at the entrance of the choir, the organ loft, the slight elevation of the chancel, the slender yet lofty columns, the mosaic painted windows, the distant prospect of the Saviour in the East window,[50] diffusing light as rising from the tomb, and over it the upper Eastern Window, with the enchanting representation of the brazen serpent,[51] all conspire to give grandeur and sublimity.[52]

Paintings in the choir vault

According to Celia Fiennes,[53] 'The top of the Quoir is exactly painted and it looks as fresh as if new done, though of 300 years standing.'[54] But in 1748 Defoe[55] says that the cathedral interior 'is certainly hurt by the paltry old Painting in and over the choir, and the whitewashing lately done, wherein they, very stupidly, have everywhere drawn black lines to imitate joints of stone'. This must refer to the backgrounds surrounding the paintings then being renewed (see below). Dodsworth[56] has an interesting comment on these paintings:

Among the efforts of a wretched taste which, in attempting to ornament, had deformed the edifice, were various paintings on the vaultings of the choir and eastern transept. These were erroneously considered as coeval with the building, and consequently highly admired by those who regard the mere antiquity of an object as a sufficient title to admiration. But on a close inspection they were found to conceal lines drawn in imitation of brick-work like those which then remained on the ceiling of the nave and principal transept, and may still be traced in the Chapter House and Cloister. Their antiquity therefore was much less remote than was generally supposed. Drawings of these were made for the Society of Antiquaries [by Jacob Schnebbelie]. Mr Wyatt judiciously coloured the arches and ribs of the choir like the original stone and contrasted the ceiling and walls with a lighter tint which gives every part its due effect.

He adds that the same treatment was later given to the main transept and nave. Gleeson White says:[57] 'The originals were . . . buff-washed. . . . Owing to the tenacity of this wash, and the friable non-adhesive quality of the paint it covered, it was found impossible to remove the . . . coating without destroying the original paintings.' So the designs were repainted by Clayton and Bell[58] from what could be seen through the wash (probably after damping?).

Did they consult the Schnebbelie drawings? Old photographs before Scott's purge show nothing on any of the ceilings except a slight darkening around the bosses. Later photographs (c. 1875?) of the choir aisles show the restoration of the filigree ornament along the apex of the vaulting in two stages – fully restored towards the east and with

dull fish-like shapes further west. This process was evidently followed in the nave which had similar decoration. The ceilings of the eastern transepts were not 'restored' when those of the choir were repainted, and a recent Royal Commission photograph of the north-east transept (west side) shows dull circles on the vault, such as might have become visible after damping and subsequent drying of the wash. From all this we may deduce the following process: first, damping the wash to induce visibility of the underlying designs, then tracing or copying these and comparing them with the Schnebbelie drawings and, lastly, the repainting from full-size cartoons.[59]

The later nineteenth century

By the 1820s the distant altar was found to be impracticable and a plain table with draped cloth was erected on the site of the old high altar, thus reverting to the ancient arrangement, but with no screen to back it up. A design was made by J. C. Buckler for a low Early English altar-screen and appended to Cassan's *Lives of the Bishops of Salisbury* (1824), but it was never erected.[60]   194

But by this time attitudes were changing. In 1830 'E.I.C.' (Edward John Carlos) could write, after commending such an altar-screen:[61] 'A throne, which might be designed after the spire of the cathedral, and an entire new set of stalls in oak, it is to be hoped will one day supply the place of the miserable woodwork which defaces the choir. The design of the present throne must have been suggested by a tile-kiln; the stalls are perfectly carpenters' "Gothic".'[62] And in 1839 Winkles wrote:[63] 'There is at this time, it is believed, but one opinion respecting the desecration which was then [1790s] called improvement.'   192

Apart from the altar-table, and the removal of the Reynolds window in the Lady chapel in 1854,[64] Wyatt's work remained unaltered until the 1860s when Sir G. G. Scott was called in. Until his death in 1878, Scott was engaged in transforming the choir and Lady chapel by casting out all Wyatt's furniture and fittings,[65] and replacing them with new work designed or directed by himself. These include the exceedingly rich encaustic tile floor, the bishop's throne, marble pulpit (and another in the nave), elaborate marble reredos and painted Skidmore metal choir-screen. All this rivalled his choir at Worcester, as the most complete surviving example of a Scott cathedral choir. As such it might well have been spared, but alas in the 1950s and 1960s Scott in his turn came under the cloud of   193 195 197 171

196

188

fashion: floor, reredos, altar-rails, pulpits, and choir-screen, together with Lady chapel reredos and wonderful seven-branched gasoliers by Sir Arthur Bloomfield[66] were ejected. This left a mongrel interior, with the upper east window of 1781, the Victorian bishop's throne, choir seating (largely new),[67] ugly unenclosed organ-pipes and the stall-canopies of 1913 (by C. E. Ponting) to compete with an open west end, an open east end (except for filigree metal altar-screen, invisible from a distance), a large new altar and altar-rails to both choir and Lady chapel (1960s), a new wooden pulpit by Randoll Blacking (1950)[68] and plain polished Purbeck marble floor in choir and Lady chapel (1962).[69] The grisaille windows in the chapter house, inserted under Clutton (c. 1860), also began to be removed until a public outcry called a halt to these new vandalisms.

Mention must be made of two more important items in Scott's 'restoration'. First, the tower and spire, which, largely untouched since Wren's time, were becoming dangerous. Once again recourse was made to iron. Scott introduced in the interior an elaborate arrangement[70] of diagonal iron bars from corner to corner which connected with bands encircling the buttresses of the Early English base of the tower, just above the parapets of the four main limbs of the church, where they can easily be seen from the ground – a notable work which probably saved the steeple from collapse. (To bring the story up to date, in 1937 the turret staircases and corner windows were built up to give extra strength[71] and in 1951 the top 9 metres (30 ft) of the spire had to be rebuilt.)

Secondly, there was Scott's restoration of the west front in 1865. Only eight of the old statues remained, much decayed. These were repaired (some drastically) by Redfern, who also designed new figures for the niches – fifty were erected by 1869 and ten more later – on the whole a creditable performance.[72]

176

The cloisters which, if old prints can be trusted, were in a terrible state of decay, with columns missing and circles broken, were restored by Bishop Denison, who died in 1854, and is buried with his first wife in the central enclosure. The original Purbeck shafts were then replaced by common stone 'to the no small detriment of the general effect'.[73] Also the chapter house, then dangerously out of repair, was restored in Denison's memory under Mr Clutton, the cathedral architect. The biblical carvings[74] round the interior were repaired or recut by J. B. Philip, with many new heads, and richly coloured; the wall beneath them was decorated with painted 'hangings' by O. Hudson,[75] but these lasted only a short time. Old photographs of the same view show some of them as brand new while others were badly flaking. Gleeson White[76] says these recolourings were 'as far as possible in the original colours', but they were all cleaned off by 1900. William Burges wrote a monograph on the iconography of the chapter house[77] in which he 'put on record the precise amount of mutilations [of the carvings] and remains of colour to be seen previous to the late restoration', and he says that the central pillar was out of perpendicular and had to be rebuilt – with, it seems, new capital and base. The base has a series of carved animals which Gleeson White[78] says 'were reproduced from the originals, which are preserved in the cloisters'.

Bibliography

Price, 1753. Francis Price, *A Series of particular and useful observations upon that Admirable Structure, the Cathedral Church of Salisbury*, 'By Author of the British Carpenter'. A remarkable book with many fine measured and other drawings. 2nd edn 1774, with some additions and 'an account of Old Sarum'.

Dodsworth, 1792. William Dodsworth, *A Guide to the Cathedral Church of Salisbury, with a Particular account of the late Great Improvements made therein under the Direction of James Wyatt, Esq.* 5th edn 1798.

Dodsworth, 1814. W. Dodsworth, *An Historical Account of the . . . Cathedral Church of Sarum or Salisbury.* Fine engravings.

* *Britton, 1814.* John Britton, *The History and Antiquities of the Cathedral Church of Salisbury.* Many fine engravings.

The Salisbury Guide, 1818 – Old Sarum, Salisbury, Fonthill, Wilton, Stourhead, Longleat etc. (The 23rd edn, it is said, was dated 1797!)

Colt-Hoare, 1843. Sir Richard Colt-Hoare, *City of Salisbury*, last vol. in History of Wiltshire.

Brown's Guide. Brown's *Illustrated Guide to Salisbury and Neighbourhood*, 1882 edn.

* *Gleeson White (Bell), 1896.* Gleeson White, *Salisbury, The Cathedral and See*, Bell's Cathedral Series. 1901 edn.

---

* see also bibliography to the Introduction.

Notes on Salisbury Cathedral, 1920. 'Prepared at the request of the cathedral.'

Fletcher, 1933. J. M. J. Fletcher, *The Story of Salisbury Cathedral.*

Smethurst, 1953. Canon A. F. Smethurst, *Salisbury Cathedral – A Guide.*

* *Smethurst (Pitkin), 1974.* Canon A. F. Smethurst, *Salisbury Cathedral*, Pitkin Pictorial. 1974 edn.

Notes

1 Letter from Bishop Jewell (1560–71) to Peter Martyr – Dodsworth (1814), 170.
2 Dodsworth (1814), 170–71.
3 Dodsworth (1814), 171.
4 Colt-Hoare, 454.
5 *The Wren Society*, XI, 25.
6 Price, 36, says: 'This is perhaps the best piece of Smith's work, as also most excellent mechanism of anything in Europe of its age.'
7 *The Wren Society*, XI, 22, 24.
8 Price, 61.
9 Daniel Defoe, *Tour through the Whole Island of Great Britain* (4th edn 1745), I, 321.
10 Price, 60.
11 Price, 61–62.
12 Gleeson White (Bell), 25.
13 *Notes on Salisbury Cathedral*, 92.
14 *Gentleman's Magazine*, 1803, 642–43.
15 *Change and the Unchanging – A Companion to Salisbury Cathedral*, anon. (c. 1960).
16 Dodsworth (1814), 184.
17 *The Builder*, 2 Nov. 1867, 812.
18 See Canon Dawson's article on Scott, Friends *Annual Report* (1962), 12.
19 Price, 67.
20 Gleeson White (Bell), 25, note.
21 Dodsworth (1814), 185.
22 Colt-Hoare, 543. On p. 592 is an exquisite engraving of the vaulted interior of this porch, looking out.
23 To the 'north-east of the city' – Murray's *Handbook* (1861–69), 110.
24 Dodsworth (1814), 182.
25 After pl. XVIII; also in Brown's *Guide*.
26 Dr Walter Pope, *Life of Seth, Lord Bishop of Salisbury* (1697), quoted by Gleeson White (Bell), 14. This pavement is shown in R. Gough's pre-Wyatt plan, reproduced in A. Vallance, *Greater English Church Screens* (1947), pl. 80.
27 Dodsworth (1814), 174. On p. 177 he says the stalls and screens were 'designed by Sir Christopher Wren', so it may reasonably be inferred that the other decorations just mentioned were also by him.
28 Defoe, *op. cit.* Second passage quoted is not specified, but quoted by Gleeson White (Bell), 54.
29 Exteriors of these chapels are shown in east views of the cathedral by Hollar (Dugdale's *Monasticon*, III, 1673,

p. 316), and T. Hearne and W. Byrne, *Antiquities of Great Britain* (1790s), II, no IX. Interiors etc. in R. Gough, *Sepulchral Monuments* (1786), II, 1, pls LXX, LXXI, LXXII, CI.
30 *The History and Antiquities of the Cathedral Church of Salisbury and the Abbey Church of Bath*, anon. (1719), 130. The omissions here stand for the inscriptions there quoted at length.
31 John Milner, *Dissertation on the Modern Style of Altering Ancient Cathedrals* (1798), 19. (Milner was the Roman Catholic author of *History and Survey of the Antiquities of Winchester*, 1798–1801.)
32 *The Salisbury Guide*, 54.
33 Dodsworth (1814), 178, note: 'A part of this screen now forms the altarpiece of St Martin's.'
34 Dodsworth (1814), 177. Vallance, *op. cit.*, 81, says that the 'cage' was formerly 'appropriated as a seat for the Mayor and Bishop in sermon time and for the judges and sheriffs during the assises'. Gough, *op. cit*, III, pl. 39, is a plan of the cathedral showing these seating arrangements and the pre-Wyatt interior generally, with its many screens (also reproduced in Vallance, *op. cit.*, 80).
35 Milner. *op. cit.*, II, 35.
36 This is curious: Gleeson White (Bell), 14, quotes from chapter minutes of 26 Aug. 1789 that Wyatt was instructed to make, inter alia, 'new iron rails to the communion', which assumes retaining the table in its old place – evidently the lengthening of the 'choir' to the E end was Wyatt's own idea and perhaps he forgot to add rails to his new altar!
37 Milner, *Dissertation on the Modern Style of Altering Ancient Cathedrals* (1798), 38, enlarges on this: 'On looking into a dark recess [the former Lady chapel, rendered so by dark glass in the side lancets] which is now added . . . to the length of the choir, a diminutive object, without size or other marks of dignity, can just be discerned . . . in short it has more the appearance of a toilet than a communion table'; in a note he added: 'A personage . . ., respectable in his habits no less than for his situation . . . declared lately in a public assembly, that it was impossible either to hear or see from the choir what was going on at the communion-table; and that, for the lack of rails, a dog some time ago ate the bread . . . prepared for the sacrament.'
38 Carter, *Gentleman's Magazine*, 1803, pp. 1021–22, enumerates and explains these solecisms, along the south side of the nave from east to west, and back along the north side – an invaluable record. (See also Laurence Gomme, *Sacred and Medieval Architecture*, 1890, I, 212–13, Gentleman's Magazine Library.)
39 Shown on Gough's pre-Wyatt plan.
40 About 1562, according to Vallance, *op. cit.*, 80, quoting the Rev. C. Wordsworth.
41 Milner, *op. cit.*, 45.
42 Murray's *Handbook* (1861), 92.
43 *The Salisbury Guide*, 55.
44 C. Winston, 'Painted Glass at Salisbury', *Report of the Archaeological Institute's meeting at Salisbury* (1849), 135.

45 *Ibid.*, note.

46 Quoted by Gleeson White (Bell), 91, 92.

47 Britton, 103–04.

48 Carter (1748–1817) was wholly dedicated in his love of our national medieval architecture, and contributed a long series of critical letters to *Gentleman's Magazine* (over the signature 'an architect') on 'The Pursuit of Architectural Innovation'. See Joan Evans, *History of the Society of Antiquaries* (1956), 206–14, for its feud with Carter.

49 *The Salisbury Guide*, 56.

50 *The Resurrection*, designed by Sir Joshua Reynolds and executed by Mr Eginton, inserted in 1790.

51 Erected 1781.

52 J. Storer, *History and Antiquities of Cathedral Churches of Great Britain* (1814–19).

53 Celia Fiennes, *Through England on a Side-Saddle in the Reign of William and Mary*, 2.

54 '300 years' seems to be freely used by the diarist for the 'later Middle Ages'.

55 Defoe, *op. cit.*, (1748 edn), I, 326.

56 Dodsworth (1814), 183.

57 Gleeson White (Bell), 54.

58 See *The Builder*, 14 Dec. 1872.

59 The Schnebbelie drawings: there were two series of 93 compartments – (1) the original sketches with two finished work drawings (in a scrap-book with the Society of Antiquaries); (2) the finished drawings, all but two now in the Bodleian Library (Gough Maps XXXII, SC 17529). See article by F. R. Horbleck, *Archaeological Journal*, 1960, p. 116, for discussion of the iconography etc; also article by Tancred Borenius, *Antiquaries Journal*, XII, 1932, p. 375, no. 1.

60 Pub. again in *Gentleman's Magazine*, July 1830, 9.

61 *Gentleman's Magazine*, May 1830, 406.

62 Carlos may have been right about the details of this furniture, but the whole ensemble of the choir – at least looking west, with the organ in its proper place – seems to the author satisfactory, if not handsome. It may be considered superior to Scott's fittings, however much better the workmanship of the latter may be.

63 B. Winkles, *Illustrations of the Cathedral Churches of England and Wales* (1838), 11.

64 This was replaced by a memorial window to Dean Lear, of bright '13th-century' colours; in 1960 it was removed to admit some original glass from behind the Gorges monument (E end of N choir aisle), of 13th-, 16th- and 17th-c. dates (Smethurst, Pitkin, 1974, 11). Seen in original position in Fletcher (1933), opposite p. 64. In place of this old glass a new window in memory of George Herbert by Christopher Webb was inserted. Another new (heraldic) window is behind the Hertford monument (E end of S choir aisle).

65 Except for the panelling from the Beauchamp Chapel – still in position in the Lady chapel. Before Scott's time the charming late 17th-c? font, seen in Biddlecombe's print of 1754, had been given up and a new one made in memory of Dean Lear (d. 1830). The old font was given in 1876 to a church in Yankalilla, S. Australia (Fletcher, *Cathedral Church of the Blessed Virgin Mary of Salisbury*, 1935, 14).

66 Brown's *Guide*, 46, says of these gasoliers: 'The bases are of foreign walnut and the whole surface is richly decorated with embossed and saw-pierced work of solid silver.'

67 *The Builder*, Dec. 1892, p. 83, says: 'The old thirteenth-century stalls, the only fittings of the choir which could be kept have been cleansed from their paint, and wait for proper canopies.'

68 Smethurst, 1953, p. 22.

69 Friends' *Annual Report* (1962), 5.

70 Planned with the help of 'the eminent engineer, Mr Shields'.

71 *Change and the Unchanging – a Companion to Salisbury Cathedral*, anon. (*c.* 1960), 8.

72 Views before the restoration show nine of the eleven niches above the central west doors as having a quatrefoil sunk panel (or window?) which was completely hidden by any statue placed in the niche. For the iconography of the new statues, see H. T. Armfield, *The Legend of Christian Art* (1869).

73 Murray's *Handbook* (1861), 101. But Carter, (*Gentleman's Magazine*, 1803, p. 643) says: 'I found, the cloisters in good hands. . . . The restoration of such parts as are decayed seem to be tolerably correct. How is this? Why, indeed, the poor man had no other superintendent than the common plodding master mason.' Storer, *op. cit.*, 8, says: 'The cloisters are in fine preservation', and in his pl. 4 and Britton, pl. 8, the only broken arcades visible are those through which the view is taken – perhaps an example of 'artistic licence'!

74 *The Ecclesiologist*, XVII, 1856, p. 375, says these 'were in many places so obliterated and decayed that little remained in many places but the impression of the shadows of the departed statuettes on the wall'.

75 Brown's *Guide* (1900 edn), 56.

76 Gleeson White (Bell), 75.

77 *The Ecclesiologist*, XX, 1859, p. 109.

78 Gleeson White (Bell), 75.

174. This 'south-west prospect' by J. Harris was published about 1715 but is possibly a copy of an earlier view. It shows the bell-tower and the complete library range adjoining the south transept.

175. The west front before 1865. Only eight of the statues remain. Note the quatrefoil windows in nine of the eleven niches over the door, hidden when new statues were provided.

176. The west front between 1880 and 1890, after the addition of the new statues.

Salisbury: the bell-tower and Lady chapel

177. The bell-tower in Hollar's etching, *c.* 1672.

178. View from the south-east (1798, Hearne and Byrne) with the two chantry chapels still shown in situ.

Far right
179. The east end from the north-east, as it is today.

180. The bell-tower in 1761, surrounded by little houses (engraving by G. B. Jackson). Of interest also is the small porch added to the north transept, later removed to the grounds of the College.

181. The bell-tower shortly before its demolition by Wyatt (Hoare's *History of Wiltshire*).

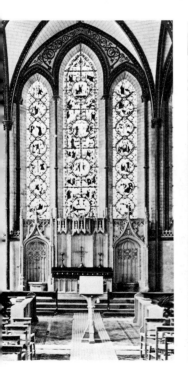

182–84. In the Lady chapel Wyatt reused fragments of the Beauchamp and Hungerford Chapels for the reredos and panelling. The former (*left*) has gone, but the latter (*centre*) remains. Scott's restoration (*right*) involved replacing the glass of the east window but for some time Wyatt's 'mosaic' glass remained at the sides.

185. The nave looking east (Biddlecombe, 1754). The Early English pulpitum was removed by Wyatt. The font (bottom left) is now in Australia.

186. The nave looking east, c. 1865. The screen is that erected by Wyatt.

189. The medieval pulpitum in its present position, against the west wall of the north-east transept. The later central niche comes from elsewhere.

190. The crossing and transepts, c. 1865, showing Wyatt's screen in detail.

187. The nave looking east in the late 19th century, with Scott's screen replacing Wyatt's.

188. The same view today, after the removal of Scott's screen and reredos, exposing the entire length of the cathedral.

Salisbury: the screen

191. Plan of the eastern arm of the cathedral in 1796, showing the position of screens and chapels before Wyatt (Gough's *Sepulchral Monuments*). The demolished Beauchamp and Hungerford Chapels flank the east end. In the nave north arcade, one bay west of the crossing, Gough shows the iron Hungerford Chapel ('the cage') which Wyatt moved to the choir and converted into a family pew for the Earl of Radnor; it appears on the left in pl. 194.

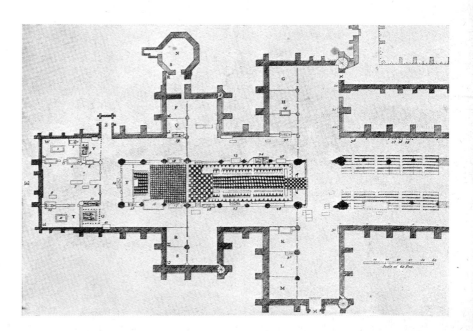

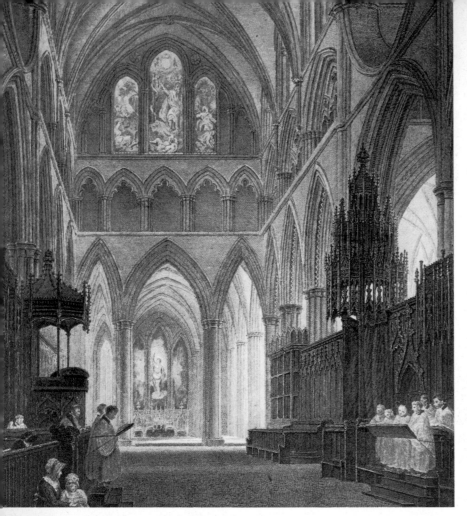

Salisbury: the choir

192. The choir looking east, *c*. 1814 (engraving from Dodsworth). The stalls and fittings are those provided by Wyatt, with his 'high altar' in the Lady chapel.

193. The same view after Scott's restoration: new fittings, new reredos, new glass.

194. The choir looking west in 1860; the furnishings are still Wyatt's, but with a new communion table added after his time, as that in the Lady chapel was found to be too remote to serve as the high altar.

195. Scott's choir looking west: screen, stalls (added 1913) and reredos formed one of the most complete Victorian ensembles of any cathedral.

196. One of Blomfield's gasoliers, destroyed with Scott's screen in the 1950s.

197. View looking west from the Lady chapel, showing the extreme height of Scott's reredos from this side, now open to the west end.

123

Winchester

UNTIL the early years of this century, the exterior of Winchester Cathedral – surely the lowliest in the world for such a major church – appears to have altered little since the Reformation, except for the roof of the tower. This is now invisible from the ground, but Daniel King's etching of 1655[1] shows a low roof running east and west with a gable each end, and in the centre a rod with cross and vane. Twenty years earlier Lieutenant Hammond[2] tells us that there was (presumably forming the vane) 'St George on horseback on the top of the flat-bottom'd steeple, to be sentinell and give notice of her Governor's prerogative Prelacy of that high noble Order.' (The bishops of Winchester were prelates of the Garter.) As King and later engravers do not show St George he was probably shot down in the Civil War. By 1773 an engraving in the anonymous *History*[3] shows a rod and vane and no visible roof, but the text says: 'the tower . . . has no proper finishing, but is covered in as if the building had been left off' – a curious statement! Lastly, Warren's *History and Antiquities of Winchester* (1836) says:[4] 'Formerly a weathercock was placed on . . . the tower, but it has recently been taken down.'

Soon after the Reformation the puritanical Bishop Horne (1560–80) purged his cathedral of 'objects of Superstition'. In 1570 he pulled down the chapter house and cloisters, apparently to save the cost of upkeep, and houses were built in their place against the church. By the early 17th century a common thoroughfare had been established through the nave and south aisle. Under Archbishop Laud the houses were demolished to remedy this desecration, and at the same time the old slype between the south transept and the chapter house was opened up by Bishop Curle (1632–47) as a public passage, entailing the piercing of the great buttress propping the transept. At the east and west entrances to the slype were Latin anagrams to direct pedestrians (removed to a nearby wall at the late 18th-century enlargement of the passage).[5]

About this time two alterations were effected in the cathedral. Firstly, in 1634 a groined wooden ceiling was erected in the tower, immediately over the four great arches, thus shutting out the former lantern with its fine Norman arcading. This late fan 'vault' is elaborately decorated with carved bosses and a medallion with portraits of Charles I and Henrietta Maria, and, as springers to the vault, there were carved busts of James I and Charles I in alternate corners. These busts were removed in the repairs of the 1820s when, newly painted, they were said to look ridiculous, 'resembling Punchinello'.[6] Was this ceiling erected to counter downdraughts?

Secondly, in 1637, the medieval pulpitum or choir-screen was rebuilt or reconstructed in a Classical manner from a fine design by Inigo Jones,[7] with two bronze statues of James I and Charles I by Hubert le Sueur (who covenanted to produce them by March 1639 for £340, and £40 to convey them to Winchester).[8] They were stolen from the cathedral in December 1642, but being deemed valuable were not destroyed. Later they were found at Portsmouth, bought by a Mr Benjamin Newland of the Isle of Wight for £10 and buried safely until the Restoration, when he sold them 'very privately' to the bishop for £100. They were then restored to the screen.[9]

In the Civil War the cathedral escaped major structural damage, although furniture and brasses suffered badly under Sir William Waller, as the following extract from *Mercurius Rusticus* will show:[10]

the monuments of the dead were defaced, the bones of the kings and bishops thrown about the church, the two famous brazen statues of Charles and James, erected at the entrance of the choir, pulled down, the communion plate, books, hangings, cushions, seized upon and made away with, the church vestments put on by the heathenish soldiers, riding in that posture in derision

198. The reredos of Winchester Cathedral, c. 1890. Though basically medieval, the canopies and figures had been only recently restored (see pls 214, 215); Christ on the Cross is still missing and West's painting of The Raising of Lazurus *is still over the altar.*

216

205
206

about the streets, some scornfully singing pieces of the Common Prayer, whilst others tooted upon broken pieces of the organs. The stories of the Old and New Testaments, curiously beautified with colours, and cut out in carved work,[11] were utterly destroyed, and of the brass torn from the violated monuments, might have been built a house, as strong as the brazen towers of the old romances.

No wonder there are no brasses in Winchester Cathedral! In fact, according to Dean Sykes,[12] 'it seemed possible at one moment that Parliament's decision to pull down the Cathedral might be carried into effect; but the townsmen successfully petitioned against such an act of vandalism'.

By the end of the 18th century the cathedral was becoming ruinous through prolonged neglect, as Carter testified in 1789:[13]

In surveying this cathedral, I was struck with the idea that it appeared in the same state as a building soon expected to be taken down to make way for a new erection. . . . At the West Front . . . the parapet of the gallery over the three grand porches was in a most ruinated state, many parts of it having fallen into the gallery. On the north side of the nave I everywhere saw broken pinnacles, architraves and mullions of the windows; innumerable quarries of the glass were wanting . . . a scene of generall devastation. . . . The appearance of the West front of the north transept is really disgraceful; here is an entrance into the transept which is connected into a receptacle for all kind of rubbish. . . . it is impossible to command the indignation raised by viewing the groins over the exquisite monumental chapel of Cardinal Beaufort, which was left in such a deplorable state that the rain often deluges this wonderful object. Nay, so little is it respected that prodigious quantities of its broken minute parts are thrown by as so much rubbish.

Milner[14] says that Beaufort's chantry is 'neglected and consigned to dust and ruin, equally by his family, his foundation, and his cathedral; to all of which he proved so liberal a benefactor . . . of the canopies . . . and of the crocketted pinnacles . . . a horse-load has fallen, or been taken down, which are kept in . . . a neighbouring chapel'. According to Vaughan:[15] 'There seems to have been originally no effigy on the tomb. The present figure in the robes of a Cardinal, belongs to the time of Charles II.' Britton[16] calls it 'a vulgar clumsy piece of workmanship, rather that of a *stonemason than a sculptor*'. In contrast, 'the opposite chantry, that of Bishops Waynflete', had the advantage 'in the attention that is paid by his children of Magdalen College, Oxford, to keep it clean and in decent order'.[17]

The nave and transepts were neglected and dusty, the transepts shut out by huge screens from the choir which, it seems, was the only part of the cathedral to be kept in decent order. Storer[18] says 'this [North] transept is now in so ruinous and degraded a state that the public have lately been denied access to it'.[19]

The reredos

Milner[20] calls this late 15th-century work 'a magnificent screen of the most exquisite workmanship in stone which this or perhaps any other nation can exhibit'. He says that the original statues in the niches, 'having been demolished in the Reformation as superstitious, their places were, with more liberality than taste, filled with Grecian urns'. But Gale's opinion in 1715 was very different:[21]

The ascent to the altar, of marble steps, and the Pavement are very curious, being inlaid with different colour'd marbles in various figures. The altarpiece is a very handsom Design of Woodwork which forms a lofty canopy, projecting over the Table, with vast Festoons hanging down from it, and all over beautified with exquisite foliage. Behind this, there is a very high skreen . . . of Stone, the work of Bishop Fox, full of antique Carving and Niches, where formerly were statues, but they being demolished, the Vacancies are filled with large vases or urns, which add an extraordinary Grandeur to the whole. This ornament was the Gift of William Harris, who by his Will bequeathed eight hundred pounds towards it, A D 1700.

This wooden altarpiece covering the screen is said to have been erected by Bishop Curle (1632–47). The lower part accorded well with the first of these dates, being 'Jacobean' in appearance: a plate in Sandford's book of 1677[22] shows the lower part with the decalogue (rare in cathedrals?) and altar-rails of this period.[23] How the Jacobean work finished above was obscured by a splendid canopy of hanging festoons, liberally gilded, and evidently of the Wren period, as E.I.C. (Edward John Carlos) pointed out.[24] It was surmounted by a delicately carved cresting, containing a 'Pelican in its Piety' and C.R. (for Carolus Rex). Milner says:[25] 'It is certain neither of these articles would have been tolerated' during the Presbyterian regime, which would mean either that they were removed for safety and later restored as he suggests or, more probably, that they had not then been added with the whole canopy. It is noteworthy that Milner does not refer to the statement in the anonymous *History*[26] of 1773 that 'in the grand rebellion, the

211

210

altar-screen was artfully protected . . . by a partition erected in a parallel line before it' – not very practical, as the soldiers would surely have torn it down! Perhaps they did so and destroyed the original summit, and hence the new canopy?

That the canopy was of the Wren period is affirmed in *The Beauties of England* (1776):[27] 'The altarpiece, which is by much the noblest in England, is the gift of Bishop Morley [1662–84]. It consists of a lofty canopy of woodwork, projecting over the Communion table like a curtain, with gilt festoons hanging down from it, and other ornaments.' (Warner, in 1795, gives the same attribution.)[28] It continues: 'On either side of the altar are stone vases with golden flames issuing up to the roof of the church'! The present splendid altar-rails (superseding those in Sandford) are also of the Wren period.

In 1782 the dean and chapter purchased Benjamin West's large painting of *The Raising of Lazarus* and placed it in front of the Commandments (it remained over the altar until 1899). Altogether the whole ensemble must have looked quite splendid, except for one thing: the stone-work flanking the reredos was painted brown to match the woodwork![29]

The early nineteenth century

Meanwhile the Gothic Revival was advancing and Classical features retreating in informed esteem, boosted, no doubt, by the publication in 1817 of Britton's *Winchester Cathedral*, with its fierce attacks on 17th- and 18th-century fittings, however distinguished. It is an interesting reflection on the Revival's rapid advance that Milner, about 1800,[30] can speak of Jones's pulpitum as 'elegant' and 'highly beautiful in itself', though inappropriate in a Gothic cathedral; while Britton in 1817[31] calls it 'a bad and unsightly object. . . . It is discordant and highly displeasing, and betrays a deplorable lack of feeling.'

Thus prepared for change, with the appointment of William Garbett as architect to the dean and chapter, the first and greatest 'restoration' of the cathedral (*c.* 1812–28) got under way, with Prebendary George Frederick Nott as leading spirit. By 1818 the urns had been removed from the niches[32] and in 1820 the 17th-century wooden reredos was taken down (a large part of which is still preserved in the cathedral).[33] From then until the 1880s to 1890s, when the stone canopies were restored and the niches repeopled, the 15th-century screen looked denuded indeed.[34]

Dean Kitchin (1883–94) takes up the story:[35]

the painted stone-work [was] washed over with whitening. Dr Nott's men cleaned it all down . . . and carved out in a rude, though not altogether unpleasing, fashion some of the larger blocks that remained behind the lost canopies; they also replaced some pedestals in a different stone apparently copying them from the work at St Albans[36] . . . he proceeded also to finish the broken crockets, finials and pinnacles in plaster,[37] not badly done at all. . . . The general result of these . . . 'restorations' has been the creation of a blank, respectable soul-less structure.

A new Gothic bishop's throne replaced Bishop Trelawney's Classical erection, which was relegated to the end gallery of the north transept. Inigo Jones's pulpitum was demolished[38] and replaced by a Gothic structure loosely copied from the west front porches, with the two royal statues in the new niches; and the organ, replaced over the north stalls, given a Gothic case.[39] These designs of Garbett were much admired at the time – the choir-screen, made by one Gillingham, deservedly so. The throne is still with us, but the screen was, regrettably, swept away by Scott. Garbett also removed the great screens that so effectively cut off the choir from the transepts, and the latter were given flat pannelled and decorated wooden ceilings (probably inspired by those in St Albans Abbey) to hide the rough timber roofs – a creditable performance, though they also hid the rose window in the north gable.

As for structural work, Garbett renewed two flying buttresses on the south side of the presbytery, and the canopies on the apex of the east and west roofs, and extensively restored the vaulting of De Lucy's retrochoir.

But the most important repair that has been effected in this, or perhaps in any other cathedral, is the restoration of one of the immense pillars . . . of the nave [adjoining Edington's chantry] To accomplish so hazardous an undertaking, it was deemed advisable to provide an artificial support for three entire arches . . . whilst the masonry of the pillar was cut away and re-constructed. Two hundred and fifty loads of timber were required for the ponderous scaffolding which supported the superincumbent mass – a weight little less than 400 tons.[40]

Lastly and strangely, the old east and west entrances to the former cloister were walled up and a new doorway constructed between them. This restoration cost 'upwards of £40,000'.[41]

The chantries

In Milner (9th edn 1830)[42] the supplement answering his complaints about Beaufort's chantry, says that it 'has not been neglected during the recent renovations by the representative of his illustrious family, and to record this becoming attention, the Dean and Chapter have attached an elegant inscription to the walls of the Chantry'. And yet, in Warren (1836) we read:[43] 'This elegant Chantry in its design . . . has been much mutilated, in so much that scarcely a pinnacle or niche is to be found entire. . . . We hope the time is not far distant when . . . it will be restored to its original perfection.'

As for Waynflete's chantry and Milner's assurance of its being repaired by his college, it in fact seems to have deteriorated so much that a major restoration was undertaken,[44] as Warren (1836) describes:[45]

It was severely mutilated during the last extensive alterations . . . in the cathedral. The iron bars, also, had been previously removed from the compartments of the screen, which the original architect had thus wisely strengthened. . . . This needless operation required immense labour, and it was not effected without severe injury to the monument, as the bars (which were of the hardest wrought iron) passed quite through the mullions and pillars. . . . The effects of age and violence . . . were very numerous. One hundred and nine pinnacles and shafts, thirty finials, and crockets of various kinds . . . have supplied the deficiencies. Nearly all the remaining pinnacles were insecure owing to the use of wooden pegs, instead of brass wire, with which the whole are now fastened. Stone of several qualities were used . . . in the monument . . . supposed to have been brought from Beere in Devonshire. The repairs have been made with Painswick and Farley Down Stone; and the whole brought to an uniform and beautiful colour. [He then says that after injury by Cromwell's troops the figure of the bishop was] clumsily repaired with putty and coarsely painted.

This was remedied, but Murray's *Handbook* (1861)[46] says that the 'great part of the effigy is modern, the head specially having been much restored.'

In 1836 Warren[47] says that Fox's chantry 'has recently been restored by Mr James Kellow, mason, of this City; and it now appears with all that freshness and perfectness [as] when first erected' and that 'the monuments of Bishops Waynflete and Fox are now the most perfect in the Cathedral'.[48] The modern figures in the lower niches of the front are by Sir George Frampton.

Of William of Wykeham's chantry, Milner says:[49]

This chapel and monument are kept in repair at the joint expense of Wykeham's two foundations, New College, Oxford, and Winchester College. It was repaired and ornamented . . . in 1664, and again in 1741, but with very little judgment. . . . again in . . . 1799 [when] the painting and gilding were executed by Mr Cave, of this city, in a very proper manner, as far as depended on his taste. The chief faults of the late work are, the gilding of so great a surface as the whole cope has a tawdry appearance; on the other hand the whole collection of the orbs in the vaulting . . . ought to have been gilded, and not few of them only.

In the south transept the 'venerable chapel' (the northern of the two in its eastern aisle) looks like a chantry, being enclosed by an elaborate stone screen, the lower part having a doorway between two Perpendicular windows, all filled by fine 18th-century iron work (given by William Eyre, Sargeant-at-Law, who died in 1714),[50] while the upper part rises to six tall crocketted pinnacles. Ball[51] states that this chapel was 'secured by a beautifully ornamental screen surmounted by funeral urns'. Could these be Dr Harris's vases removed from the altar-screen?

The choir

Bishop Fox's fine glass in the east window, removed at the Civil War and badly replaced, was in Milner's time 'covered with dust and cobwebs'. Under Garbett 'the whole was properly arranged and the mutilated parts judiciously restored'.[52] But Pevsner says:[53] 'The east window is essentially of 1852 (by David Evans)', and for what original glass remains, he refers us to Le Courteur.

Views of the altar-screen soon after Garbett's repair are hard to come by but it remained unaltered to at least 1854, if we can trust a large wood engraving of the choir in the *Illustrated London News* (15/4/1854), which shows the screen in all its meagreness. By 1859 'the whole [sic] of the overhanging canopies' had 'been restored by Mr Forder, the Cathedral architect'.[54] But photographs of the 1860s and 1870s show 'the whole' to be incorrect – only two canopies under the arms of the great cross completed; and a notable addition – four new and elaborate canopies and bases to match the original work, one above the other each side of the central compartment. And so it remained until 1885, when J. D. Sedding was appointed architect to superintend the final restoration.[55] Exact copies of the canopies just mentioned were gradually repeated over the rest of the reredos and eventually, after careful consideration of the icono-

214

198 graphy by Dean Kitchin,[56] peopled with statues, culminating in the figure on the great rood in 1899 by Farmer and Brindley. In that year West's picture was removed[57] and its place taken by a
215 carving of the Holy Family and six saints (also by Farmer and Brindley). And so, at long last, the Winchester screen became once more a splendid object and superior to its rival at St Albans (where the statues by Harry Hems differ in colour from their background).

The other statues on the reredos were the work of four sculptors – all the upper and outer large figures and several small ones by Boulton of Cheltenham; four large statues by the cross by Nicholls of London; and the rest of the small figures by Geflowski of London and Miss M. Grant. The surveyor was John B. Colson.

209 In 1873 Garbett's substantial choir-screen was swept away by Scott,[58] who replaced it by the
208 present feeble screen – just copies of the return stalls (1876) – seemingly his only work at Winchester Cathedral. Besides the poorness of the idea, the lack of depth east and west of Scott's screen has left untidy Norman remains on the piers each side of it – formerly hidden by the greater width of its three predecessors and so never converted to Gothic.

In Milner's two plates of the choir, and the western views of it in Britton (1817) and Winkles (1836), the 15th-century pulpit of Prior Silkstede's time is shown with an ogee crocketted canopy. But in the afore-mentioned engraving in the *Illustrated London News* of 1854 there is a new and more
8, 215 elaborate ogee crocketted canopy. This balanced well with Garbett's bishop's throne, and together they framed the view of the sanctuary from between the stalls in a very satisfying way. We are not told who designed it, but it remained in position until around 1970. Then the pulpit, sans canopy, was placed one bay eastwards, thus spoiling this veritable *coup d'oeil*.

De Lucy's retrochoir, in spite of several attempted repairs, remained insecure until 1905, by when its condition, and that of the whole eastern end of the cathedral, had become alarming. The original builders had failed to reach the solid gravel bed beneath the marshy peat and had laid trunks of trees as a raft on which to build, which then sunk, thus dislocating the fabric.[59] Its repair was now got underway:

Mr J. B. Colson, FRIBA, Mr T. G. Jackson, R.A., and Mr Francis Fox, the eminent engineer, reported to the Dean and Chapter as to serious cracks and settlements in the transepts and eastern parts of the Cathedral, and in 1906 the underpinning of the walls down to the gravel beds

and repairs of the vaulting were entrusted to Messrs Thompson and Co. of Peterborough, who have employed divers to work beneath the Cathedral, in some 14 foot of water, to dig out, at selected points, the logs of timber, and peat, and to lay bags of cement and masses of concrete prior to pumping out the water, so as to enable the bricklayers to lay good foundations on the gravel 14–18 feet [4·2–5·4 metres] below the level of the ground.[60]

De Lucy's retrochoir, the Lady chapel and the transepts were thus underpinned; and the south wall of the nave was strengthened against the thrust of the vaulting by new arched buttresses
201 (which incidentally improved the otherwise bald south side of the cathedral – so rendered by the demolition of the cloisters in 1570). Completed in 1912, this great undertaking cost £113,000.[61]

Lastly, in the retrochoir a new piece of furniture was added – 'St Swithin's Shrine, 1962, by Brian Thomas and Wilfred Carpenter Turner, a strangely thin, delicate piece, inspired by the Swedish style of the twenties. Black silver and brass.'[62]

Bibliography
Gale, 1715. Samuel Gale, *History and Antiquities of the Cathedral Church of Winchester*, 'Begun by . . . the late Earl of Clarendon, and continued to this time by Samuel Gale, Gent'. With 17 copper pls.

History, 1773. *History and Antiquities of Winchester*, anon. 2 vols.

* Britton, 1817. John Britton, *The History and Antiquities of the See and Cathedral Church of Winchester*. 30 splendid engravings.

Ball, 1818. Charles Ball, *An Historical Account of Winchester with Descriptive Walks*. With 12 aquatints.

Milner, c. 1830. Rev. John Milner, *Milner's Historical Account of Winchester with a Supplement describing the alterations and repairs*. Reprint of his description of the cathedral. 9th edn has a supplement answering his charges of neglect, etc., and another on the Lady chapel paintings (dated 1830).

Warren, 1830s–1920s. The Warren family of Winchester issued a series of excellent guide- and picture-books of the cathedral and city. In addition to those mentioned in

* see also bibliography to the Introduction.

the text and notes, a small *Antiquities of Winchester* (c. 1836) is noteworthy.

Willis, 1846. Rev. R. Willis, *Architectural History of Winchester Cathedral*.

Kitchin, c. 1890. G. W. Kitchin, DD, *The Great Screen of Winchester Cathedral*. Printed by Warren's.

* *Sergeant (Bell), 1898*. P. W. Sergeant, *Winchester, the Cathedral and See*, Bell's Cathedral Series.

Vaughan, 1919. John Vaughan, *Winchester Cathedral, Its Monuments and Memorials*.

Le Couteur, 1920. J. D. Le Couteur, *Ancient Glass in Winchester*. Printed by Warren's.

* *Cathedral Records* (Friends of Winchester Cathedral): Frank Warren, 'The lost panels of the choir-stalls', no. 4, 1935; J. D. Atkinson, 'The Quire-Screen', no. 7, 1938, p. 5; G. H. Blore, 'The Cathedral in 1820', no. 7, 1938, p. 12; H. S. A., 'A Major Restoration' (c. 1820s–40s), no. 33, 1964; J. M. G. Blakiston, articles on 'The Inigo Jones Screen', pts I, II (apparently a fuller version of pt II and later history of the screen can be found in the chapter library), no. 45, 1976, p. 10, and no. 46, 1977, p. 13.

* *Sykes (Pitkin), 1969*. Rev. N. Sykes, *Winchester Cathedral*, Pitkin Pictorial.

Notes

1 In W. Dugdale's *Monasticon Anglicanum*, I (1655).

2 The diarist of *Topographical Excursions* (1634, 1635). For details see bibliography to Introduction; see also under Bristol, Ely and Lichfield.

3 *History* (1773), I, 32, 33.

4 Warren, *History and Antiquities of Winchester* (1836), 80.

5 Milner (2nd edn 1809), I, 107, note 3.

6 *Gentleman's Magazine*, Oct. 1823, p. 313.

7 See Blakiston (1976, 1977): he reveals from the diary of the then dean (Yonge) that this reconstruction originated from Charles I who 'much dislikes the placing of the [pulpitum] which stands cross the navis ecclesiae before the west dore of the Quier at such a distance that a good space of the church is thereby lost'. The dean recommends rebuilding it 'close up to the west end of the Quier'.

The now exposed Norman remains on the 2 N piers W of the choir entrance show that the original pulpitum and rood-loft occupied 2 whole bays of the nave in width (see type 3 in St John Hope, 'Quire-screens in English Churches', *Archaeologia*, 58, 1916–17, p. 69). Would that be wide enough to justify the statement of its stretching 'at such a distance' etc? If the words indicated, as they seem to, any greater width, it would surely be a unique and inexplicable departure from medieval practice.

8 A. Vallance, *Greater English Church Screens* (1947), 51, quoting Gotch's article in RIBA journal (24 Nov. 1928).

9 Vallance, *op. cit.*, 51–52, quoting letter from Bishop Brian Duppa, Dec. 1660. For subsequent fate of statues and screen, see below, note 38.

10 Bruno Ryves, *Mercurius Rusticus* (1646), quoted in Milner (1809), I, 408.

11 Milner (1809), II, 34, suggests these came from the medieval pulpitum, while Sykes (Pitkin), 20, maintains they were originally under the stall-canopies and 62 in number. Lt. Hammond lists the subjects.

12 Sykes (Pitkin), 20.

13 *Gentleman's Magazine* supplement, 1798, p. 1105.

14 Milner (1809), II, 60.

15 Vaughan, 52.

16 Britton, 81.

17 Milner (1809), II, 61.

18 Storer, 9.

19 Carter (*Gentleman's Magazine*, 1812, p. 7) shows the hazards of cathedral exploring early last century: 'There is in this church a kind of griping avaricious propensity with the officers deputed to show the same to strangers. Artists and others are most unfeelingly pressed in this sort'. He speaks of the extreme difficulty of obtaining permission from the dean and chapter to study its antiquities. Are they so poor that the vergers 'must seek their wages from the accidental payments of . . . travellers?'

20 Milner (1809), II, 42. This is extravagant language, although he probably means the *delicacy* of the work was unique. But he ignores the nearly identical screen at St Albans which retained (as comparison of prints before the modern restorations shows) far more of his much admired lace-like enrichments than Winchester. For there, original work was almost confined to the top of the screen and the two doorway canopies, whereas at St Albans most of the canopies and crusting were intact.

21 Gale, 28.

22 Francis Sandford, *Genealogical History of the Kings and Queens of England* (1677), 22.

23 These rails have been reconstructed to a modified design and are now in the Lady chapel (Pitkin, 1972 edn).

24 *Gentleman's Magazine*, 1828, p. 311.

25 Milner (1809), II, 40, note.

26 *History* (1773), I, 42.

27 *The Beauties of England* (1776). Quoted in Warren, *Winchester Illustrated* (1905), 36.

28 Warner, *History of Hampshire* (1795), I, pt 2, 254.

29 Kitchin, 12.

30 Milner (1798–1801), 32.

31 Britton, 80.

32 Ball, 109.

33 In the N transept. Woodward, *Hampshire* (c. 1870?), I, 60, note, says: 'where the curious may see [it in] becoming state of ignomy and neglect'.

34 In Milner (9th edn 1830), 176, the editor says of the urn's removal: 'whatever may have been gained *in correctness* by this alteration is certainly lost *in effect*, as the vacant spaces have now a very naked appearance. It will perhaps be found that, unless the deposed saints had been restored to their niches, no ornament could have been substituted so little at variance with the feeling of the age, and with the rules of architectural propriety. As good Protestants, we should prefer the *ashes* of the saints, to the saints themselves; and then, by an easy transition, the Grecian vases formerly so repugnant to scientific eyes, would become *cinerary urns* of many very memorable personages.' This is the only expression of regret for their removal I have met with.

35 Kitchin, 12, 13.

36 Warren, *Small History and Guide to Winchester* (1836), 132, has a more contemporary account of these works: 'In this, canopied niches which had been chisled down to a plain surface, have been reconstructed; the concavities of others, which had been filled up, cleared out; and the damage . . . done by the addition of a canopy and carving displaying the architecture of Wren and the sculptors of Grinlin Gibbins (sic), as well as by the paint . . . bestowed by way of embellishment, have been carefully repaired.'

37 As against this, E.I.C. (Edward John Carlos), *Gentleman's Magazine*, Oct. 1828, p. 313, says: 'I cannot better conclude this long letter than by saying the whole of the works have been executed in solid wood and stone, and that roman cement, compo[sition] or other expedients have very properly been avoided.' But, p. 311, he says: 'Two of the engaged columns which ornamented this new pier have been constructed in cast iron, and tinted uniform with the stone; this appears, in any point of view, an absurdity.'

38 When taken down in the 1820s, the stones were preserved in the N transept triforium where, as a convenient quarry for stone, they became depleted (Vallance, *op. cit.*, 52). But in 1908, when Jackson was underpinning the building, he ordered their removal as too heavy for their weakened position. After lying on the grass, protected from frost by straw, the remains were offered to the town council. Ultimately, the central part was offered to and accepted by Cambridge University and is now in the Museum of Archaeology there. (*Country Life*, 22 May 1909, and *Winchester Cathedral Record*, no. 7, 1938.) The statues did duty on Garbett's screen until its demolition *c.* 1873, when they were placed in their present position at the W end of the nave.

39 Garbett made his screen substantial in case it was decided to place the organ in its traditional position upon it, but after hot debate this was decided against (Milner, 9th edn 1830, p. 173).

40 *Ibid.*, 170. E.I.C. (*Gentleman's Magazine*, Oct. 1828, p. 311) says the need for this great quantity of timber (1300 ft or 260 loads according to Warren, *op. cit.*, 130)

was questioned at the time and led to controversy. But *Gentleman's Magazine*, July 1827, p. 412, states that there were *two* faulty piers, the inner core of which 'was in the most appalling state of separation'. So perhaps the quantity of wood was justified after all? – and the statement above, that three arches were shored up.

41 E.I.C., *Gentleman's Magazine*, Oct. 1828, p. 314.

42 Milner (9th edn 1830), 174.

43 Warren, *op. cit.*, 120.

44 In 1828, under direction of Mr Buckler (B. Winkles, *Illustrations of the Cathedral Churches of England and Wales*, 1836, p. 143).

45 Warren, *op. cit.*, 121–23.

46 Murray's *Handbook* (1861), 23.

47 Warren, *op. cit.*, 114, 123.

48 Milner (2nd edn 1809), 57, says: 'the beauty and solitude of [Fox's] oratory must have been greatly heightened by the painted glass which, we are informed, filled all the open work of the arches until destroyed in the Grand Rebellion' (see Wharton, *History of English Poetry*, I). If true, surely a unique feature?

49 Milner (1809), II, 26.

50 In his will he directs 'to enclose with iron work . . . the little chapple where my relations are and may be buried'.

51 Ball, 103.

52 White, *History, Gazetteer and Directory of Hampshire and the Isle of Wight* (1859), 81.

53 N. Pevsner, *Buildings of England: Hampshire*, 679.

54 White, *op. cit.*, 80.

55 Sedding's report to the Archdeacon Jacobs Memorial Committee (*Building News*, 24 Apr. 1885) says of this new work: 'The four pedestals [and canopies] in the lower part were executed in modern time in indifferent stone and were weak copies of work at St Albans Abbey.' They were certainly not weak work, and, as comparisons of old and modern photographs will show, they were later copied *exactly* over the rest of the screen. Sedding introduced new work – lines of smaller niches between the large ones – where old photographs show only a plain hollow shaft next to a smaller one with tiny canopies at intervals (which still remains – seen clearly in Britton's pl. XV: screen cleared of urns and wooden altarpiece). In 1891 Sedding produced an elaborate design for completion of the whole reredos (*The Builder*, 10 Oct. 1891), but it was not adopted.

56 Kitchin, 9–12.

57 W. T. Warren, *Illustrated Guide to Winchester* (1909), 30, says it was purchased for New York Cathedral in 1899.

58 Vallance, *op. cit.*, 52.

59 Article by J. G. Jackson, *Transactions of St Paul's Ecclesiastical Society*, VI, 1910, p. 229.

60 Warren, *op. cit.*, 120.

61 Warren, *Guide to Winchester* (1922), 120.

62 Pevsner, *op. cit.*, 676.

Winchester: exterior and north transept

199. The south side of the nave in the 1880s.

200. Jackson's design for buttressing the south aisle of the nave and restoring the cloister (*The Builder*, 1910).

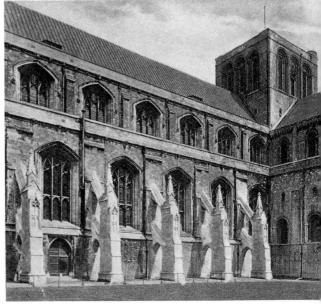

201. Jackson's flying buttresses as built; the cloister was never restored.

202. View from the north-west, *c.* 1860, showing the old tombstones, now nearly all removed.

203. Britton's engraving of the north transept in 1817, with its open timber roof. (Storer shows the gallery with a battlemented top.)

204. Winkles's view of the same transept in 1838, with flat panelled and painted ceiling; the old bishop's throne has been placed in the gallery.

Winchester: the pulpitum

205. The nave looking east in 1817, with Inigo Jones's pulpitum in place.

Opposite
207. The nave looking east about 1870, with Garbett's screen replacing that by Jones.

208. The nave looking east in 1890, with Scott's screen replacing Garbett's.

206. An early 18th-century drawing of Inigo Jones's screen, now partially re-erected in the Cambridge Archaeological Museum (G. Woodfield del.).

209. Garbett's screen, based on the west front (see pl. 202), but retaining the earlier statues of James I and Charles I by Le Sueur.

Winchester: the reredos

210. The earliest view of the reredos (Sandford's *Kings and Queens of England*, 1677) shows the two side doors and their canopies intact, but the rest of the lower part covered with Jacobean panelling, the Decalogue over the altar, and Jacobean altar-rails.

Below left
211. The choir in 1808 (Milner). Urns have now been placed in the niches of the reredos; the central part is still covered with panelling, now including West's *The Raising of Lazarus*.

212. Detail of Britton's section across the cathedral, 1817, showing the reredos behind Inigo Jones's pulpitum – practically the same as pl. 211, but Britton omits the urns.

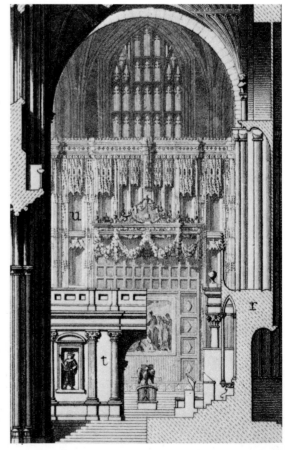

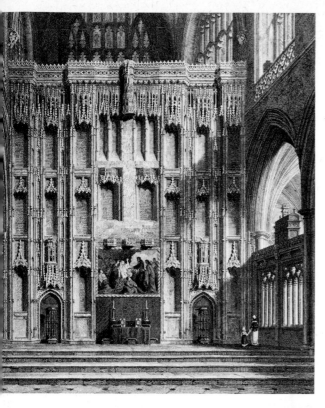

213. Drawing by Blore in 1817 (for Britton), showing the reredos 'as it would appear if divested of the tasteless urns and carved work now before it'.

214. Blore's reconstruction carried into effect. The canopies above and beside West's picture are later.

215. The reredos, *c.* 1910 (the stage between pl. 214 and this one is shown in pl. 198). The whole screen is now restored, with canopies, statues, and Christ on the Cross, and a carving of the Holy Family and six saints replacing West's painting.

Winchester: the choir and Lady chapel

216. Cave's engraving of the choir looking west in 1808, showing Bishop Trelawney's throne, Silkstede's pulpit with ogee tester, and return stalls against the back of Inigo Jones's pulpitum. The ceiling of the crossing is that inserted in the 17th century; the central circle now has a different design. Note the tall coved blocking to the transepts, with fine organ on the north.

217. The Lady chapel altar in 1876, showing the Jacobean altar-rails removed from the high altar (see pl. 210). The monument is that of Bishop Brown, now moved.

218. The Lady chapel as it was later. The panelling each side is now removed.

219. The choir looking west before 1873, with return stalls against Garbett's screen.

220. The choir looking west after Scott's restoration. The bishop's throne is Garbett's; the pulpit still Silkstede's, but with a new ogee tester, since regrettably removed. The pulpit has also been moved east, thus destroying the fine balance of the woodwork framing the stone reredos, as in pl. 215.

221. Detail of Britton's engraving of Langton's chantry showing its heavy crested screen.

222. Langton's chantry as it now appears; the cresting has been moved to go round the inside walls and the screen set back.

Lichfield

THE GRACEFUL three-spired cathedral of Lichfield, originally full of superb craftsmanship, without and within, has suffered two major disasters. In the Civil War, its close was fortified and besieged, bringing the great church to almost complete ruin. And then, from about 150 years later, the restored church underwent 'ordeal by Wyatt' and other indignities.

The architectural history of the cathedral between the Reformation and the Civil War is scanty. Britton tells us:[1] 'Early in the sixteenth century, some extensive repairs appear to have taken place; and Bishop Blythe [1503–31] contributed fifty oaks, and the sum of £20 towards the same.' So, the building itself might not have needed another repair for many years. This is confirmed by Erdiswicke in the late 16th century:[2] 'In the Close is a goodly Cathedral Church . . . one of the Fairest and best repaired in *England*, being thoroughly Builded and Finished, which few are.'

The earliest description of the cathedral is in *The Itinerary of John Leland* (c. 1535–45). Lichfield is one of the very few cathedrals he notices. He mentions the 'three pyramids' but, according to him, 'the glory of the church is the worke of the west end that is exceedinge costly and fayre' – as usual with early 'discriptions', not very enlightening!

Erdiswicke's description of the west front is quaintly verbose:

There are also outwardly builded three Pyramids, or Steeples of a good convenient height, all very well wrought with Free Stone and especially the two Gemmetts [sic][3] that stand Westwards, very well cut, and cureously wrought. The which West Part is . . . exceeding finely and cunningly set forth, with a great number of Tabernacles, and in the same, the Images or Pictures of the Prophets, Apostles, Kings of *Judah*, and divers other Kings of this Land, so well embossed and so lively cut, that it is a great pleasure for any man that takes delight to see Rarities, to behold them.

In 1634 the Norwich Tourists in their *Topographical Excursion* (see bibliography to Introduction) similarly describe the front, only adding that the statues (about a hundred in number) did 'grace it much, especially in time past, when, (as they say) they were all gilt'. There are said to be five original statues on the north-west tower and another very fine one is on a south choir-aisle buttress.

Holler's etching of the west front in Thomas Fuller's *Church History* (1655) – but evidently drawn before the Civil War[4] – shows a seated figure, doubtless of Christ, in the central gable. Its place was later taken by a statue of Charles II and, since 1869, by a new statue of the Saviour. In an article in the *Connoisseur*, 'Some traditions of a Medieval Statue of Christ', W. Norman Furnival states he was asked by W. R. Lethaby if he knew of such a statue, reputed to have come from Lichfield; and that he at length located one at Swynnerton, about twenty-four miles from the cathedral, but not far from Eccleshall Castle, the bishop's palace from 1290 until the early 19th century. Apparently some time before 1813[5] this fine statue was unearthed when a vault at Swynnerton church was being repaired. Pevsner dates it to about 1260–80 and calls it 'worthy of Westminster Abbey or Lincoln Cathedral'. It is a seated sandstone figure, 2·1 metres (7 ft) high, and fashioned to be seen from below. In view of this, its high artistic quality, and that such a figure is shown in situ by Hollar, it seems reasonable to assume that it did come from the west gable of Lichfield Cathedral and that it was taken by some devoted Royalist to the safety of this village near Eccleshall Palace. Should not this fine sculpture, still at Swynnerton, be housed at the cathedral, even if its venue cannot be certainly established?

223

225

---

223. The west front, engraved by Hollar, as it was before the Civil War – medieval tracery in the west window, a statue of Christ in the gable and the full complement of statues. Note old library on left.

LICHFIELDENSIS ECCLE-
SIÆ CATHEDRALIS, (IN AGRO
STAFFORDIENSI IN ANGLIA)
FACIES OCCIDENTALIS.

RESURGAM

EN VNO OMNIA.

Eliæ Aſmole Arm:
Mercurio-phylo Anglo
Accepta refundit.
T. F

Sem: Ryck pinxit. W: Hollar fecit.

141

The medieval interior

In 1634 the Norwich Tourists also record: 'As soon as we arrived in the City the Cathedral knell call'd us away to prayers; there we entered a stately neat Fabricke, the Organs and Voyces were deep and sweet, their Anthems we were much delighted with, and of the voyces, 2 trebles, 2 counter-trebles and 2 basses that equally on each side of the Quire, most melodiously acted and performed their parts . . . the inward part [of the church] is neat and glorious with fayre pillers, rich windows, and the Quire beautify'd with 6 fayre gilt statues, 3 on each side.' Pennant[6] says these statues are 'now much mutilated, placed in beautiful gothic niches, and richly painted; the first on the left is *St Peter*, the next is the *Virgin*; the next is *St Mary Magdalene*, with one leg bare, to denote her legendary wantonness. The other three are *St Philip*, *St James* and *St Christopher*, with Christ on his shoulder.' Wild,[7] quoting from 'the MS ascribed to Dr Stukeley', says the ten niches round the Lady chapel were formerly filled with statues said to represent the Wise and Foolish Virgins.[8] The Tourists also saw 'rich Coapes of Tissue, a fayre Communion Cloth of Cloth of Gold for the High Altar', and in the Lady Chapel 'eight stately fayre painted windowes'.

The medieval altar-screen is described as follows by Stukeley:[9] 'the partition . . . betwixt the two choirs is a fine piece of architecture, but demolished [sic] also in time of war; and although the figures are destroyed, and at the foot of the same every cherub defaced, yet it may be perceived to be a fine piece of work; for though it be uniform from top to bottom, yet every capital and pedestal are different works within and without'. Pennant[10] describes it as built by Bishop Langton (1290–1321)[11] and as 'a stone screen, the most elegant which can be imagined, embattled at top and adorned with several rows of Gothic niches of most exquisite workmanship; each formerly containing a small statue. Beneath them are thirteen stalls with Gothic work over each.' In the *Gentleman's Magazine* (1801) John Carter wrote of it: 'I but too well remember the divine beauties of that superb decoration, which I had classed with those of Winchester and St Albans in their affinity of design and luxuriousness of enrichments.' For by then it had, sadly, been ruined by Wyatt (see p. 145).

Under Henry VIII the cathedral was despoiled of its shrines and ornaments. Browne Willis (1742),[12] writing of the many brasses formerly there, says:

'These seem to have been all of them spoiled of their brasses about the beginning of Queen Elizabeth's Reign, who was forced to publish a proclamation to prohibit defacing monuments.' The Tourists take up the story:

Many fayre and ancient monuments that were in this stately Minster we were curteously guided to the sight of them, and these especially we observed: Bp Langton's, who built the Lady Quire, and part of that stately Castle belonging to this See [Eccleshall Castle] where the last day we were so kindly entertayn'd; he also wall'd the close.
Bp Haynes, and Bp Butlers; and many other of Bishops, Deans, Prebends, and Canons in alabaster.
Of the Layite, 3 monuments especially we observed.
The Ld Bassets of Drayton Basset, in his coat of Maile, and Armour of Proofe, ye wild Bore at his head and Feat.
The Ld Pagets of Beaudsert and his Lady
The Ld Paget his son, and his Lady; with the Tiger at the Top on a large and rich monument of 8 fayre black marble Pillars, which monument cost a good summe of money; which and more (as they report) was got from that fayre and ancient church.

In the 'Life of Sir William Dugdale', written by himself in the third person,[13] we read that in the summer of 1641 (encouraged by Sir Christopher Hatton 'who timely foresaw the neere approaching storm'), he visited St Paul's Cathedral, Westminster Abbey and a number of other Greater Churches, including Lichfield, 'having with him one Mr William Sedgwick (a skilful Armes-paynter) . . . and there made exact draughts (trickt by Mr Sedgwick) of all the monuments in each of them'. Of his drawings of Lichfield, Browne Willis writes:[14]

in the College of Arms or *Herald's Office, London*, and in the *Musaeum Ashmoleanum* at *Oxford* and also in Lord *Hatton's* Library are excellent draughts handsomely delineated of all the arms and effigies in the windows and tombs in the Church which were in being *an.* 1641. . . . Here were then about a hundred coats of arms; five raised tombs of Bishops, with their effigies . . . besides tombs of the Lord *Basset*, Lord *Paget*, Chancellor *Masters*, Captain *Stanley*, Deans *Yotton* and *Heywood* and about five other tombs of Canons, all neatly represented tho' they are now mostly perished.

240–243

Lastly, of the 'Gravestones robbed of their inscriptions', Browne Willis says 'there were no less than sixty-seven; but as there have been divers of them remov'd from Place to Place, on new Paving of the Church, there is no ascertaining to whom they belonged. Tho' it is plain four of them belonged to bishops.'

The Civil War

The close at Lichfield, fortified by walls and bastions, was a place of considerable strength – early in 1643 it was 'garrisoned by the inhabitants under the command of the Earl of Chesterfield', and was then attacked by the Parliamentarians under Robert, Lord Brook. 'This Lord', says Dugdale,[15]

being strangely tainted with fanatic principles, by the influences of one of his relations, and some schismatical preachers (though in his own nature a very civil and well-humoured man) became thereby so great a zealot against the established discipline of the church, that no less than the utter extirpation of episcopacy, and abolishing all decent order in the Service of God would satisfy him. To which end he became the leader of all the power he could raise for the destruction of the cathedral. . . . In order whereunto, when he had marched within half a mile of Lichfield, he drew up his army and there devoutly prayed a blessing upon his intended work; withall, earnestly desiring that God would by some special token manifest unto them his approbation of that their design: which being done, he went on, and planted his great guns against the south-east [west?] gate of the Close, himself standing in a window of a little house near thereto, to direct the gunners . . . but it so happened, that there being two persons placed in the battlements of the Chiefest steeple, to make shot with long fouling guns at the Cannoniers; upon a sudden accident which occasioned the souldiers to give a shout, this Lord, coming to the door (compleatly harnessed with plate armour cap-a-pie) was suddenly shot into one of his eyes . . . whereupon he suddenly fell down dead. Nor is it less notable that this . . . fell out upon the second day of March.

This was the festival of St Chad, the fifth Bishop of Mercia and first Bishop of Lichfield (669–72), and widely regarded as the founder of the diocese. Lord Clarendon says the musket was fired by a common soldier. Other accounts and uniform tradition give the merit of it to a person called Dumb Dyott, a deaf and dumb member of a well known and long established Royalist family in Lichfield.[16]

The siege lasted three days with the Roundheads victorious, but later in the same year the close was retaken for the king after a ten-day siege. Lastly, in 1646 it was again taken for the Parliament after a desultory siege of about four months. Dr Plume, Bishop Hacket's biographer, says 'two thousand shot of great ordnance and fifteen hundred grenadoes had been discharged against' the great church.[17]

By this time the cathedral was reduced to near ruin, with the west window smashed, the central spire battered down,[18] much of the roof destroyed and the vaulting broken. Both by the gunfire and the wantonness of the soldiers, all the stained glass was shattered and most of the monuments destroyed. This last atrocity was intensified by 'one of the soldiers raising the corner of a tomb containing the remains of Bishop Scrope and finding a silver chalice and a crozier of considerable value. This discovery naturally excited the soldiers, and every tomb was at once taken to pieces and its contents scattered.'[19] We are told that here, as at a number of other cathedrals, the soldiers indulged in horse-play and blasphemous behaviour (hunting a cat in the church and 'baptizing' a calf at the font – see Introduction, p. 10). Browne Willis says:[20] 'and indeed the Church was so totally demolish'd An. 1646 that it may be truly said there is not now remaining the least Piece of Brass, Glass, Iron, Arms, etc. but what appears to have been put up since 1661'. Shaw[21] says that the cost of damage to the cathedral in the Civil War was estimated at £14,000, 'an immense sum in those days'.

1660–1788

At last the Restoration of the monarchy brought the prospect of a restored cathedral. Among the Ashmolean mss is the following minute: 'June 16, 1660: This morning Mr Rawlins, of Lichfield, told me that the Clerks Vicars of the Cathedral had entered the chapter-house, and there said service; and this, with the vestry, was the only place in the church that had a roof to shelter them'.[22] On 18 July 1660, we learn from the same source that the prebends were induced to contribute 'half of their profits towards the repair of the fabrick', and under the superintendence of Canon William Higgins the Precentor[23] and Mr Zachariah Turnpenny the sub-chanter – the only two members of the foundation who had known the cathedral well in its former glory – the work of reparation was commenced. It was not until December 1661 that the famous John Hacket was appointed bishop, and at once threw himself energetically into the scheme, contributing largely from his own purse.[24] He collected money and in 1665 took the entire direction of it into his own hands.[25] He lived to see the repairs completed in 1669, at a cost of over £9,100; with a splendid rededication of the cathedral on Christmas Eve that year. He died in 1671, in time to hear the sound of the tenor, the first of the six new bells eventually installed – he called it, according to Dr Plume, 'his own passing bell'.[26]

To this great repair Charles II gave 'one

hundred fair timber trees out of Needwood Forest', and his brother the Duke of York (later James II) gave money for new tracery to the great west window[27] (removed 1869). Above this was a statue of the king, 'grotesque' according to Wild, which is still in the cathedral. It was given by Hacket and 'was the work of Sir William Wilson, originally a stone-mason from Sutton Coldfield, who after his marrying a rich widow, arrived at the honour of knighthood'.[28] Inside, Hacket paid for new stalls and a new organ, costing £600. The pulpit, of 'fair wainscoat', was given by Prebendary Fr. Bacon in 1671.[29] Wild[30] tells us that the old altar-screen, 'having suffered great injury in the Civil Wars, was encased by Bishop Hacket in wood painted with an inappropriate Grecian design'. A drawing of the woodwork, said to have been designed by Sir Christopher Wren, may be seen in the Salt Library at Stafford.[31] Remains of it were extant in the sacristy in 1813, according to *The Beauties of England and Wales* (vol. XIII, pt 2) published that year.

We learn incidentally from Harwood[32] that a new pavement was laid down in the choir in 1668. This was doubtless the same as that described in 1738 as 'lozengy black and white, with Cannel Coal for the black, and Alabaster for the white . . . [which] being kept clean, looks like black and white marble';[33] but under Wyatt grey and white lozenges were substituted. Harwood[34] tells us the nave was formerly covered with gravestones and Shaw that it was floored with 'brick' but 'much defaced and mutilated'; and now 'entirely renovated with the excellent Derbyshire Hopton stone, in the execution of which the gravestones were all removed, but an exact account was taken of their situations'.

Shaw[35] tells us that up to Wyatt's alterations in 1788, 'the inhabitants of the Close, as soon as the morning prayers were ended, went into the nave to hear the sermon, where they were met by many inhabitants of the City for the same purpose . . . this was attended with many inconveniences'. The old stalls (Hacket's) which, Shaw says, 'correspond with no order or style, still remain [1798], but have received a fresh complexion by the painter having given them the appearance of new oak'. The number however was reduced to forty-eight from the fifty-two mentioned by Browne Willis.[36] Willis adds that 'the names of the donors are put up over each respective stall, in letters of gold . . . with the title of the Prebend' – he then lists them all.[37]

'In 1749, at the instigation of . . . archdeacon Smallbrook . . . the dean [Penny] was prevailed

upon to remove several of [the west front] images to the great deformity of this very beautiful west end.'[38] The exterior of the cathedral was further impoverished by the substitution of slates for lead on the roofs (apparently at a lower pitch) between 1774 and 1778, when there were twenty-two separate sales of lead and a corresponding purchase of slates.[39] Pennant[40] says the lead was 'so out of repair that the Dean and Chapter were obliged to substitute slates instead of metal' as mending it would be beyond their narrow resources. He also tells us that the 'lost pillars' of the chapter house wall arcade 'instead of being restored, are now supplied with an uniform plaster'. Of this immediate pre-Wyatt period, Britton rather surprisingly writes:[41]

The general appearance of [the cathedral] was considerably improved by several judicious alterations . . . about the year 1760; when the Cathedral library built by Dean Heywood [1457–92], and an adjoining house very incommodiously situated between the church and the deanery, were demolished; the ground of the cemetery was at the same time levelled; the tombstones laid flat; some useless walls and gates removed [including the fine gate of the Choristers' House in 1773];[42] and slates substituted for the old leaden covering of the roof.

James Wyatt

In 1788 Wyatt was called in and 'a thorough and substantial repair was . . . commenced . . . and was completed, with many improvements in the year 1795'.[43] Shaw[44] says of Wyatt's work: 'Amongst the various necessary repairs, five of the groins of the nave (stone) were taken down and replaced with plaster',[45] to save the walls from collapsing. 'The roofs of the aisles were raised, which give additional support to the walls, and the roof of the nave is now rendered perfectly secure.[46] The middle spire has been lately taken down a considerable way and rebuilt [which does not reflect favourably on the rebuilders of the 1660s!] and new buttresses erected to support the south transept', as the former abutments, shown in Hollar's and later views, leant forwards, it is said, by about 3 metres (9 ft)! (Surely an exaggeration!) But although Wyatt's new buttresses were built on old bases and were undoubtedly impressive, they were 'offensive to the eye, both in size and colour'. The lowered and slated roofs are also an eyesore.

The medieval altar-screen had been sadly mutilated in the Civil War, and not repaired by Hacket, only covered by a wooden Baroque altarpiece. Shaw in 1798[47] says it was 'much

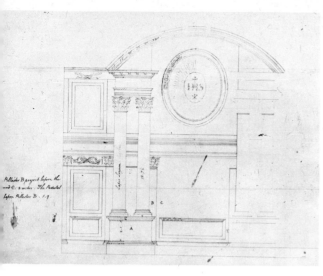

224. Wyatt's drawing of Bishop Hacket's reredos, a design attributed to Wren.

blemished and covered by a plaster of whitewash, but cleaned and well repaired by the present dean, Proby' (1776–1807). To do this, he must have demolished Hacket's work (which Shaw calls 'a mass of deformity' and 'properly removed') which would leave the ancient screen sans altarpiece, to be eventually taken down by Wyatt. So Shaw's statement seems to refer to a period shortly before 1788. But as Wyatt is said to have found the screen 'in a very mutilated state' (which would not have been the case if just repaired) and 'restored it with the assistance of Roman cement',[48] these two statements seem to be incompatible. On the other hand, John Carter's comments quoted above, praising the screen in 1782, could not have been written if the screen were still hidden behind Hacket's altarpiece – against which, had it been there, he would certainly have animadverted.

In any case, Wyatt removed the newly repaired screen (thus throwing choir and Lady chapel into one) and broke it up, using the canopies to decorate his new altarpiece in the former Lady chapel, and his new choir-screen, on which he placed a fine organ; while on the nave side he erected a huge glass window with Perpendicular tracery stretching up to the vaulting. Murray's *Handbook* (1864) says rather maliciously: 'It is satisfactory to record that after all this transformation, the Canons still complained of cold.'[49]

253
254

245

Of Wyatt's greatest interior innovations, Britton says:[50] 'The present choir is noted for its length and narrowness, the former of which is occasioned by

the whole extent from the organ-screen under the tower to the east end being an uninterrupted open space; and the latter, by the filling up of the side arches to the aisles. These two great innovations . . . were advised by Mr Wyatt in 1788 and have been much censured by some antiquaries'. Shaw,[51] speaking of the 'disproportionate length of the new choir', says: 'Some have, too justly I fear, called it a melancholy fact that Milton's "long drawn aisle" is transferred to the choir till it is *wire-drawn*' and made to be 'all seeing and no hearing'. In 1806 Harwood says:[52] 'It is an acknowledged principle of architecture, that where the proportions of any building have been well calculated, to alter any one of them is to destroy the effect of the whole. This cannot be denied to be the effect of lengthening the choir of Lichfield Cathedral.'

Criticism of Wyatt's alterations was widespread. In the November 1795 issue of the *Gentleman's Magazine*[53] a letter signed 'Viator' roundly condemns Wyatt's treatment of the cathedral:

Methinks, Mr Urban, as there is a fashion in all things, our affection for the externals of cathedral worship is to be drawn off by making playthings of the sacred structures which our forefathers were at so great an expense to render magnificently solemn. Would it not redound more to the honour of the bishops, deans and chapters, if they would spare some of the ample sums they subscribe in modernizing their churches, for the augmentation of small livings, and the salaries and incomes of the poorer clergy of their respective dioceses? Or would a prelate or dignitary be more reluctant to add 20l per annum to the comfort of a poor brother and his family, than to give 500 or 1000l in a lump to a whimsical architect who were better employed in keeping things in their places, than pulling them to pieces and putting the wretched fragments out of their places? Far be it from me to abet the modern doctrine of Equalty, which, after a short reign, is gradually wearing out, but it may safely be said that equalization is nowhere more needful than in the incomes of the clergy of the Church of England.

The following humorous, though equally damning, account by John Carter[54] – that valiant champion of our medieval architecture – of a visit he paid in 1801 to Wyatt's 'improved' interior, also makes good reading:

The entrance into the choir, taking in its general space from the pavement line to the point of the groins, is entirely shut out from the nave by the new screen and the *glazier's work*. Much of this screen is of fresh manufacture, and the rest is made up from the remnants of the demolished high altar-screen, as a communicative person who thought fit to attend my steps informed me.

Indeed, I but too well remembered the divine beauties of that superb decoration, which I had classed with those of Winchester and St. Albans in their affinity of design and luxuriousness of enrichments. Here it will be no great difficulty to conceive in what sense I commented on this national loss. Yet, as my attendant observed, 'This altar-screen is still in being, as there is no morsel of it but what has been preserved by being stuck up in one place or other. Here is a niche, there a buttress; observe that cornice, that pinnacle, and those ornaments. But come with me – I will show you all the rest of them as we look about. Now, sir, we are under the organ-loft; here on each side are more of the high altar niches. Ah! you need not doubt but your notes shall have each particle that you are in quest of.' Willing to listen to every intelligence in this scene of transformation, by way of bringing back my astonishment to some sort of account-able point, I still remained silent; which my attendant, no doubt, conceived was the effect of unutterable delight at beholding something *new*. 'Now, sir,' he went on, 'we are in the choir, where you see all its beauties at once from one end unto the other; not, as when the altar-screen was up, to trouble strangers in their inquiries about other sights, still lengthening out their charms, as they called it, by peeping over the screen, or prying behind it for founders' chapels, chantries, monuments, and I know not what, as they said were to be found in other un-un-*improved* [ah! that was the word] cathedrals. Do not mind those stalls; we have not got new ones yet – all in'good time. But look at the fine painted east window which, to give an effect like some exhibition transparency, we have darkened all the surrounding ones. I observe your eyes are not very clear, therefore you must come quite close to see our new pretty little altar-piece. It is rather in obscurity, to be sure; but this part of our show is not of much consequence. Now turn round. There you shall behold all and everything in pomp and state, as the organ, its screen, the stalls before it, and the glass window behind: this is our grand display, which from this shadowed spot is seen to the finest advantage of light and shade.' Recovering at last my speech, I begged to know what could possibly be the cause why the arches above the stalls, and those in continuation opening into the side-aisle, had been stopped up, whereby those diversity of lines given by intervening windows, columns, and groins were hid from the inquiring sight, ever most pleased at such diversifying objects. 'Ah! sir,' my attendant answered, 'did you but consider the strict service of this choir twice a day, and how desirable a thing it is to be snug and warm, although little more than half an hour does the business, you would not be surprised at this stopping-up, as you are pleased to call it, to keep out the cold; whereby we are rendered as comfortable as any public room in the kingdom could make us.' 'Very good,' I rejoined; 'now show me into the side-aisles.' 'This way, sir. And pray how do you like this closet doorway opening into the aisles? Quite handy. Take care; we are somewhat at a loss for want of light in these aisles, but they are of no use now; so give me your hand, and I will lead you to the chapter-house. Here again we are made comfortable; good wainscoting keeping the chills and damps from the walls and the columns which are hid behind it. All is improvement in this cathedral; everything is so smart, with white-washing, painting, and glazing. Ladies and gentlemen can now attend without the fear of taking cold, or the dread of seeing anything to make them think about dying and all that.'

Condemnation of Wyatt increased as time went on. In the *Gentleman's Magazine*, Dec. 1824,[55] a letter from 'B' says:

The choir of Lichfield Cathedral has throughout been deformed and defaced; and the altar in particular removed and destroyed by James Wyatt. This is an irretrievable injury; and the glazed or plastered arches are not likely soon to be relieved of their defilements. Such tasteless havoc as this in a Cathedral, is worse than the barbarous injuries of the Puritans who mutilated without mercy whatever they touched.

Wyatt was also instrumental in placing the stained glass in the east window. To quote again from the *Gentleman's Magazine*, 1795:

Lichfield, June 13th. This day the beautiful and elegant cathedral of this city, on the improvement and embellishment of which the Dean and Chapter with the most laudable munificence, have expended not less than 8000l, received its last finish, by the addition of a painted window at the east end of the choir. The subject is the Resurrection of Jesus from a design of West's, and the execution of it reflects the highest praise on Mr Eggington of Handsworth near Birmingham.[56] The chaste but brilliant effect of the preater-natural light, the graceful form of the abscending [sic] Savior, and the animated expression of the countenance, have excited the warm approbation of numerous visitors of judgment, taste and fashion, who have bestowed unqualified commendations upon the unrivalled skill of the artist who has thus perpetuated his ingenuities and abilities to time's remotest bound.

Alas for this pious hope – Eggington's work was removed within a dozen or so years of its setting up!

'Viator' commented on this glass (*Gentleman's Magazine*, Nov. 1795) and was answered by 'Richard George Robinson' in the December issue:

Viator: Instead of the fine masses of colour of the antient glass-painters with their blended tints, some blaze of one or two colours predominate; and all the lights on either hand of it are put out, to set off a single window. This I have actually seen at Lichfield.
Robinson: The painted window at the east end of the church, finely executed by Mr Eggington of Birmingham, is a representation of the Resurrection, immediately after it took place 'when it was yet dark'. The

introduction of different colours, therefore, would have been absurd. The divinity of our Saviour could not be better expressed than by the glory which shines around him. . . . The frames covered with paper in the adjacent windows, are to be temporary only. The two other windows at the end are to be glazed with stained glass in mosaic; and three others on each side are to have curtains before them; one fault of the choir being too great a degree of light[!]. They will give a better effect to this beautiful picture.

192 It is interesting that under Wyatt, Eggington painted a similar window of the Resurrection at Salisbury, with the side windows of the former Lady chapel there darkened in the same way with 'mosaic' glass.[57]

The glass in the Lady chapel

254 We now come to the happy seizing of an opportunity which eventually transformed this gloomy east end into one of great splendour. The seven eastern windows of the Lady chapel are filled with early 16th-century glass from the dissolved Abbey of Herkenrode, near Liège, which was discovered by Sir Brooke Boothby of Ashbourne, Derbyshire, in 1802, who bought it for only £200, and generously sold it for the same amount to the dean and chapter. These at least are the facts given in A Short Account, first published in 1811, less than ten years after the glass was purchased. A later edition[58] adds that the glass consisted 'of 340 pieces each about 22 inches [·55 metres] square (besides a large quantity of tracery and fragments).[59] . . . The short Peace of Amiens afforded an opportunity of safely importing this treasure, which . . . may be estimated at the value of Ten Thousand Pounds. The total expense of purchasing, importing, arranging and repairing the glass, and of fitting the windows may have cost about one thousand pounds.'

But Hugh Bright's book on the Lady chapel windows[60] tells quite another story. Sir Reginald Hardy writes to Bright:

I cannot remember how my theory of the windows first impressed my mind. I may have heard the story from my mother, whose great grandfather was Dean Woodhouse [1807–33]. She knew the cathedral very well. My story was that Sir Brooke Boothby informed the Dean that a ship was lying in the docks and contained the Herkenrode glass captured on its way to South America to adorn a cathedral, and advised the Dean to buy it for a very small sum, which the Dean carried out.

Bright thought this a more likely story, but set against it the earliness of the generally accepted account. The 'Chapter Acts' books which he

quotes are singularly unhelpful. So it seems the real story is veiled in mystery.

The two western windows of the Lady chapel were filled after 1802 with armorial glass commemorating dignitaries and benefactors of the cathedral; but in 1895 these were superseded by the present glass, said to be Flemish work of the mid-16th century (provenance unknown). But uncertainty prevails about this glass also.[61] It belonged to the family of the Marquess of Ely, having, it was said, been brought from France in the mid or late 18th century; and after being at Rathfarnham Castle, Ireland, it was sent to be sold at Christie's about 1845. It remained in Christie's cellars until 1895, when it was purchased for Lichfield Cathedral for £2,000. The marquess was also the owner of the fine Jesse window now in St George's, Hanover Square (acquired c. 1840) and Sir Eric, in his appendix, mentions a theory propounded by M. Jean Lafond that the glass now in the western windows of the Lady chapel at Lichfield originally flanked the St George's Jesse window and that all three probably came from a church in Malines, and he ascribes them to Arnold of Nÿmegen (fl. c. 1490–1538).

1813 to 1856

248 Wyatt's narrowing of the choir was later rectified, as Britton tells us:[62] 'Since Mr Wyatt's time [he died in 1813] an essential improvement has been adopted, by widening the choir. This celebrated architect had directed a plain walled skreen to be raised flush with the inner face of the arches and thus forming a flat surface[63] on each side of the choir. This wall has been removed and re-erected further back', thus showing the whole of the inner mouldings of the arches, with the stalls placed in the newly found spaces.

245
248 As mentioned before, Hacket's stalls were retained by Wyatt, but painted as new oak, and these are just visible in Wild's plate of the 'Choir West' (1813). But in Britton's same view, of 1820, we see Gothic stalls, and this is confirmed by Harwood:[64] 'The choir has been lately ornamented with stalls in imitation of the richest style of pointed architecture.'

In Storer we read:[65]

We cannot terminate this brief sketch without paying our humble tribute of respect and gratitude to the present Dean. . . . Since Dr Woodhouse's accession to the deanery his attention both to the internal decoration and external repairs of his church has been unremitting. The deep trench that, except in front, surrounds the

Cathedral has wonderfully preserved it from damp; but the dean's great object was to remove the common objection that the choir was too narrow for its length. The year 1815 beheld the accomplishment of this important and difficult attainment. After a year's cessation from choral service, though not from parochial, the choir has been recently opened; the large massive stalls [Hacket's] of carved wood, which with the chorister's seats projected into the choir, are now entirely removed; the [new] stalls are inserted *within* the arches, which [stalls] are richly and appropriately decorated,[66] and a width equal to that of the former . . . choir is thus gained, with extreme ingenuity, but with great expense. No eye can behold this extraordinary improvement, without instant delight; no heart can approach it without quickened feeling; no mind can contemplate it without religious gratitude.

The deteriorating condition of the exterior of the cathedral induced the dean and chapter to bestir themselves. According to *A Short Account*:[67] 'To restore the whole of [the] western front . . . has long been an object to the Dean and Chapter, which they have at length accomplished by bestowing their utmost efforts upon it during the summers of 1820, 1821 and 1822.' Unfortunately, they chose the then popular Roman cement as material for repair and for new work. And they further showed their poor judgment in appointing a 'Mr Robert Armstrong, Statuary'[68] to carry out the work, whose productions, especially his new figures, were deplorable. But, also according to *A Short Account*, the statues of kings immediately over the portals (the only row of ancient statues then remaining on the exterior) were carefully restored. 'These statues in their former decayed state have been supposed to represent the Monarchs of Israel and Judah.' But the writer considers they portray St Chad in the centre with English kings, William I to Richard II on the north, and Saxon Kings, Penda to Edward the Confessor, on the south. He goes on: 'Every ancient linament in face and figure and attitude has been carefully preserved; and the parts totally lost have been supplied from acknowledged portraits, or the seals and coins of the Kings'; and he details their former condition and what was done to each of the English monarchs (but not of the Saxons – evidently no 'portraits' to hand).

Concern at the methods of restoration employed was expressed in a letter signed 'B' in the *Gentleman's Magazine*, Oct. 1824:[69]

Surely everyone must lament the manner in which the West Front of Lichfield Cathedral has lately been restored. The whole of that beautiful façade is now of plaster [as 'B' constantly calls the Roman cement]. . . .

The figures of the Kings . . . have, however, been repaired with tolerable accuracy. . . . The fashion of repairing stone buildings with plaster is mean and despicable. The operation a structure must necessarily go through before it is coated with this detestible substance is more destructive to its appearance than the united injuries of time and violence.[70] The west front of Lichfield Cathedral was hacked and chipped until it resembled a huge rock in which one could here and there discover a feature that seemed to proclaim a work of art. Thus prepared, the walls were plastered and the arches and ornaments formed in some instances according to ancient authorities and in others according to the judgment of the plasterer.

This was very true, as old photographs, compared with Britton's fine engraving of the central porch, will show. The beautiful outer moulding seen in the latter, with its many small statues in niches, was ruthlessly replaced by a monotonous succession of square flowers – a very great loss – beside a general down-grading of design in all three west doorways. And, except for the central figure of the Virgin and Child in the central porch, which was not too bad, the new statues were really frightful.[71] Equally queer new figures were placed over the south doorway and one on each side of the north.

Lastly, an assessment of 1850:[72] 'The beauty . . . of Lichfield is greatly diminished by the barbarous use of Roman Cement . . . the whole has the appearance of a plaster copy of what Lichfield Cathedral once was, and is indeed the most disappointing Cathedral elevation that we know of.'[73]

To recall the interior just before Scott's restoration, here are a few items from Lonsdale:

In 1856, nave and transept were devoid of furniture of any kind, except that the South Transept contained the fittings of the Consistory Court, and in the North Transept stood the statue of Bishop Ryder [1825–36] on a high pedestal. . . . The whole interior was covered with a dead yellowish whitewash. The nave was unused – indeed, except during service hours, the verger's silver key alone gave admission to any part of the church – and during service in the choir, the nave was used as a promenade by nursery maids with their babies! Wyatt's screen filled the whole of the first bay of the present choir and contained vestries for the Lay Vicars and the choristers. The organ was on top against a window of glass stretching to the ceiling – this for warmth – but as such it was a dismal failure as both nave and choir were bitterly cold. From the organ-screen to the entrance to the [former] Lady Chapel were pews of oak, lined with green baize studded with brass nails.

In 1842 Sydney Smirke was engaged by the dean and chapter to undertake urgent repairs to the

231

232
234
237
239

cathedral exterior, and for the next ten years was at work on the nave and north transept.

Scott and his followers

In 1856 Scott was called in. The great restoration which started under him, and was carried on by his son Oldrid and others, continued to 1908 at a total cost of £98,000.[74]

First, the choir arcade was opened out and restored, and although no remains of the six statues already mentioned were found, Scott perpetuated their memory with new figures of the same saints (made by Farmer and Brindley); but he introduced angel stops to the vaulting shafts. He designed a splendid reredos and placed it in the ancient position, thus giving back to the choir its proper proportions. He demolished Wyatt's choir-screen and organ, substituting the finest of his metal screens – a superb work of art, made by Skidmore of Coventry, the figures on both the reredos and screen by Birnie Philip.[75] Also by Scott and Skidmore is the remarkable pulpit in the nave, of similar open metalwork. Scott also designed new (uncanopied) stalls and an elaborate bishop's throne made by Evans of Ellaston, and the fine inlaid stone pavement in the choir. In 1869 the great west window was taken out and new tracery, designed by Scott, was inserted, but the Charles II statue in the gable remained until the renewal of the west front from 1877 to 1884 which cost £40,000. The figures were designed by Scott (he died in 1878) and Oldrid, and were executed by 'Miss Grant [who was responsible for the Christ], Mr Seale and Mr W. R. Ingram, all of London, and Mr Bridgeman of Lichfield who carried out the largest part of it'.[76]

Under Oldrid Scott the following repairs and additions were undertaken. In 1879, in memory of Bishop Selwyn (1867–78), the three curious chapels on the south side of the Lady chapel were restored and their outside recesses received new gables and pinnacles. The central chapel contains his tomb-effigy by Nicholls, the walls lavishly decorated by Clayton and Bell and tiling by William de Morgan. In 1895 the Lady chapel exterior was renewed with statues of holy women of the Old Testament above and of the New Testament below[77] and three of the windows each side, which had 'debased' tracery, were given new tracery of better and more correct design. In the same year statues of ten female saints, designed by C. E. Kempe and made by Farmer and Brindley, were placed in the Lady chapel.

In 1881 the north transept doorway was restored in memory of the first wife of Dean Bickersteth. 'Several of the vesicas in the mouldings of the [arch], which with their figures had been much weather-worn, have been replaced with excellent carving by Mr R. Bridgeman, who also executed the beautiful figure of Christ in glory in the head of the gable. A little ideal figure of St Anne immediately over the doorway presents . . . a likeness of Mrs Bickersteth.'[78] Until 1892 there was a great Perpendicular window above this doorway, similar to that still in the south transept front. It was in bad condition and it was decided to rebuild it. But 'on taking out the . . . window, and removing such stone work as was defective on either side, the headings of the fine Early English lights, which had unquestionably composed the original window were discovered'.[79] This design was followed in the restoration incorporating sound fragments, and the beauty of the transept much enhanced.

In 1897 the chapel of St Chad's Head over the consistory court was restored under Dean Luckock at his own charge. Between about 1890 and 1900 the plain battlemented parapet of the central tower was replaced by an arcaded, plain-topped parapet.

In 1946 St Michael's war memorial chapel was dedicated. In 1961 under George Pace, consulting architect, it was redesigned and refurnished as the chapel of the newly formed Staffordshire regiment.

Also in 1946 an appeal was launched which enabled the dean and chapter to restore the northern nave buttresses, recast and rehang the bells, clean the choir and repave the close. In 1950 the central tower and spire were renovated and a new summit cross erected.

Under Dean Macpherson (1954–69), in consequence of an appeal which brought in £200,000, a major restoration of roof and fabric was achieved. And lastly, in 1974, the cathedral organ was restored at a cost of £34,000.[80]

Bibliography

Erdiswicke, c. 1593. Sampson Erdiswicke, *A Short View of Staffordshire.* . . . Pub. from William Dugdale's transcript of the original 1723.

* *Browne Willis, 1727.* 2nd edn 1742.

Pennant, 1782. Thomas Pennant, *Journey from Chester to London.*

---

* see also bibliography to the Introduction.

Shaw, 1798. Rev. Stebbing Shaw, *History and Antiquities of Staffordshire*, I.

Harwood, 1806. Thomas Harwood, *History and Antiquities of the Church and City of Lichfield*.

A Short Account, 1811. *A Short Account of Lichfield Cathedral, more particularly of the Painted Glass . . . Intended . . . for the Information of Strangers*, anon. 3rd edn 1823, with additions and an engraving.

Wild, 1813. Charles Wild, *Lichfield Cathedral*. Fine aquatints.

* *Britton, 1820*. John Britton, *The History and Antiquities of the See and Cathedral Church of Lichfield*. Fine engravings.

Harwood's Erdiswicke, 1844. Erdiswicke's work (*c.* 1593), ed. Thomas Harwood.

Lonsdale, 1850s. Canon Lonsdale, *Recollections*.

* *Clifton (Bell), 1898*. A. B. Clifton, *Lichfield, The Cathedral and See*, Bell's Cathedral Series. (Not always reliable, especially pp. 26–28.)

Bodington, 1899. Canon Bodington, *Lichfield Cathedral*.

* *Wallis (Pitkin), 1956*. Canon J. E. W. Wallis, *Lichfield Cathedral*, Pitkin Pictorial. 'Revised and enlarged by Olwen Hedley, 1970.' Wallis and Hedley, 1974.

Notes

1 Britton, 28.

2 Erdiswicke, 100–02.

3 Harwood's Erdiswicke (1844) has 'Gemmels' (twins) which must refer to the W towers.

4 Signed 'Samuel Kyrk, pinxit. W. Hollar sculp.' James J. Irvine, in an interesting article on the W front, *British Archaeological Association Journal*, Dec. 1882, says: 'This etching must have been taken from a larger and really admirable drawing [painting?], by Samuel Kyrk which was made for Elias Ashmole, prior to the Civil War, probably in 1620. This drawing [had it survived] would, from its extreme accuracy, have been the most valuable representation left us of any English cathedral of so early a date.'

5 It is mentioned in *The Beauties of England and Wales*, XIII (1813), 960.

6 Pennant, 107, 108.

7 Wild, 10.

8 Harwood (1806), 74, says: 'upon the buttresses on the outside of the Lady choir, are places for twenty-four figures supposed to have been the twelve patriarchs and twelve apostles' – but gives no reference. Counting the niches (now filled with modern statues, *c.* 1890) it is hard to see how 24 was arrived at.

9 Quoted in Clifton (Bell), 102.

10 Pennant, 108.

11 But some canopies from this which still survive in the cathedral (over the sedilia and Bishop Howard's monument) are patently Perpendicular in character – perhaps a century after the bishop's death. So we may assume the screen had been either rebuilt or enlarged at a later date.

12 Browne Willis (2nd edn 1742), III, 374. He seems uncertain as he later says: 'They were all gone before 1644.'

13 *Heraldic Miscellanies, consisting of the lives of Sir William Dugdale, Garter and G. King Esq. . . .*, (n.d., *c.* 1800?), 6.

14 Browne Willis, *op. cit.*, 373, 377.

15 Sir W. Dugdale, *Short View of the late Troubles in England* (1681), 117, quoted by Harwood (1806), 20–21.

16 *Ibid.*, 22, note 61.

17 Quoted in Bodington, 36.

18 In the Bodleian Library (ms Ashmole, 1521, 147) there is a pen-drawing of the close from the south (very poor) showing the stump only of the tower.

19 Clifton (Bell), 18, where he adds: 'The crozier was later sold to Elias Ashmole.'

20 Browne Willis, II, 374.

21 Shaw, 242.

22 Quoted by Harwood (1806), 56.

23 To him we owe the survival of St Chad's Gospels, which he took and kept safe until 1660. Originally, it seems, from Llandaff, this superb 8th-c. Celtic ms came to Lichfield in the late 10th c. and so has been the cathedral's great possession for a thousand years.

24 Said to have totalled £1683-12s.

25 H.E.S., *The Story of Lichfield Cathedral* (8th edn, revised and enlarged 1951), 10.

26 Quoted by Harwood (1806), 67.

27 The following quotation from Ashmole ms is given in Harwood (1806), 67: 'October 6, 1671, were arms in the Great West window, of Charles II and James, Duke of York. The Arms of the Seas of Canterbury and Lichfield, and of Richard Newdigate de Arbore in Com. Warwick.' The etching of the W front in W. Dugdale's *Monasticon Anglicanum*, III (1673), shows the king's arms at the top of the great 'rose' and those of the duke in the centre of it. The bishops' arms are below the transome, but there is no indication of Newdigate's armorials. How long these five arms remained in situ does not appear, but when Dean Addenbrook (1745–76) filled the window with painted glass, Wild (pls 7, 8) and photographs before 1869 show only a royal arms (the duke's?) in the centre; the rest appears to be abstract patterns only.

28 Harwood (1806), 72.

29 Harwood (1806), 67. Turned out by Wyatt, this pulpit was purchased for Elford church in 1789.

30 Wild, 9.

31 Bodington, 30. This drawing, half finished, shows a simple design with fine carving round the central oval, and above the pediment the words 'King's Arms'.

32 Harwood (1806), 111.

33 *Magna Britannia et Hibernia, Antiqua et Nova* (1727),

V, 4. A specimen of the cannel coal squares is let into the consistory court floor with some ancient tiles (Clifton, Bell, 108).

34 Harwood (1806), 74.

35 Shaw, I, 260.

36 Browne Willis, 375.

37 Three of Hacket's stalls survived Wyatt's and Scott's renewals and form the chancellor's seat in the sacristy, now used as the consistory court. They seemed to have been formed from the bishop's throne and two lesser canopies.

38 Shaw, 244.

39 Bodington, 47.

40 Pennant, 107.

41 Britton, 31.

42 *Gentleman's Magazine*, May 1782, p. 506, has engraving of it.

43 Britton, 32.

44 Shaw, 260–61.

45 How did Wyatt suspend the heavy stone bosses? Did he hang them from the cross-beams of the roof?

46 This raising of the aisle roofs was, aesthetically, one of Wyatt's best performances. Early views show that they were too low to cover completely the triforium arcades, the tops of which appeared outside, below the clerestory, and were glazed.

47 Shaw, I, 260.

48 Britton, 42.

49 Murray's *Handbook* (1864), 269. See also Lonsdale's remarks below, note 66.

50 Britton, 42.

51 Shaw, 261, quoting letter by 'Viator' in *Gentleman's Magazine*, May 1795.

52 Harwood (1806), 92.

53 *Gentleman's Magazine*, 1795, pp. 924–25.

54 *Ibid.*, 1801, pt I, 311–13.

55 *Ibid.*, 1824, supplement, 582.

56 Shaw says: 'two adjoining windows will be filled with suitable paintings by the same excellent artist as soon as sufficient money can be collected.

57 Viator also condemns the lengthening of the choir. The reply states the reason was to include in the choir those people who assembled only in the nave, waiting for the sermon. Viator and Robinson actually agree on the ugliness of the S transept buttresses, but later excuse it on the grounds of expense.

58 *A Short Account* (3rd edn 1823), 8, 10.

59 J. Storer, *History and Antiquities of Cathedral Churches of Great Britain* (1814–19) says that before Dr Woodhouse's 'elevation to his high office, it was his incessant and almost unassisted care to separate and arrange the countless fragments of painted glass that arrived from the continent in many huge packing cases'. But Bodington, 52, states: 'It was laid out on the floor of the nave and sorted and arranged by the Dean's daughters.'

60 H. Bright, *Lichfield Cathedral – the Lady Chapel Windows* (3rd edn 1950) 9, 10.

61 See Bright, *op. cit.*, 20–21, and appendix by Sir Eric Maclaren, 24–25.

62 Britton, 42.

63 Wild's engraving shows this surface ornamented with vertical lines in relief.

64 Harwood's Erdiswicke (1844), 290.

65 Storer, *op. cit.*

66 A dubious exchange! For Lonsdale says of these stalls in 1856 that they were all composed of 'plaster, wood, rope, nails and much else, which the old verger of that day used to call "beautiful tabernacle work" ' – *imitative composition*, probably not without a certain charm (cf. Wyatt's similar stalls at Salisbury), instead of *sound original craftsmanship*, albeit inharmonious with Wyatt's other furniture.

67 *A Short Account* (3rd edn 1823), 103.

68 *A Short Account*, 102.

69 *Gentleman's Magazine*, Oct. 1824, p. 295.

70 But in a later letter (*Gentleman's Magazine* supplement, Dec. 1824, p. 582) he forgets his animosity: 'I too well know what has been done within the last thirty years in the interior of Lichfield Cathedral, and I also know how to appreciate "A.C.'s" favourite composition [Roman cement] when used judiciously on the inside of a building; and, looking a little beyond Lichfield for an example, I can inform him that the choir screen of York Minster is an admirable and *lasting* monument of the beauty and durability of plaster.' In view of the extensive restorations in stone there by Shout (or Shoult), clerk of the works, on the W front and chapter house, 1802–28, is it likely that artificial stone would be employed on the choir-screen – or elsewhere – in York Minster? (Unless 'B' is referring to *before Shout's time*.)

71 Murray's *Handbook* (1864), 273, says these four statues 'were restored in 1820, as Mary Magdalene, Mary the mother of James, St Peter and St John. These restorations were, however, very uncertain; and from the decay of the material then used, it has been found necessary to renew the figures, with some slight alteration of detail' – renewal within forty-four years, thus confirming B's contention in the above letter, that 'it has proved by more instances than one that external reparations in plaster are not attended . . . with success.'

72 Poole and Hugall, *Guide to York Cathedral and Its Antiquities* (1850), 71.

73 In 1943 the statue of Charles II and several of the stucco figures from the W front were standing in the interior of the NW tower. In 1977 it was standing on the ground just west of the S transept.

74 Wallis and Hedley (Pitkin), 24.

75 N. Pevsner, *Buildings of England: Staffordshire* (1974), 184. On p. 186, he says: 'Let Salisbury and Hereford be vandals and remove their Scott-Skidmore screens, Lichfield must hold out till High Victorianism is at last fully appreciated in its best work.'

76 *Our National Cathedrals*, anon. (1888), II, 142.

77 Clifton (Bell), 50.

78 *Our National Cathedrals*, II, 141.

79 Clifton (Bell), 69, quoting Lonsdale.

80 Wallis and Hedley (Pitkin), 24.

225. The presumed original statue of Christ, removed from the gable before or during the Civil War and now in the church of Swynnerton, Staffordshire.

Lichfield: the west front

226. The statue of Charles II, placed on the gable after the Restoration, was removed in 1877, and stored ignominiously with other statues in the north-west tower.

227. In the 1860s, the 'debased' tracery of the 17th century still filled the great west window. The kings had been repaired in 'compo' in the 1820s and new statues by Armstrong had been placed in the centre porch and over the transept entrances.

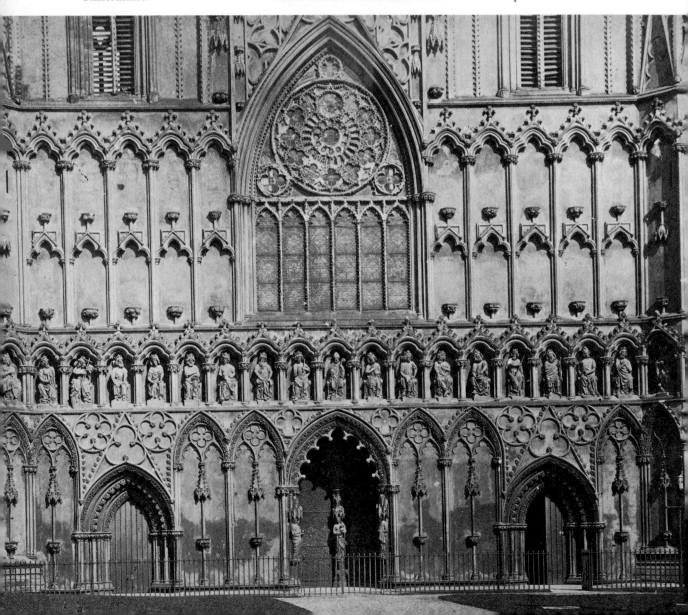

228–30. Three views of the west front. *Left*: Samuel's view from the north-west in 1810. The west window is that inserted after 1660. Charles II now occupies the gable and all the rest of the statues have disappeared with the exception of three high up on the north tower, and the row of kings over the doorways. *Centre*: after Scott's new west window had been inserted in 1869, but before the provision of the statues. *Right*: the front complete with its statues as it is today.

231. The central west doorway in 1820 (Britton), before any restoration.

232. The same doorway about 1860, with Armstrong's very poor figures and bunchy foliage round the arch.

233. The same doorway after Scott had provided new, better figures and restored the arch to something like its original appearance.

153

Lichfield: three portals

234. The south-west portal before Scott, with Armstrong's oppressively crude foliage mouldings and sprouting capitals.

236. Portal to the north transept in 1813: medallions worn (more worn than they actually were?), sculpture missing (Wild).

235. The south-west portal as restored by Scott, purged now of its grosser elements and with an ornately hinged new door.

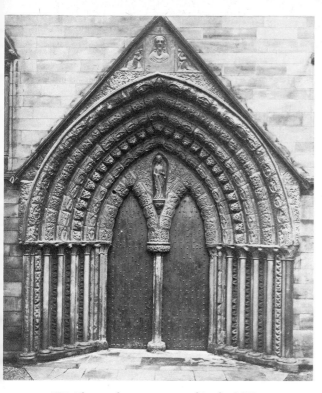

237. The north transept portal in the 1860s: Armstrong's sculpture in the spandrel and gable.

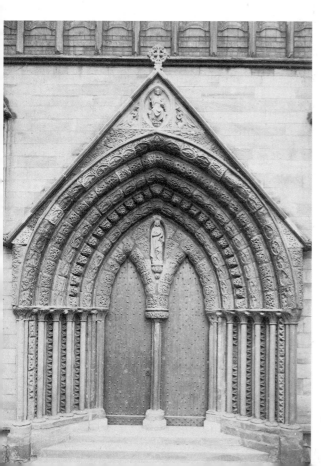

239. The south transept portal in the 1860s. The voussoir foliage carvings are clearly the inspiration for those in pl. 234. The curious heraldic carving in the spandrel dates from Bishop Hacket's time; above them, Armstrong's statues.

238. The north transept portal in 1880: new sculpture replaces Armstrong's.

155

240–43. Five of the monuments, dating from medieval and Tudor times, that were destroyed during the Civil War, from drawings preserved in the College of Arms.

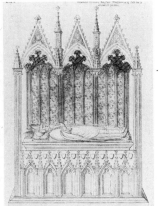

Lichfield: the choir

245. The choir looking west in 1813 (Wild). Bishop Hacket's stalls can just be seen at the far end. Beyond them are Wyatt's screen and organ. Wyatt filled the crossing arch with a huge glazed and traceried screen to keep the choir warm, and for the same reason closed up the arches of the arcade by solid walls flush with the piers.

244, 246. After the Civil War, new stalls (*above*) were paid for by Bishop Hacket (drawing by Wyatt). Removed about 1814, the Bishop's throne and two lesser seats were combined to form the Chancellor's seat in the consistory Court, as at present (*right*).

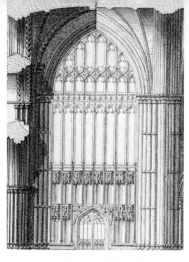

247. Detail of Britton's section through the crossing, 1820, showing Wyatt's screen from the west.

248. The choir looking west (Britton), a few years later than pl. 245, but closer to the screen. The throne, pulpit and stalls are Wyatt's. The walls that he placed between the arches of the arcade have now been set further back and his new stalls set in the added space.

249. An engraving from the *Illustrated London News* of 1866 showing the choir from the east. Scott's screen and stalls are already in position, but work has not yet been begun on the west window.

250. Scott's choir looking west, with throne, screen and west window as they remain today. The window rises higher than the vaulting – the 1670 window fitted better (see pl. 249).

Lichfield: the screen and Lady chapel

251. One of Scott's most splendid pieces of ecclesiastical furnishing was the screen, executed by Skidmore of Coventry. Happily surviving changes of taste, it has recently been cleaned and restored.

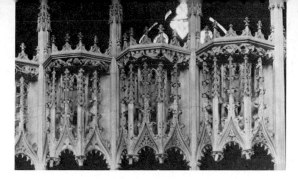

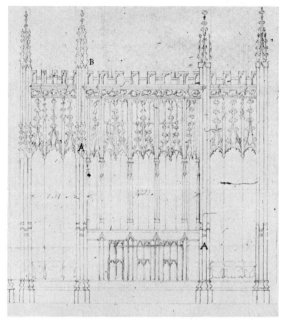

252–4. A reredos for the Lady chapel was designed by Wyatt, partly reusing material taken from the medieval altar-screen covered up by Bishop Hacket. Drawings survive (*above left*), but the reredos as built (*above*, from Britton) was slightly different, with two storeys instead of one. When Wyatt's work was demolished, the surviving parts of the old altar-screen were incorporated in the sedilia (*top left*).

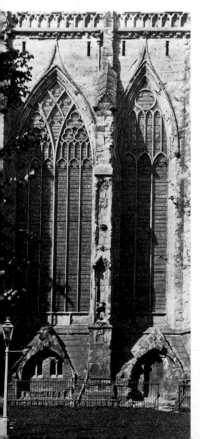

255, 256. Exterior of the Lady chapel from the south, *c.* 1875 and in 1890. The 'debased' tracery of two of the windows has been replaced and the tomb recesses restored rather too thoroughly. Another window to the left was also altered.

Worcester

The west view of the cathedral as seen from across the Severn is a fine one, but the thorough Victorian refacing of the whole exterior renders other views, aesthetically, most disappointing.

One of the earliest views is Daniel King's 'smudge' drawing (in the Society of Antiquaries library) for his etching in Sir William Dugdale's *Monasticon*, vol. I (1655), which shows short pinnacles at east, west and transept fronts, and a tower with pinnacles and battlemented parapet, but omits the 'clochium' or detached bell-tower. Hollar's engraving for Dugdale's *Monasticon Anglicanum* vol. II (1672), shows similar details, but more accurately, and includes the clochium, but omits the narrow lower windows in the tower![1]

In 1647 the leaded spire was removed from the bell-tower – 18·2 metres diameter and 64 metres high (60 × 210 ft) – which stood detached near the north-east corner of the cathedral; and thereafter the stone structure (walls 3 metres, 10 ft, thick) became ruinous. It was patched up in 1688 for the casting of lead, and was not finally cleared away until the 1750s.

Brown Willis says:[2] 'The whole fabric [of the cathedral] is in excellent repair, several thousands of pounds having been expended of late years by the Dean and Chapter, who are yet generously going on in new casing the outward walls, which being built of a soft reddish stone have mouldered. The said Chapter have rebuilt four neat pinnacles on the top of the tower.' These are stated by Britton (1835) to have been 'altered and repaired'. Willis also shows a new parapet, without battlements. Of the tower itself, Wild (1823) says:[3] 'About twenty years ago its surface, being much decayed, was subjected to a process professionally known as "scaling" ' (paring the stone to the depth of several inches and so finally destroying what little remained of its original ornaments).

In spite of all this repair and destruction, Winkles (1842) has this appreciation:[4] 'The tower, which is by far the most dignified and important external feature of this Cathedral, seems hardly to belong to it, from the great superiority over every other portion of it. It is indeed worthy of a better body. It is lofty, and divided into two stories, the lower of which is adorned with an elegant arcade . . . [and] the upper storey is divided from the lower by a graceful band of quatrefoil tracery.' Yet, only twenty-two years later, Murray says:[5] 'the existing central tower dates from 1374, but the general design alone remains. The soft sandstone of which it is built has crumbled away to such an extent that all the details have perished.' But old photographs seem not to bear this out.

Early in the 18th century new very tall pinnacles were erected all round the cathedral at the extremities of the nave, transepts and east end, during, Green[6] conjectures, the repairs of 1712: 'that handsome set of spires, so ornamental to the external appearance of the Cathedral and which distinguishes it from every other in Europe'. These were all gradually removed after 1832 and replaced by others, shorter and more 'correct', and the tower was completely 'restored' to good Gothic Revival standards, but much to its aesthetic detriment, by Perkins. The top with its pinnacles, parapet and many needle-like spires is said to have been claimed by Sir Edmund Beckett (later Lord Grimthorpe) in 1865 as his own design.[7] Between the wars the 'needles' were removed, much to the improvement of the tower.

In the alterations of 1748 to 1756 the north transept front was rebuilt and its two windows – medium-sized above, smaller below – were replaced by one long one of five narrow lights; this

257. View from the north-west, *c.* 1865.

258. The same view *c.* 1880, showing Perkins's 'restorations': new fashioning of the tower and its pinnacles, new west window and west door.

259. The cathedral about 1935. Perkins's pinnacles along the tower parapets have been removed.

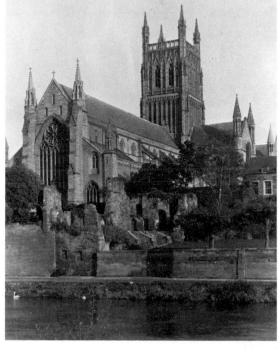

269   was again altered in 1865, to good four-light Geometrical.

265   Between 1727 and 1795 six great flying buttresses were erected, two at each corner of the east

267   end, and two diagonal ones against the south-east transept front (all removed c. 1860). In the 1790s Westmoreland slates were substituted for lead, apparently over the nave and certainly over the whole eastern half of the cathedral.[8]

275   In 1789 the eight-light Perpendicular west
276   window was renewed to a different design, as was
284   the nine-light Perpendicular east window in 1792.
285   Green says these two windows were 'built, by Mr Thomas Johnson, architect of this City'. They were again renewed sixty to seventy years later by A. E.
287   Perkins – the present east window of ten lancets (a
288   good effort) before 1857 and the present west
277   window after 1864. He also opened the west entrance (long walled up), which was given a new doorway and carving by Boulton. In 1864 he removed the Perpendicular tracery from the
271   eastern transept lancets, thus completing the work of converting all the Perpendicular intrusions in the eastern limb of the cathedral to Early English. Lastly, he superintended the refacing of the north porch with its many niches, which he filled with statues by Hardman.[9] The result of all this renewal has rendered the whole exterior flat and uninteresting.

    In 1762 the cloister openings were reduced by
290   partial filling-in around poor new tracery.
291   This was all removed, and Perpendicular tracery substituted about a hundred years later.

The interior

At the Reformation the cathedral suffered a purge of its altars, shrines, images and other furniture. Much of the splendid stained glass in cathedral and cloisters escaped destruction only to succumb to the attacks of the Earl of Essex's troops in 1642, when practically every bit was destroyed and the great organ of 1613 hardly escaped destruction (only to be demolished soon afterwards – see below).[10] The roofs of the cathedral and cloisters were denuded of their lead (and the latter of their wooden roofs too) no doubt to make bullets, and at the Restoration of the monarchy in 1660 were becoming ruinous. Noake[11] describes at length the journeys of Mr Oley, treasurer, and Clarke, plumber, into Derbyshire and other counties to buy new lead, by then scarce and expensive. New plate and service-books for the choir had to be bought and new fittings constructed. The repairs

and replacements cost at least £6,000 which Noake in 1866 reckoned would amount to 'little short of £30,000 . . . in our coin' – how much more now?

The choir

Up to the Dissolution of the monasteries (1539–40) the choir appears to have been under the tower and extended one bay into the nave, with the pulpitum taking up the next bay westwards. But in 1550–51, two pairs of organs (in chapels) and the 'great organ' were taken down by Dean Barlow;[12] and in 1556 the whole choir was moved into its present position, east of the tower, with a new pulpitum or choir-screen under the eastern tower arch. The old stalls of 1397 with their misericords, which had been stored in the clochium since 1551, were re-erected, but with new canopies (of Renaissance design?) and a new bishop's throne with pillared tester. The 'whole order of the choir [was] restored; at the same time the upper part of it, from the end of the stalls to the foot of the altar, was enclosed with stone, grated with iron and two doors on each side'.[13] (Part of this enclosure is shown, incidentally, in Britton's pl. VI.)

    These fittings which, it seems, largely survived the Civil War, are lukewarmly remarked on by Browne Willis:[14] 'the stalls . . . are of good oak, and being regular and uniform, look decent; and were here a good Altar and Bishop's Throne, the whole choir would appear handsome'. From this it would seem that the stalls were superior to the throne, but Green says of the latter:[15] 'it is a plain, respectable and characteristic object, on the top . . . is a mitre on a cushion, below which are the emblems of peace denoted by an olive branch. The whole with the stalls are made of fine Irish oak with an abundance of carving dispersed about the seats [the medieval misericords?], pillars and cornices'. These stalls, he says elsewhere, were the same as those erected in 1556. From this extract and from a study of Wild's engraving of the choir looking 281 west, the stalls and throne appear to be en suite – were they avant-garde work of 1556 or old-fashioned work of 1660? Murray says:[16] 'The present canopies date from the reign of Charles II, but are of no great interest'. (Parts of these are now in Sutton Coldfield church.) Green[17] adds that 282 'above these stalls are two spacious galleries on each side, furnished with seats for ladies'.

    In James I's reign the 1556 choir-screen was greatly altered and enlarged to accommodate a 273 huge new organ, made in 1613 by Thomas Dallam, organ-builder, at a cost of £211, as recorded by

Green,[18] the case and work on the organ-loft costing another £170 or so:

The case and joiner's work about the loft . . . £68-14-8 to Robert Kettle
The floor and loft in carpenter's work, about . . . £13-0-0
The gilding and painting . . . £77-18-0 to William Peacy
For painting the escutcheons about the loft . . . £11-0-0 to John Davys of Worcester.

(this last item refers to the arms of the subscribers to the cost).

Green[19] says the great organ escaped with little damage in the Civil War, and that there is 'no account of its being either removed or repaired occurring until the early part of Dean Waugh's time' (1751–65), but it seems he was badly mistaken in both statements. For Noake[20] gives the articles of agreement between Thomas Harris of New Sarum and the dean and chapter of Worcester, on 5 July 1666, for making within eighteen months a double organ of great and 'chair' organs to cost £400, the cases 'to be designed after the manner of Windsor Church before the Wars', which are then described in detail. Harris's receipt of the £400 (plus £33 extra) is also given. So it appears from this that while the organ gallery dated back to 1614, the organ and case were made in the late 1660s, with which period the design as shown on all the engravings well accords; but the crocketted spires were obviously a gesture of later date to accord with the Gothic surroundings.[21]

Little is known of the original altarpiece, but Brakspear[22] says that before the alterations of 1812 (he says 1792) 'there remained parts of the original 13th-century reredos, formed of an arcade similar to the wall panelling of the aisles of the Lady Chapel'; but he gives no reference. He implies it was hidden behind the 17th-century altar-wainscot now to be described by Green:[23] 'The altar-screen is an object not otherwise noticeable as a part of the garniture of the Cathedral than that, like others hastily set up to cover the outrage committed on the ancient altar, and to be as much dissimilar to them or to any other part of the church as possible. . . . it stands . . . a Greek among Goths. . . . The screen is formed of plain oak divided into large panels by a series of Corinthian pilasters.'

The early eighteenth century

Green[24] says new iron gates were set up at the entrance to the choir, under the organ-loft, with the arms of Dean Talbot as Bishop of Oxford and Dean of Worcester and the date '1701'. Soon afterwards, between 1712 and 1715 suggests Green,[25] a number of alterations and additions were effected, including a square pier and two unchamfered arches (which he calls 'modern') built across the south-east transept to strengthen it. Green also includes in this period the erection of a curious wall, incorporating several fine monuments, and pierced by four large cusped circles or quatrefoils, stretching between the north-east and north-west piers of the eastern crossing, which were leaning inwards. But the superior finish and Gothic quatrefoils of this wall suggest an earlier date than the 18th century.

One other strange alteration (not noticed by Green) was to the first pillar from the west crossing, on the north side of the choir. Murray[26] says that, having shown signs of weakness, it was 'recased and enlarged in Jacobean Gothic, with a curious base of masonry in the shape of a tulip'. Noake[27] is more explicit, describing it as 'cased in an extraordinary form, having new caps in imitation of the general forms of the old foliage, and its base fortified by gigantic consoles of the Italian form and in a kind of tulip shape'. (It is well shown in Browne Willis's plan.)

Green says that about this time 'the greater part of the church was whitewashed' and it appears that in the later 1720s the wooden roofs over the eastern limb of the cathedral were mostly renewed.[28]

1748 to 1818

Green[29] and Noake[30] say the choir and its aisles were newly paved in 1748, and Green adds that 'the present floor of the choir has been laid over the old one which lies about eight inches beneath; it is . . . party-coloured . . . blue and white. . . . The old floor of the great cross ile, and of the nave and its side iles were taken up, together with all the sepulchral stones, and several monuments and tombs, and in its stead was laid the present white stone floor, which has rendered this part of the church eminently beautiful; and since which time no graves are suffered to be made in it.' This was in 1750 when, according to Noake, 'Mr Wilkinson procured Painswick stone to pave the cathedral' after workmen had been sent to view the pavement of Gloucester Cathedral – 'a beautiful white stone' from 'the quarries at Painswick'. Green adds that 'in the floors of the side iles [of the choir] gravestones, that had been removed from the nave and great cross ile, have been laid by their walls'. He then proceeds:

286

288

The steps leading to these iles, and to the choir at the west end from the great cross ile, and those leading from the east end into the Lady's Chapel, together with the iron gates that enclose them, were formed and set up at the same time; also the passage round the west end of the Cathedral leading on the left into the cloisters . . . was laid open, by which improvement the indecent annoyance of passengers conveying every sort of burthen through the principal north entrance across the nave . . . to the cloisters, even during divine service . . . was effectively removed.

The following quotation, also from Green,[31] poses several questions:

There was anciently in the churchyard a lofty stone cross. At this place the sermons were wont to be delivered in the open air. At the south side of it, near the church walls, there were seats . . . for the principal citizens. On its demolition in the civil wars . . . the place for sermons was within doors, at the bottom of the cathedral, and was continued there till the new floor of the nave was laid [1750]. A stone bench, set up under the great west window, and covered with fine blue arras cloth was appropriated to the chief citizens. The bishop's chair was placed under the second lowermost pillar on the south side; the pulpit stood beneath the opposite corresponding pillar. Near the bishop's chair were the seats of the dean and prebendaries, on a stone bench, covered also with blue arras cloth; on which was wrought a design of Robert Alchurch, sub-prior of, and a considerable benefactor to, this church. Near these, under the third arch on the south side, was an organ, long since removed from the church.

The pulpit mentioned above, Green says, was now removed to its present position in the choir[32] and, until Scott's rearrangement there, was corbelled out from a panelled stone pier attached to the pillar. It retained a delightful wooden tester with carved drapery round the perimeter upheld by hands and on the supporting backboard was a carving of the Heavenly Jerusalem under an elaborate open canopy.[33] On the stone pulpit itself are carved four open books each with the symbol of an Evangelist above. Its generally Gothic appearance suggests an early 16th-century date but certain details, such as cartouches of arms, seem to betray a later origin, and various dates to as late as 1748 have been suggested. But in 1968 Dean Milburn confirms a Carolean date: 'The stone pulpit originally set up in the nave . . . is by Stephen Baldwin, 1641.' (Pevsner says 1642.)

In Green's description of the furniture removed in 1750, a query arises concerning the blue arras with the 'design of Robert Alchurch', which if newly set up during the Civil War seems a remarkable thing for a Puritan to include in the fittings? Which leads to a second query – when were the nave services established? It appears this was earlier than the Civil War as the following statement by Dr W. Moore Ede, Dean of Worcester (1908–34), in a booklet entitled *Worcester Cathedral, Its History, Its Architecture, Its Library, Its Schools* (4th edn 1937), will show: 'A pulpit was erected at the west end of the nave, and of Sunday afternoons a puritan divine expounded the Scriptures and the scheme of salvation as formulated by Calvin.' This preacher was appointed and paid for by the Corporation. A resolution passed in 1614 appointed a lecturer 'to preach at the College every Sunday so long as it seemeth good to this Corporation'. Seats were placed for the congregation and there, said the dean, the senators and their wives sat in pomp and more state than in their Guildhall. 'They would not go into the Choir, where the Prayer-book services were conducted by the Cathedral body, but walked about the nave chatting with one another until the preacher entered the pulpit.' But Dr Ede does not mention the preaching-cross.

Green[34] says that the ancient font had stood at the second pillar, nearly opposite the upper entrance from the cloister into the south aisle. It was of black marble, with this inscription: 'Hic fons est Vitae / Mundani quicunque venite / Suscipit ista reos / Et parit unda deos.' We are not told why it was discarded, but a new font was made and placed in the Jesus chapel, then newly laid open to the north nave aisle, and was first used on 12 July 1770, Green informs us.[35] He proceeds: 'Its form is that of a term,[36] elevated on a double plinth, making an ascent of two steps. . . . The whole is of marble, and from its elegant simplicity, is very ornamental.' Noake states:[37] 'The font cost £24. 12s, and was furnished by Mr P. Hoare, Statuary, of Bath' and he hopes it 'will soon give way to something more worthy', while Murray calls it 'singularly hideous'. Where is it now? Its successor, the present font, in the westernmost bay of the south aisle, is by Bodley, and has a stupendous spired cover with niched statues and pinnacled canopies.

Green says that the altar was wholly unadorned until 1792, when the dean and chapter 'did the author the honour to accept a copy of [Rubens's] Descent from the Cross . . . 9 feet high by 7 feet wide [2·7 × 2·1 metres] painted by Mr Thomas Phillips', which was added to the 17th-century altar-screen.[38] In 1812 this screen was removed and

281
285

1

285
288 its place taken by a fine stone erection of nine
traceried Perpendicular windows or bays formed
from the 15th-century enclosures of the north-east
287 and south-east transepts. When Scott's reredos
superseded this screen, four of the bays were
preserved (but cut down) and placed under the
south-west transeptal Norman arch. (In 1936 they
were returned to their original position in the
north-east transept to form, with some new work,
its enclosure as before – now St George's memorial
chapel.)

Up to the early 19th century the pulpitum or
choir-screen of 1613 was still in situ, and showed
its Elizabethan or Jacobean character on its east
side by the richly carved arches on the organ
281 gallery front (see Wild's pl. 12 of the choir looking
west). These arches, and canopies from the stalls,
were thrown out by Scott 'in a moment of
inattention' as he describes it,[39] and some of them,
made into a screen, may be seen today in Sutton
282 Coldfield Church, Worcestershire. Until 1818 the
west front of the pulpitum was plain and nonde-
script, with an eliptically headed entrance to the
273 choir – see the plate of the nave in Green, who thus
describes the organ and screen in 1796:[40] 'The
organ . . . is esteemed a fine instrument . . . and
forms a magnificent object, viewed either from the
nave or choir.' On the west front of its gallery, on
the cornice, is the following inscription: 'These
honourable and worshipful gentlemen, whose arms
are here placed were contributors towards this
gallery, anno Domini, 1614', and he then enumerates fifty-seven coats. Of the organ-case he
says:

On a plane in the centre of this front, is a painting of the
Virgin Mary with our Saviour in his arms; underneath
which the arms of the see are represented, displayed by
two naked boys withdrawing a large drapery from
before them.

The east front of the gallery towards the choir has a
good imitation of a marble parapet or screen, inclosing
the floor of the gallery over the [return-] stalls of the
choir. On this side the lesser or chair organ is seen. . . . In
[the great organ's] painted decorations, the arms of the
see [occurs] as on the west front, over which, answerable
to the situation of the Virgin and Child, as already
described, an angel is seen sounding a trumpet, and
holding an olive branch in his left hand. The carvings on
the top are the Kings Arms, without the supporters, from
which, on each side, a bold festoon, richly composed of
flowers, fruit, etc., is suspended. At the bottom of the
larger pipes, on each side, are carved heads of cherubim.
The pipes of the chair organ have their tops inserted
behind the expanded plumes of a large cherub's wings,

which spread over the whole line; a pretty design, but
indifferently executed.

(Wild's view of 1823 shows an eagle between two
urns on top of the choir organ, and neither his nor
Green's plate shows the Virgin and Child or the
angel – only a niche. But Britton's west view (his pl.
V) shows a seated figure in the niche probably
meant for the Virgin.)   278

In 1818,[41] under Mr St John as treasurer, the
west front of the choir-screen was remodelled in   274
cement to his own design – a Gothic arrangement of
three pointed arches,[42] surmounted by panelling,
to the cornice of which he fixed many of the
misericords from the stalls (these are shown in
Britton's pl. V), and they remained there until the   278
restoration of 1857–74. He also removed the old
doors from the north porch and replaced them with
new ones fashioned from the old altar-screen. The
old doors were, according to Noake,[43] 'no doubt
those, a portion of which remains in the crypt, and
said to be covered with human skin'.

Perkins and Scott

The following interior changes were effected by
Perkins, and after 1864 with G. G. Scott: the
removal of whitewash from walls and pillars,
revealing much fine carving of caps and so on,
preserved underneath it; the laying-down of new
pavements, black and white in the nave and west
transepts and coloured tile-work in the eastern
limb; the elaborate decoration of the vaultings of
choir and Lady chapel; the repair or renewal of the
much decayed sculptures of the wall arcading and
triforium by R. J. Boulton, who also carved the
spandrels of Perkins's great east window and
the new arcading beneath it; the removal of the
pierced wall north of the altar and the arched
braces in the south-east transept and rebuilding of
the affected pillars. All choir fittings were removed
(including the altar-screen and stalls) and replaced   283
by new designs, except the stone pulpit of 1641,   287
but this was altered and deprived of its charming
wooden tester, although the top of its stone
support with its canopy and remarkable carving of
the Heavenly Jerusalem was preserved and is now
in the north chancel aisle.

Last but not least, Perkins took down the old
choir-screen and organ. In its place Scott's metal   280
enclosure was erected, and a new organ was built
in the south transept, with a small pipe case on the
north side of the choir (later duplicated on the
south side).

Bibliography

* *Browne Willis, 1727.* 2nd edn 1742.

Green, 1796. Valentine Green, *History of Worcester*, 2 vols.

* *Wild, 1823.* Charles Wild, *Worcester Cathedral*. Superb aquatints.

A Concise History of Worcester, c. 1830.

* *Britton, 1835.* John Britton, *The History and Antiquities of the Cathedral Church of Worcester*. Splendid engravings.

Report of the Transactions and Excursions of the British Architectural Association, at their 5th Congress at Worcester, 1848. Pub. for private circulation (only 25 copies) in 1851. By A. J. Dunkin.

Noake, 1866. John Noake, *The Monastery and Cathedral of Worcester*. A mine of information.

* *Strange (Bell), 1900.* Edward F. Strange, *Worcester, The Cathedral and See*, Bell's Cathedral Series.

Brakspear, 1937. Harold Brakspear, *Worcester Cathedral Booklet*.

* *Milburn (Pitkin), 1968.* Dean Milburn, *Worcester Cathedral*, Pitkin Pictorial.

* *Kemp (Pitkin), 1975.* E. W. Kemp, *Worcester Cathedral*, Pitkin Pictorial.

Lockett, 1978. R. B. Lockett, 'The Victorian Restoration of Worcester Cathedral' in *Worcester Cathedral* (B.A.A.)

Notes

1 It is curious that photographs of the present, restored tower show that from certain viewpoints and in certain lights these windows can be quite invisible.

2 Browne Willis, 628.

3 Wild (1823).

4 Winkles, III, 56.

5 Murray's *Handbook* (1864), 232.

6 Green, 139.

7 Peter Ferriday, *Lord Grimthorpe* (1957), 68.

8 Noake, 339, says 1796; Brakspear says 1799.

9 Of the unrestored porch, Britton says: 'On each side within is a dwarf wall of unusual design', and these are shown on his plan of the cathedral. Murray, *op. cit.*, says: 'The dwarf wall either side of the steps . . . descending to the nave is a peculiar arrangement.' But *The Builder* (12 May 1866) is more explicit: 'The floor of the great north porch (which had been raised by a series of gradations, apparently in modern times, with an odd-looking dwarf wall on each side, the use of which has puzzled many . . .)

has now been levelled to the bases of the shafts, and nearly on a line with the floor of the nave. This has increased the apparent height of the porch. It has also been deemed advisable to lower the approaches to the North porch in the College yard, so that they might run into the porch on a level, or nearly so. The carved enrichments of the exterior . . . have not yet been completed by the insertion of the statuary in the niches [which it says were to be] by Messrs Hardman of Birmingham.'

10 Noake, 478–80.

11 Noake, 323–31.

12 Noake, 474.

13 Green, 135, quoting ms of Bishop Blandford.

14 Browne Willis (1742), 626.

15 Green, 135.

16 Murray's *Handbook* (1864), 208.

17 Green, 136.

18 Green, II, appendix VI.

19 Green, 115.

20 Noake, 482–83, 484.

21 The late 17th-c. organ-cases in both Exeter and Gloucester Cathedrals, still happily extant, were also furnished with similar spires in the 18th-c. – now removed.

22 Brakspear, 57.

23 Green, 137–38.

24 Green, 138.

25 Green, 139.

26 Murray's *Handbook* (1864), 207.

27 Noake, 333.

28 Noake, 335.

29 Green, 140.

30 Noake, 336.

31 Green, 141.

32 When the rest of the above furniture was also removed.

33 See pl. 45 in N. Pevsner, *Buildings of England: Worcestershire*.

34 Green, 110. The inscription quoted from Leland.

35 Green, 141.

36 Or 'terminal pillar' – apparently a pier composed of 4 consoles back to back (cf. altered pillar in choir, p. 163).

37 Noake, 337.

38 Noake, 618, adds: 'What can have happened in nine years after this to induce Mr Green to ask for the return of the picture is not known, but probably the work of restoration going on at the cathedral about that time was thought to require its removal, and hence an order appears in the books for its return to Mr Green, free of expense to him.'

39 Milburn (Pitkin), 22.

40 Green, 114–15.

41 *Gentleman's Magazine*, Mar. 1821, p. 214; Noake, 341.

42 See Wild, pl. 5, and Britton, pl. V (elevation and section looking east).

43 Noake, 341.

* see also bibliography to the Introduction.

260–63. Four views of the tower:
in 1672 (Hollar); *c.* 1860, before
Perkins's restoration; *c.* 1880, after
Perkins; and as it appears now.

WIGORNIENSIS
Ecclesiæ Cathedralis
Ab Aquilone Prospectus

Worcester: the exterior

264. Hollar's view from the north, 1672. Note particularly the separate octagonal bell-tower, and the fact that the main transept has two windows, later altered (see pl. 268).

265. *Right*: Wild's view from the north-east, 1823. The very tall pinnacles to the transepts and the east and west ends were added probably in 1712; the east window is of 1792. (Houses actually existing in the foreground are omitted by the artist.)

266. Storer's distant view of the west front, *c.* 1817, with the tall pinnacles matching those of pl. 265.

267. *Left*: Storer's view of the south side, 1817, with houses close to the cathedral and Perpendicular windows in the aisles and clerestory.

272. *Right*: The same view in the late 19th century: the houses cleared away, new pinnacles and new Early English windows.

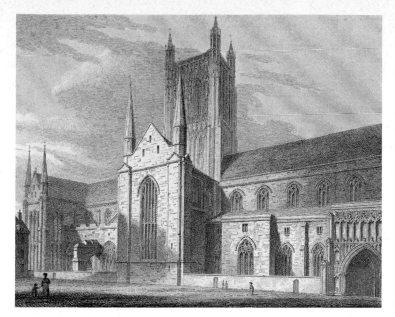

268. The north transept in 1817 (Storer), showing the large single window built between 1748 and 1756.

269. The north transept, c. 1870, with the new four-light Geometrical window and new pinnacles.

270. *Above left*: View from the north-east, c. 1833. In the ten years since 1823 the tall pinnacles have been taken down. This view also shows the old houses and church of St Michael, omitted by Wild in pl. 265.

271. *Above right*: The same view after the 1860s: St Michael's demolished, a new east window of ten lancets by Perkins, new pinnacles added, the clerestory windows changed from Perpendicular to Early English and all tracery removed from the old lancets.

169

273. The nave looking east, 1795 (Green), showing the fine organ and the choir-screen erected in 1613.

274. The nave in 1823 (Wild), with the new Gothic screen of 1818.

275–77. Changes to the west window. First, the medieval window (Green); second, that of 1789 (Britton); and third, Perkins's new window and west door.

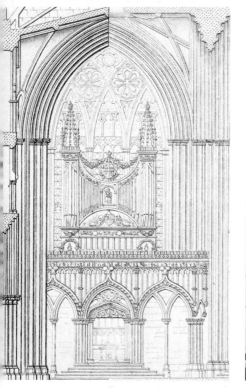

278. Detail of Britton's section through the cathedral looking east. The screen is that of pl. 274 but Britton shows, as Wild does not, the misericords from the choir-stalls fixed to the cornice. Behind it is a detailed representation of the 1792 east window.

279. Looking east from the crossing after Scott's restoration: Scott's pulpit, screen and reredos; at the back, Perkins's east window.

280. Scott and Skidmore's magnificent screen.

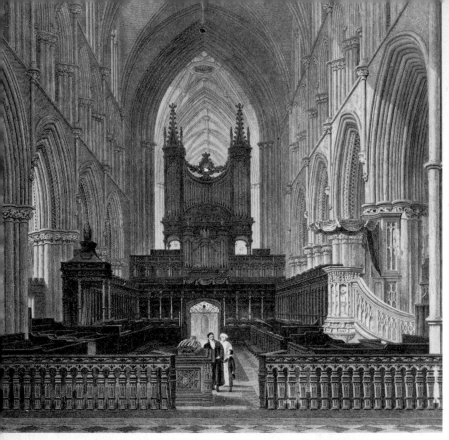

282. Woodwork from the old choir-screen and return stalls reused in the church of Sutton Coldfield. (See 281, *left*)

281. *Left*: Wild's engraving of the choir looking west, 1823; note the pulpit with its delightful tester, the bishop's throne and Jacobean altar-rails.

283. The choir looking west, *c*. 1880, with Scott's furniture and screen.

Worcester: the choir

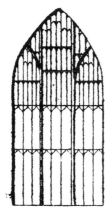

284. The medieval east window, a detail from Green's plan of 1795

285. The choir looking east, 1823 (Wild), with the window inserted in 1792, the pulpit with tester (see pl. 1) and the altar screen of 1812.

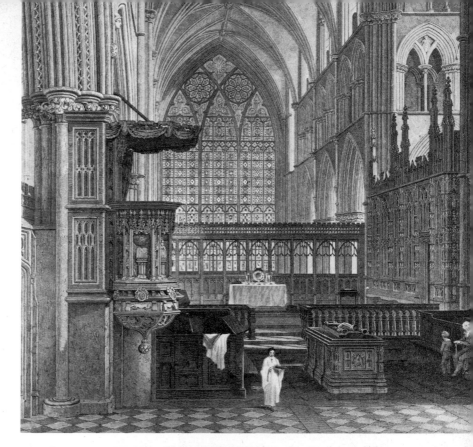

286. In the 18th century a pier supporting two round-headed arches was built across the south-east transept – one arch is glimpsed in this detail from Coney's plate.

287. The choir as left by Scott. The east window is by Perkins; the pulpit, as in pl. 283, is the early 17th-century one minus its tester.

Worcester: choir and cloister

288. View of the choir in 1862 (Murray's *Guide*), showing a wall, of uncertain date, built across the north-east transept pierced by four cusped holes.

289. The same view after Scott's restoration, the wall replaced by a gabled arcade.

290. The cloister garth about 1860, with crude tracery of the 18th century in the arches.

291. The same view today, with the Perpendicular tracery restored.

Index